Gesture, Speech, and Sign

Gesture, Speech, and Sign

Edited by

LYNN S. MESSING

Gesture and Movement Dynamics Laboratory
University of Delaware and duPont Hospital for Children

and

RUTH CAMPBELL

University College, London

OXFORD
UNIVERSITY PRESS

OXFORD

UNIVERSITY PRESS

Great Clarendon Street, Oxford OX2 6DP

Oxford University Press is a department of the University of Oxford
and furthers the University's aim of excellence in research, scholarship,
and education by publishing worldwide in

Oxford New York

Athens Auckland Bangkok Bogotá Buenos Aires Calcutta
Cape Town Chennai Dar es Salaam Delhi Florence Hong Kong Istanbul
Karachi Kuala Lumpur Madrid Melbourne Mexico City Mumbai
Nairobi Paris São Paulo Singapore Taipei Tokyo Toronto Warsaw

and associated companies in Berlin Ibadan

Oxford is a registered trade mark of Oxford University Press

Published in the United States
by Oxford University Press Inc., New York

British Library Cataloguing in Publication Data
(Data available)

Library of Congress Cataloging in Publication Data
Gesture, speech, and sign/edited by Lynn S. Messing and Ruth Campbell.
Includes bibliographical references.
1. Gesture.   2. Speech.   3. Sign language.   4. Deaf–Means of
communication.   5. Human-computer interaction.   I. Messing, Lynn S.
II. Campbell, Ruth, 1944–   .
P117.G469   1999   419–dc21   99–18289

ISBN 0 19 852451 X (Hbk)

Typeset by Footnote Graphics,
Warminster, Wilts

Printed in Great Britain
on acid-free paper by
Bookcraft (Bath) Ltd.,
Midsomer Norton, Avon.

This volume is lovingly dedicated to Lynn's mother Susan Messing and to the memory of our parents Ralph A. Messing, and Hugo and Balbina Droller, who fostered our curiosity and encouraged us to pursue our dreams.

Acknowledgements

Ruth Campbell: The work reported in this chapter is based on many collaborations, only a few of which can be acknowledged here. The work has been supported financially by the Economic and Social Science Research Council of Great Britain, The Leverhulme Foundation (UK) and the Medical Research Council (UK). I particularly thank Edward De Haan, Barbara Brooks, Simon Wallace, Mairead MacSweeney, Bencie Woll, and Phil Benson for their collaboration in the experimental work, and Bencie Woll, Tony David, Gemma Calvert, Phil McGuire, and Mike Brammer for collaboration in neurophysiology.

Justine Cassell: Thanks to Norm Badler, Mark Steedman, Catherine Pelachaud, Scott Prevost, Matthew Stone and the other members of Gesture Jack who were co-authors of Animated Conversation, and heavy contributors to its description here, and thanks to the entire GNL-humanoid group for their work on Rea. The research described here has been funded by the NSF VPW and STIMULATE programs, by Deutsche Telekom, and by other generous sponsors of the MIT Media Laboratory.

David Corina: I thank Susan McBurney for insightful discussion and assistance in the preparation of this chapter. This work was supported by a grant from the National Institutes on Deafness and Communicative Disorders (R29-DC03099).

Paul Ekman: Preparation was supported by a Research Scientist Award from the National Institute of Mental Health (MH06091).

Karen Emmorey: This work was supported by the National Science Foundation (Linguistics Program, SBR-9510963) and the National Institute of Deafness and Other Communicative Disorders from the National Institutes of Health (R37 HD13249). The paper has benefited greatly from discussions with Edward Klima and Judy S. Reilly. I also thank Brenda Falgier and Steve McCullough who provided invaluable insights as native ASL signers. Address correspondence to Karen Emmorey, Laboratory for Cognitive Neuroscience, The Salk Institute for Biological Studies, 10010 North Torrey Pines Road, La Jolla, CA 92037; e-mail: emmorey@axp1.salk.edu

Pierre Feyereisen: Gratitude is expressed to Lynn Messing for her careful editorial assistance, as well as to Ruth Campbell, Marc Crommelinck, and Brigitte Tilmant for other helpful comments on a previous version of this chapter. During his work, the author was funded as Research Director of the National Fund for Scientific Research, Belgium.

Susan Goldin-Meadow: The research described in this chapter was supported by BNS 8810769 from the National Science Foundation, RO1 DC00491 from the National Institute of Neurological and Communicative Disorders and Stroke, RO1 HD18617 from the National Institute of Child Health and Human Development, and a grant from the March of Dimes.

Robert M. Krauss and Uri Hadar: We gratefully acknowledge the contributions of the collaborators whose names are noted in connection with the research in which they participated. Our thinking about these matters benefited greatly from conversations over the years about speech, gesture and how they might be related with Sam Glucksberg, Julian Hochberg, Ezequiel Morsella, David McNeill, Lois Putnam, and the late Stanley Schachter. Of course, they bear no responsibility for the uses we made of their ideas. Finally, we thank the editors for their astute and helpful comments, their support, and their exemplary patience. The research described here was supported by grants SBR 93-10586 from the National Science Foundation and 92-00059 from the US-Israel Binational Science Fund.

David McNeill: The first part of the title was suggested by the editors. Preparation of this chapter was supported by research grants from the Spencer Foundation and the National Science Foundation. I am grateful to the University of Chicago community of gesture enthusiasts, including especially Susan Goldin-Meadow, Susan Duncan, Karl-Erik McCullough, Nobuhiro Furuyama, Gale Stam, and Lisa Miotto. I wish especially to thank Shaun Gallagher for his comments on the consciousness section.

Lynn Messing: Both the co-editing of this book and the writing of my chapters were made possible by funding from the Interdisciplinary Research Training in Rehabilitation Technology Grant Number H133P30003-96 from the National Institute on Disability and Rehabilitation Research of the US Department of Education, and the Nemours Foundation. I also wish to thank my boss, Richard Foulds, for his permission and encouragement to work on this book, and my friends and colleagues Margot Kinberg and Shirley Peters for their support and suggestions.

Preface

Gestures and actions

Human actions seem to fall naturally into two types. Firstly, there are actions designed to interact with the external world, such as picking up a cup, throwing a ball, walking to the postbox, or sitting on a chair. The objects or locations implicated in such actions moderate them; as a hand reaches towards a cup, its fingers anticipate the correct shape, orientation, and force to lift it. The spring in one's step is partly determined by the surface below one's feet, and the air temperature and strength of the wind will help to determine whether one walks straight-backed or hunched up.

In contrast, the second class of actions is controlled primarily by internal factors. Examples include pretending to pick up a non-existent cup (e.g., to indicate to someone the desire for a cup of tea), or beating one's head with one's hand upon realizing that one has done something stupid. In these two gestures, events in the head 'lead' the action. Gestures work communicatively in ways that other actions do not. For example, we can interpret a woman lifting a cup to her mouth as, 'Ah! She wants a cup of tea,' but it is only the gesture—her smile of contentment as she takes the first sip—that communicates her state of mind and indicates her intentions.

Gestures, then, are a special sort of action: they link closely to the individual's plans, moods, and desires; they intertwine in communication. Even when they are instrumental (the child pulling her parent to look at a toy in the shop once the gesture of pleading looks has failed), they operate under different sorts of constraints than other actions—constraints of a psychological and cognitive nature. Spoken language is conceived by some as gestural in its structure: while its sound patterning transmits the structured information, the ease with which we perceive utterances may lie in their structure as vocal action patterns—as vocal gestures. Because of this, questions about gesture may lead us directly to the roots of human language and human behaviour.

In the last two to three decades, one form of gestural communication has been the focus of intense interest by linguists, neuroscientists, and engineers. This is sign language or, more correctly, the various natural signed languages that are acquired by many people born deaf.

How intimately are gesture and language connected? Did the one evolve from the other? To what extent are they similarly processed in the brain? In what ways are signed languages akin to spoken languages and to gestures? Is the line between language and gesture as clearcut as it first appears? These questions are all easy to ask, but far more difficult to answer. The authors in this book address these and other questions regarding the relationships among gesture, spoken languages, and signed languages.

Gestures and signs

Until the 1960s, signed languages were not considered to be 'real' languages. At best, they were thought to be quasilinguistic systems—incomplete visual representations of spoken languages. At worst, they were looked upon as 'merely gestures'— non-linguistic, pantomimic presentations of concrete concepts. Research by Stokoe (1960) and others has proven American Sign Language (ASL) to be as complex and systematic a language as any spoken one. Similar research has shown other signed languages (e.g., British Sign Language) to be 'real' languages.

There is linguistic, psycholinguistic, and neurological evidence in favour of sign languages being true language. In the introductory chapter, Messing sets the scene with an introduction to this evidence for those unfamiliar with the area. Emmorey (Chapter 8) discusses the linguistic evidence in greater detail in relation to the most basic, yet also the hardest, question that can be posed about signed languages: to what extent do signed languages and gestural communications share common ground and to what extent do they differ? While the last ten years have seen an acceptance of sign languages as fully formed languages, there has been some reluctance to examine the nature of the relationship of sign to gesture, probably because of a fear that such considerations would lead to a downgrading of the hard-won language status of sign. However, Emmorey starts to answer this question by indicating a number of ways in which sign fits the constraints observed in spoken language and the ways in which gesture fits different schemes of classification and categorization. From this, it is possible to describe how sign and gesture may co-occur in a signer's communicative utterance. There is also evidence here for some common aspects of sign and gesture. In Chapter 2, Corina provides converging evidence from neurolinguistics. Although left-hemisphere damage in a deaf signer typically produces a language-related disorder, such as aphasia, sign does not always break down in a manner that mirrors the breakdown of spoken language: sometimes its roots in gestural communication are laid bare. Stokoe and Marschark (Chapter 9) take the 'primacy of gesture' idea even further and contemplate the possibility that the first language may have been signed, and that it may have arisen from gesturing.

Goldin-Meadow (Chapter 7) examines the gestures of children who have little linguistic input—deaf children in non-signing environments. She argues that their gestures develop language-like properties not seen in the gestures of other children or adults. Emmorey (Chapter 8) also considers the conditions under which new signed languages can arise when such children have the opportunity to interact and communicate with one another. Campbell (Chapter 4) examines how face acts may be perceived differently when they are part of a signed utterance than when they are 'merely' gestural—and how experiments might reveal how sign users respond to such distinctions.

Because speech and gestures are presented in different modalities, it is possible to articulate both simultaneously. In contrast, signs and gestures are both articulated in the same mode. Emmorey provides evidence that native signers do, in fact, gesture: but how do they do this? How is the single output stream of hand and face actions managed, when both language and gesture occupy the same channel? Messing (Chapter 10) examines the manual output of hearing female signers speaking with one another. She shows that these women, who learned ASL as a second language, intermix signs and gestures while they are speaking.

Gestures and speech

While the relationship between sign and gesture has occupied several research programmes, the relation between speech and gesture is not often considered within a single programme. Linguistics itself has not generally considered gesture to be central to its concerns. Much research on the relationship of language and gesture has thus been conducted within rather different frameworks, including those of neuropsychology, ethological or evolutionary psychology, and cognition (especially the cognition of action).

The neuropsychology of gesture has long intrigued clinicians, neurological patients, and caregivers: one common result of localized brain damage can be apraxia, i.e., impairment in the control of actions. In some patients, goal-directed actions (such as drinking from a cup) may be affected, while gesture (miming the same action) may not be; in others, the converse pattern of impairment may arise. Neurological damage can affect components of gesture specifically, as well as in association with language and other disorders. To what extent are such impairments reflections of a common deficit? (For example, the ability to plan or articulate a sequence of actions would affect both speech and gesture.) To what extent can neurological data inform questions on the separability of speech and gesture and of speech and sign? Feyereisen (Chapter 1) addresses the neuropsychological evidence on the relationship between gesture and speech, complementing Corina's review of the neuropsychology of gesture and sign (Chapter 2).

The function of speech-accompanying gestures has been hotly debated and two chapters in the present volume vividly convey the flavour of this debate within a broadly cognitive context. Both ask: where in the representation and planning of action do speech and the specific gestures that accompany it arise? Krauss and Hadar (Chapter 6) argue that the purpose of such gestures is to facilitate lexical access for the speaker. McNeill (Chapter 5), in contrast, claims that gestures are themselves lexical: They are alternative manifestations of specific concepts that are realized both linguistically and gesturally, and it is possible to use both outputs to determine the timing and unfolding of the growth points of how ideas are 'made flesh'. A full resolution of this question awaits much further research.

A different approach is exemplified by Ekman's chapter (Chapter 3). Ekman pioneered the comparative study of gestural expression, contrasting expressions and gestures in different communities, in order to show the common biological source of human gesture. This is part of an evolutionary–ethological approach to gesture which has not only clarified and systematized gesture, but which has also had some useful practical applications. A well-known example is that psychiatrists can observe the gesturing of their patients and the possible mismatches between the gesturing and the speech to aid them in their diagnoses and to gauge the severity of illness. The validity of this use of gesture for diagnosis is supported by academic research. Ekman and Friesen (1969) noted that depressed patients cover their eyes far more frequently than non-depressed individuals; however, eye-covering ceases by the time the depression has lifted. In his chapter, Ekman updates his typology of gestures and mentions in passing several interesting findings, some possible applications of which would be readily discernible to the reader. For instance, by imparting to their classes a knowledge of the types of gestures used or considered taboo in the target cultures, foreign language instructors can help their students to avoid miscommunications abroad (Morris *et al.* 1979; Carty 1980).

The chapters in this book explore gesture and language scientifically. A great part of this enterprise is the development of explanatory models. Such models, even simple symbolic ones, have the potential to be implemented; that is, by programming computers both to interpret and to produce human-like gestures, we can assess the feasibility of our theories about gesture and language. This is currently a growing topic of interest for a cross-disciplinary research programme. Cassell's chapter (Epilogue) shows us how far this research has advanced and how simulations of humans may allow us a virtual testbed in which to explore the effects of changing different model parameters to simulate different varieties of, or breakdowns in, communication. Computational research has brought the engineer's perspective to communications and language research in new ways: the engineering of smooth, efficient computer gesture and speech should give us useful insights into the design principles that have evolved in natural communication between people.

Intent of this book

This book was written with an eye toward professionals, graduate students, and upper-level undergraduate students with an interest in gesture and a background in languages, linguistics, psychology, or computer science.

The scope of the book is intentionally broad. It includes the most well-received, sometimes conflicting, views on the relationships among gesture, speech, and sign, in order to provide an adequately balanced presentation so as to permit the readers to form their own educated opinions. The intent is not to provide definitive answers to any of the readers' questions; but rather to give the readers sufficient background so that they will be in a position to ask more informed questions.

This volume aims to present some first steps towards a genuinely interdisciplinary scientific study of gesture. Insights from a wide range of disciplines are starting to inform each other, and with these insights, advances will occur in understanding the scientific basis of human action.

References

Carty, M. (1980). *Strategies used by native speakers in native-non-native conversations.* MA Thesis. Northeastern University. (Eric Document no. 207 323)

Ekman, P. and Friesen. (1969). The repertoire of nonverbal behavior: categories, origins, usage, and coding. *Semiotica* 1, 49–92.

Morris, D., Collett, P., Marsh, P., and O'Shaughnessy, M. (1979). *Gestures: their origins and distribution.* Stein and Day, New York.

Stokoe, W. (1960). *Sign language structure: an outline of the visual communication systems of the American deaf.* Studies in Linguistics: Occasional Papers 8. Department of Anthropology and Linguistics, University of Buffalo, Buffalo, NY.

Contents

Contributors

Ruth Campbell, *Professor of Communication Disorders, Department of Human Communication Science, University College London, Chandler House, 2 Wakefield Street, London WC1 1PG, UK. E-mail: psa01@gold.ac.uk*

Justine Cassell, *MIT Media Lab, E15-315, 20 Ames Street, Cambridge, MA 02139, USA. E-mail: justine@media.mit.edu*

David P. Corina, *Department of Psychology, Box 351525, University of Washington, Seattle, WA 98195, USA. E-mail: corina@u.washington.edu*

Paul Ekman, *University of California, San Francisco, 401 Parnassus Avenue, San Francisco, CA 94143, USA. E-mail: ekman@itsa.ucsf.edu*

Karen Emmorey, *Laboratory for Cognitive Neuroscience, The Salk Institute for Biological Studies, 10010 North Torrey Pines Road, La Jolla, CA 92037, USA. E-mail: emmorey@axp1.salk.edu*

Pierre Feyereisen, *Cognitive Neuropsychology (NECO), 10 Place du Cardinal Mercier, B-1348 Louvain-la-Neuve, Belgium. E-mail: feyereisen@neco.ucl.ac.be*

Susan Goldin-Meadow, *Department of Psychology, University of Chicago, 5730 S. Woodlawn Avenue, Chicago, IL 60637, USA. E-mail: sgsg@midway.uchicago.edu*

Uri Hadar, *Department of Psychology, Tel Aviv University, Ramat Aviv 69978, Israel. E-mail: uri-h@freud.tau.ac.il*

Robert M. Krauss, *Department of Psychology, Columbia University, New York, NY 10027, USA. E-mail: rmk@psych.columbia.edu*

Marc Marschark, *Center for Research, Teaching and Learning, National Technical Institute for the Deaf, 52 Lomb Memorial Drive, Rochester, NY 14623-5604, USA. E-mail: memrtl@rit.edu*

David McNeill, *Department of Psychology, University of Chicago, 5848 S. University Avenue, Chicago, IL 60637, USA. E-mail: mcneill@dura.spc.uchicago.edu*

Lynn S. Messing, *CIS Department, Delaware Technical and Community College, Wilmington Campus, 333 Shipley Street, Wilmington, DE 19801, USA. E-mail: lmessing@hopi.dtcc.edn*

William C. Stokoe, *3519 Cummings Lane, Chevy Chase, MD 20815-3235, USA. E-mail: bill.stokoe@erols.com*

An introduction to signed languages

Lynn S. Messing

Gesture and Movement Dynamics Laboratory of the University of Delaware and the A. I. duPont Hospital for Children

Introduction

This chapter is intended to provide background information on signed languages which will be useful in understanding later chapters. The information presented is, for the most part, common knowledge among signers. American Sign Language (ASL) is referred to throughout this chapter both because it is the signed language on which the most research has been conducted and because it is the one with which the author is most familiar. Many of the remarks made about it can be generalized to other natural signed languages. For an excellent, if slightly outdated, introduction to the linguistics of ASL, see Klima and Bellugi (1979).

No universal signed language

ASL is just one of the world's many signed languages; a very rough approximation is that every country has its own signed language. Moreover, one cannot tell how similar two countries' signed languages are by comparing the similarity of their spoken languages. For example, ASL is descended from, and therefore closely related to, French Sign Language. These two languages are more mutually intelligible than are ASL and the more distantly related British Sign Language, even though the United States shares a dominant spoken language with Great Britain rather than with France.

ASL as a real language

American Sign Language is a full language distinct from English. It has its own phonology (system of mental representations of articulatory units), phonetics (system of articulation), morphology (system for building words/signs), syntax (system for constructing sentences), and lexicon (vocabulary). It is not a monolithic entity, but has all the variation to which natural languages are prone. It also meets other criteria set forth to distinguish language from non-linguistic communication systems.

ASL phonology

William Stokoe was the first linguist to recognize and analyse ASL as a language in its own right. In 1960, he published a ground-breaking work in which he stated that signs are in fact decomposable into smaller units. He proposed that each sign is made up of one or more 'dez' (handshape), 'sig' (movement), and 'tab' (location). An ASL dictionary which he co-authored and which was based on this analysis was published five years later. Other researchers have since elaborated on his analysis or have developed alternative ones more in line with a variety of more current linguistic theories, including moraic analyses (Perlmutter 1993), tier analyses (Liddell and Johnson 1989; Sandler 1993), and feature geometry analyses (Corina and Sagey 1989). This cursory presentation suffices to indicate that the field is quite active and that signed languages can be analysed in the same way as spoken ones.

ASL syntax

The syntax of ASL differs greatly from that of English. For example, questions in ASL are distinguished from statements by means of facial expressions. There are three types of questions in ASL: yes–no questions (which can be answered by a simple affirmative or negative), WH questions (which need information other than 'yes' or 'no' for their answers), and rhetorical questions (which are questions which the signer himself intends to answer). A yes–no question is signalled in part with raised eyebrows and a forwardly tilted head. A WH question is indicated in part by lowered eyebrows and a forwardly tilted head. A rhetorical question is indicated by raised brows and a backwardly tilted head.

   ASL also differs greatly from English in its inflection of verbs. For example, the beginning and ending locations of many directional verbs in ASL indicate the subject and/or object of a sentence. Consequently, subject and object pronouns can be omitted in places where English would require them; they would be used in these situations only to add emphasis. ASL verbs can also be inflected to include information on whether the action involved was continuous, repeated, or took place over a long period of time. On the other hand, ASL verbs do not have inflections to indicate tense: time frames are established via the use of separate signs.

   The order of signs also differs from English word order. English is relatively rigid about maintaining a subject–verb–object ordering. ASL can also use topic–comment ordering, in which the topic of the sentence (which, syntactically, is often the direct object) is presented first, and then the rest of the sentence follows. Topicalized signs are accompanied by raised eyebrows.

Variation within ASL

ASL, like other languages whether signed or spoken, exhibits the variation inherent in any living language: ASL signing varies by dialect, by the age, race, and gender of the signer, by the degree of formality in the conversation, etc. The variation can range from minor differences in the articulation of individual signs or choices of lexical items to entirely different accents.

Other criteria

Valli and Lucas (1992) set forth a series of criteria by which one can differentiate languages from non-linguistic communication systems. ASL satisfies all of their criteria for a language. Several of these criteria were indirectly addressed in the discussions above, specifically: systematicity, variation across time and across communities, a means of showing relationships among symbols, and an organized use of symbols, iconic or arbitrary, which are composed of meaningless subparts.

Valli and Lucas show that ASL also meets these additional criteria for language:

1. It has a means for coining new symbols.
2. An infinite number of messages can be communicated in ASL. These messages can be on any topic, and can refer to items which are neither temporally nor spatially present.
3. More than one meaning can be assigned to an ASL utterance. For example, the signer's message might be serious or sarcastic. A given utterance might have a variety or pragmatic functions. A signed version of, 'Are you cold?' might be an enquiry after the health of the addressee, or a polite request to turn on the heater or shut the window.
4. The roles of addresser and addressee can switch. This contrasts, for example, with the one-way communication provided by street lights.
5. Signers pay attention to their ASL output, and make corrections to their productions as they see fit.
6. At least part of ASL must be learned. Humans seem to have an innate capacity for language but, as with other languages, one must be exposed to and learn ASL before one can use it.
7. ASL can be used as a meta-language; i.e., one can have a discussion about ASL in ASL.

This section includes only a cursory recounting of evidence that ASL is a real language in its own right. Elsewhere in this volume, Emmorey (Chapter 8) provides a much more thorough treatment of this topic.

English-based visual communication systems

Manually Coded English

Within the USA, there is considerable variation in signing. In addition to the natural language of ASL, there are also several artificial systems of Manually

Coded Englishes, or MCEs. These systems, also called Signed Englishes, were devised by educators to make the morphosyntax of English visible. They draw heavily from ASL for their lexicon, and augment their vocabulary with initialized signs and signs invented for the systems. Initialized signs change the handshape of an existing ASL sign to be the shape of the fingerspelled letter representing the first letter of the English word. For example, the sign for 'daffodil' in MCEs is the ASL sign FLOWER made with a 'd' handshape. In MCEs, each English morpheme, or unit of meaning, has its own sign, and signs are made in English morpheme order.

Contact signing

In addition to using 'pure ASL' or 'pure MCEs', people can use a variety of contact signing. Contact signing most typically occurs between a deaf signer who is fluent in ASL and a hearing signer who knows an MCE or has learned ASL as a second language. It is not a consistent or conventionalized system, but rather changes from person to person and from utterance to utterance. Contact signing may vary with respect to how closely it follows ASL or Signed English morphosyntax, but typically it omits many of the morphosyntactic markers of both English and ASL. Contact signing has until recently been called Pidgin Signed English (PSE); however, the new term arose because of arguments that PSE is not a true pidgin (Bernstein *et al.* 1985; Bochner and Albertini 1988), and that it is actually composed of several different types of signing (Lucas and Valli 1989). ASL, PSEs, and MCEs have been described by early researchers (Stokoe 1969; Woodward 1973; Woodward and Markowicz 1980) as falling along a linguistic continuum. The precise relationship among these varieties of sign has since been argued to be more complex (e.g., Lucas and Valli 1992); however, this conceptualization is a useful first approximation.

Fingerspelling

Fingerspelling is a part of ASL in which each letter of the alphabet is represented by a sign. Words from spoken languages, including but not limited to English, can be represented in ASL via fingerspelling (Battison 1978; Johnson 1994). Other signed languages have their own systems of fingerspelling, although many such systems are closely related and share large portions of their alphabets.

Simultaneous communication

Simultaneous communication (simcom), called bimodal communication in some parts of the world, is the process whereby an individual presents an entire message by speaking and, simultaneously, by a visual means. The visual means used can be a variety of contact signing, an MCE, or fingerspelling; however, the term 'simultaneous communication' is usually used only when the visible mode is contact signing or an MCE. In theory, simcom could also be used with ASL, although in practice it is extremely difficult to articulate any but the simplest sentences in two different languages simultaneously. A more detailed discussion on the processing of simultaneous communication can be found in Chapter 10.

Cued speech

Cued speech is not signing at all, but is rather a system of handshapes and positions devised to make the sounds of a spoken language visible. This contrasts with MCEs, which are an attempt to make visible the morphosyntax of English. Eight handshapes and four locations near the mouth are used to represent consonants and vowels, respectively. A given handshape or location is used to represent between two and four distinct phones, which are chosen because their visible articulations are maximally distinct. For example, the phones [t], [m], and [f] share a single cue. See Cornett and Daisey (1992) for a more complete description of cued speech.

Conventions for writing signed languages

Several systems for writing sign languages have been developed, although none have been accepted as a standard. The earliest commonly used means of referring to signs in writing, and one that is still frequently used, is with glosses of their nearest spoken language counterparts. Such glosses are written entirely in capital letters. So, for example, the sign referring to a pet feline would be written as CAT. The ASL sentence meaning, 'Is this a cat?' might be transcribed as:

$$\overline{\text{q}}$$
THIS CAT

The interrogative is represented in ASL via a facial expression. The line over the words indicates the duration of the expression, and the 'q' indicates which expression is being used. Additional information about how a sign is inflected can be indicated with subscripts. For example, plus symbols (+) indicate that a sign is repeated; each repetition of a sign is indicated by a plus symbol. A fingerspelled word is represented by a gloss in which the letters are separated by dashes; e.g., C-A-T. Cokely and Baker (1981) give a more complete description of this system. A major drawback to this system is that it can give the uninitiated the impression that ASL is merely a 'broken' version of English, and does not enlighten the non-signer about what the signs so transcribed look like. However, the system still persists, probably due to its ease of use with standard fonts and the rapidity with which people familiar with the relevant spoken and signed languages can decode the gloss.

William Stokoe created the first writing system based on the phonology of a signed language. He employed his system in his aforementioned signed language dictionary. He created a small symbol set to represent the locations, handshapes, and movements of ASL, and imposed a lexicographical ordering on the symbols, thereby permitting dictionary users an easy way to look up signs based on the values of each of their parameters. Stokoe's system was a remarkable breakthrough; but it, too, has some drawbacks. It was designed to describe individual manual signs in citation form, and cannot be used to represent facial expressions or inflected signs. It also requires a higher learning curve than does either glossing or the next system to be discussed here, Sign Writing.

Sign Writing is a system which uses relatively iconic, picture-like symbols to represent the positions and movements of the hands, and the expressions used by the face. Unlike the other systems described here, Sign Writing was designed to be used by lay people in actual written communications, rather than merely as a means for linguists to represent small amounts of data. Although it has not yet been widely accepted, it is being used in a school for the deaf in Nicaragua, as well as in small pockets elsewhere in the world.

Other systems of sign transcription also exist. Among these are SignFont and HamNoSys. This introduction presents the reader a taste of the variety of orthographies available, as well as emphasizing the fact that there is no single widely-accepted standard means of transcribing signs.

Summary

This introduction was intended to provide basic information which will be presupposed in other chapters of this book. It discussed natural signed languages, artificial signed systems, contact signing, fingerspelling, and cued speech. The variety within and among signed languages was emphasized, and some of the transcription systems for signed languages were mentioned. The interested reader is referred to the references at the end of this chapter for further reading.

References

Battison, R. (1978). *Lexical borrowing in American Sign Language.* Linstok Press, Silver Spring, MD.

Bernstein, M., Maxwell, M., and Matthews, K. (1985). Bimodal or bilingual communication? *Sign Language Studies*, **47**, 127–40.

Bochner, J. and Albertini, J. (1988). Language varieties in the deaf population and their acquisition by children and adults. In *Language learning and deafness* (ed. M. Strong), pp. 3–48. Cambridge University Press.

Cokely, D. and Baker, C. (1981). *American Sign Language: A student text. Units 10–18.* T. J. Publishers, Silver Spring, MD.

Corina, D. and Sagey, E. (1989). Predictability in ASL handshapes and handshape sequences, with implications for features and feature geometry. Unpublished manuscript. Salk Institute, San Diego, CA.

Cornett, R. O. and Daisey, M. E. (1992). *The Cued Speech resource book for parents of deaf children*. The National Cued Speech Association, Raleigh, NC.

Johnson, R. (1994). The structure of fingerspelling American Sign Language. Videotaped lecture presented to Waubonsee Community College on April 8, 1994.

Klima, E. and Bellugi, U. (1979). *The signs of language*. Harvard University Press.

Liddell, S. and Johnson, R. (1989). American Sign Language: the phonological base. *Sign Language Studies*, **64**, 195–277.

Lucas, C. and Valli, C. (1989). Language contact in the American Deaf community. In *The sociolinguistics of the Deaf community* (ed. C. Lucas), pp. 11–40. Academic Press, San Diego, CA.

Perlmutter, D. (1993). Sonority and syllable structure in American Sign Language. In *Phonetics and phonology: Current issues in ASL phonology 3* (ed. G. Coulter), pp. 227–61. Academic Press, San Diego, CA.

Sandler, W. (1993). Linearization of phonological tiers in ASL. In *Phonetics and phonology: Current issues in ASL phonology 3* (ed. G. Coulter), pp. 103–29. Academic Press, San Diego, CA.

Stokoe, W. (1960). *Sign language structure. Studies in Linguistics*, occasional papers, Vol. 8. Department of Anthropology and Linguistics, University of Buffalo, Buffalo, N.Y.

Stokoe, W. (1969). Sign language diglossia. *Studies in Linguistics*, **21**, 27–41.

Stokoe, W., Casterline, D. C., and Croneberg, C. G.. (1965). *A dictionary of American Sign Language on linguistic principles*. Linstok Press, Silver Spring, MD.

Valli, C. and Lucas, C. (1992). *Linguistics of American Sign Language: a resource text for ASL users*. Gallaudet University Press, Washington, DC.

Woodward, J. (1973). Implication lects on the deaf diglossic continuum. Unpublished Ph.D. dissertation, Georgetown University.

Woodward, J. and Markowicz, H. (1980). Pidgin sign languages. In *Sign and culture* (ed. W. Stokoe), pp. 55–79. Linstok Press, Silver Spring, MD.

A

The neurobiology of human communication

CHAPTER 1

Neuropsychology of communicative movements

Pierre Feyereisen

Department of Experimental Psychology, University of Louvain

Introduction to the neuropsychology of communication systems

Broadly speaking, communication is the use of signals to influence other individuals and thus, it is dependent on a social context. Reaching, for instance, may be used as a request or as the preliminary phase of object handling. Similar actions can either be addressed to another person or be performed for various private purposes, and depending on the motor intention, several details of the realization may differ. This is the issue of task relevance. Moreover, several means such as gestures, words, or signs may be used to elicit some expected responses from communication partners or to change their states of mind. For instance, we can refer to an object by pointing to it with the hand or the chin, by naming it, or by performing a gesture that illustrates its shape or its function. This is the issue of equifinality. Various acts may convey the same core meaning and allow one to obtain the same result. However, their forms differ from each other and they are processed through specific devices. Spoken and signed languages, in particular, rely on a complex machinery which allows for the transformation of meanings into sounds or hand movements and vice versa. One of the goals of the cognitive sciences is to understand the mechanisms by which communicative acts are performed and perceived; more specifically, the goal is to identify which processes are unique and which are common to several equivalent acts or are shared by various tasks. In recent years, some controversies have arisen about the proper distinctions to be made among information processing systems. Are we right to oppose verbal and nonverbal gestures, emotional and referential signals, sentences and hierarchically organized actions? Neuropsychology is one way to address these questions empirically.

The main assumption underlying current neuropsychological research is that the brain is built from several specialized systems and subsystems. These components are sensible to particular classes of input and they are designed to produce a particular output in relation to motivational or central states. There is, for example, a complex system that controls eye saccadic movements in order to bring to the fovea of the retina a target detected in the visual field. Systems and sub-systems are defined by a set of connections with other parts of the brain (afferences and efferences); and thus, they cannot rapidly substitute for each other. Even if many cognitive functions are not precisely localized in 'centres' but depend on multiple spatially distributed structures, different regions play different roles through specific neural connections. This cerebral organization has been shaped by natural selection during phylogeny, and several hypotheses have been proposed about the progressive specialization of some cortical regions for language pro-cessing and manual skills. The kernel of the debate concerns the possible links between linguistic and motor competence. These human achievements may rely on quite separate bases or one may imagine that they derive from a common primitive ability, such as an increased precision in movement execution. More-over, the brain is not solely the product of species evolution. Experience during ontogeny (i.e. development of an individual) also intervenes in the elaboration of input-specific and output-specific devices. Regular patterns of cerebral activation result in structural changes, especially during the earliest years of life, so that some networks become selectively devoted to some aspects of the performance: guid-ance of action, socio-emotional communication, language use, etc. Because of this, it is unnecessary to specify in the genome all the information concerning cerebral functions, and some reorganizations are possible during the life span as con-sequences of practice. These evolutionary and developmental issues are frequently discussed in the journal *Behavioral and Brain Sciences*.

There are several means of analysing the components of human communication. These include developmental studies (because different systems or subsystems grow at different rates), experimental studies (because selected external variables have different effects on different processes), and the study of brain functioning. In recent years, the techniques of neuropsychology have evolved considerably and we can now disentangle cognitive processes in various ways. The most classic one is still to describe the selective consequences of brain damage (according to the principle of double dissociation: if task I is impaired in case A and preserved in case B and if an inverse pattern of results is observed for task II, then tasks I and II must rely on separate mechanisms). Several neuroimaging techniques are also available to show interactions between cerebral regional activity and specific operations. The aim of the present chapter is to review a part of that literature in order to identify different components of the human manual communication system.

In the first part, we shall focus on the control of action. Apparently simple move-ments, such as pointing to, holding, or showing how to manipulate an object, involve complex transformations of visual information into instructions for arm and hand muscles. Together with other neurophysiological data, the study of brain damaged patients shows that these movements can be disturbed in various ways. For instance, distinctions are made among the different cognitive spaces that intervene in interactions with the physical world. There is a personal space defined by egocentric bodily references, a reaching space in which objects are located at distance from the body, a larger extrapersonal space for walking, throwing, etc. Some patients cannot point to objects or to parts of another person's body despite being able to point normally to parts of their own body (Degos *et al.* 1997). Other patients show the reverse breakdown (Sirigu *et al.* 1991a). Thus, despite our experience of a homogeneous spatial environment, the brain has multiple task-dependent representations of space which may be selectively impaired by lesions (see, e.g., Stein 1991; Rizzolatti *et al.* 1994; Goodale 1996). The second part of this chapter will be devoted to the analysis of limb apraxia, a particular impairment in the control of action. This deficit mainly affects pantomime and imitation tasks, but actual use of objects may also be disturbed. Finally, in the third part, we shall discuss the relationships that may exist between these disorders of the action system and the disorders of language processing in cases of aphasia. In this review, for the sake of concision, only data on adult human behaviour will be considered; although in recent years, many interesting studies have investigated the brain mechanisms that control manual and vocal movements in monkeys. Priority will also be given to recent studies not previously reviewed (Feyereisen 1991).

Brain mechanisms underlying human manual activity

Human communication relies on visual and auditory signals that are produced by movements of various organs. Gesturing, signing, and speaking involve precise motor coordination of multiple parts forming the musculature of the hands, the face, and the vocal apparatus. Some investigators have suggested that the neural systems involved in the control of vocalization and manual activity are closely linked. Kimura (1993), for instance, claims that 'knowing something about the neural mechanisms controlling arm and hand movements may elucidate the characteristics of human communication systems in general' (p.4). She posits that some regions of the left cerebral hemisphere are specialized for motor selection and intervene both in the repetition of nonsensical syllables and in the imitation of meaningless hand movements. Likewise, Lieberman (1991, 1992) has suggested that the human syntactic ability evolved from the capacity to combine several nonverbal movements into complex sequences. However, similarities between the domains of action and language may be only superficial; to demonstrate the intervention of a general purpose control mechanism, one has to scrutinize the processes by which manipulation of tools, execution of gestures referring to objects in their absence, and speech production are made possible.

Pointing to, grasping, and handling objects

Two central ideas emerge from recent neuropsychological research on the control of action (Jeannerod 1994, 1997). First, limb movements are guided by some mental representations of movements before their execution. Spatiotemporal parameters are largely predefined during a planning phase and only partially corrected by local adaptations to the environment through feedback processing. People can also imagine gestures without performing them and it has been suggested that motor imagery and motor preparation are identical (for a review, see Decety 1996). Thus, purposive movements result from a series of complex transformations of the information that is available before a command is given to the effector organ. Second, multiple task-dependent representations have to be distinguished. Performing a representational gesture such as pretending to drink from a glass involves several processes. The hand is placed in a location that is defined in reference to bodily coordinates. It is shaped around an imaginary object. The speed and amplitude of its rotation are fixed in relation to the movement's goal. We know now that transporting, catching, and manipulating rely on separate cerebral mechanisms.

The representations of movements in the brain may be affected by lesions in different ways, as shown by a comparison of performance in different tasks. The control of hand direction in space has been extensively studied through simple pointing and reaching tasks in which subjects are requested to indicate positions or to take objects in front of them. In a syndrome called optic ataxia, these movements become very inaccurate, although the patients have no problem in visually identifying objects and in touching named parts of their own bodies. Conversely, some patients may have problems in visual object recognition (visual agnosia) without being impaired in visually guiding and positioning the hand, for instance when they are instructed to 'post' a card in slots that vary in orientation (Milner and Goodale 1995, Chapter 5). Thus, it is proposed that there are at least two visual cortical pathways, one for reaching (the dorsal action system, which involves specific structures of the parietal and frontal lobes) and one for recognizing objects (the ventral identification system, in the temporal lobe: see Fig. 1.1). This proposal is a refinement of a previous distinction made between structures concerned with the 'where' and the 'what' questions. Object grasping requires information not only about location, but also about shape, weight, solidity, etc. (the 'how' question). Some patients may have difficulties in using this visual knowledge to control personal movement but not in perceptual or verbal tasks. Furthermore, some dissociations are observed within the action system. For instance, A.F., a patient with optic ataxia, was able to orient her hand toward the object, but she did not grasp it normally. By contrast, with her eyes closed and when familiar objects previously shown were named, A.F. was able to indicate the size of the objects through the aperture of her thumb and index finger (Jeannerod *et al.* 1994). Conversely, in D.F., a case of visual form agnosia, actual grasping was intact, as was pantomime, i.e. a verbally driven movement, but the subject was severely disturbed when a delay of two seconds was imposed between the vision of the object and the grasping, or when the subject had to show with the thumb and the index finger the size of a visually presented object without grasping it (Goodale *et al.* 1994). In other cases, such as L.L., movement direction and simple reaching were normal, but the hand was not shaped according to object use; for

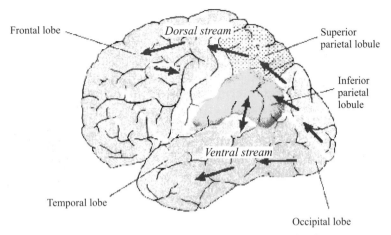

Frontal lobe

Dorsal stream

Superior
parietal lobule

Inferior
parietal
lobule

Ventral stream

Temporal lobe

Occipital lobe

Fig. 1.1 Lateral view of the left cerebral hemisphere with partial indications concerning the two visual pathways, the dorsal action system and the ventral identification system (redrawn from Jeannerod 1997, Milner and Goodale 1995, Stein 1991).

instance, the fingers were not correctly inserted into the rings of a pair of scissors (Sirigu *et al.* 1995). Less frequent are the cases in which actual use of objects is impaired but pantomime and naming are intact, as reported by Motomura and Yamadori (1994). Converging evidence for partially separate neural pathways involved in object recognition, pointing, and grasping tasks has been provided in normal human subjects through the technique of positron emission tomography (e.g. Grafton *et al.* 1996; Faillenot *et al.* 1997). Thus, various observations support the notion that different specific neural structures are devoted to the translation of visual information about object location, size, and shape into motor commands.

Gesture imitation and comprehension

Similar distinctions between systems for action and recognition have been made when the visual input is a hand movement instead of an object. Seeing a gesture to reproduce it and seeing it to understand it constitute two different tasks. Decety *et al.* (1997) have analysed regional cerebral activity in normal subjects observing movements under two conditions: subjects were instructed to memorize gestures either for further recognition or for further imitation. Two kinds of gestures were also compared: actions which the subjects would find meaningful (e.g., sewing on a button) and those which they would find meaningless (e.g., items of American Sign Language unfamiliar to them). Both the task and gesture factors had main effects on regional cerebral activity. Encoding for further imitation activated several sites of the dorsal action system (e.g., dorsolateral prefontal cortex or supplementary motor area), whereas encoding for further recognition activated a structure of the right temporal lobe (parahippocampal gyrus). Regardless of the task, presentation of meaningful gestures mainly influenced activity in regions of the left hemisphere and presentation of meaningless gestures, activity in regions of the right hemisphere. It is likely that when instructed to imitate, subjects mentally prepare the movements to be reproduced. The finding that the presentation of meaningful pantomimes activates structures which also intervene in visual semantic tasks is consistent with the results of other investigations, as is the finding that the presentation of meaningless gestures activates the right occipitoparietal areas.

These results suggest the possibility of double dissociations between gesture imitation and recognition in brain damaged patients. Selective impairments of imitation have been described and called conduction apraxia by analogy with the syndrome of conduction aphasia, in which patients are unable to repeat words they can understand (Ochipa *et al.* 1994). Goldenberg and Hagmann (1997) proposed the more neutral term of 'visuo-imitative apraxia' for the same disorder. Conversely, in the two cases of pantomime agnosia documented by Rothi *et al.* (1986), patients were able to reproduce the movements performed by the experimenter but could not discriminate between two visually presented gestures or match gestures to pictures of objects.

The systems for gesture imitation and recognition are not independent, however. First, one may assume that knowing the meaning of a gesture can facilitate its execution in an imitation task (indirect reproduction may be mediated by the semantic system). Accordingly, some patients were found to be impaired in the imitation of meaningless hand positions but not in pantomimes elicited by verbal commands or by instructions to imitate object use (Goldenberg and Hagmann 1997). Second, in a large sample of left-hemisphere damaged patients, an association was found between the presence of substitution errors in production and in recognition tasks (McDonald *et al.* 1994).

Subdivisions can also be made within the recognition system according to the nature of the material that is presented in matching and naming tasks: words, pictures, and gestures (I assume that naming objects and actions requires identification of the input). In matching tasks, subjects are given a target word or pantomime together with a series of pictures of objects. They have to point out the picture of the correct object from among the distractors. A critical aspect of the task is the similarity that may exist between the target picture and the foils. In word-to-picture matches, the most frequent errors are due to semantic similarity and concern the choice of a coordinate (a member of the same category, e.g., a trumpet when the word *piano* is presented). In gesture-to-picture matches, errors are mainly due to motor similarity. They occur when the actions performed with different objects resemble each other, such as piano playing and typewriting (Bell 1994). Thus, different factors influence performance in word and gesture processing. Dissociations between the comprehension of words and gestures were also found in cases of pantomime agnosia with preserved spoken word identification (Rothi *et al.* 1986). In some cases of visual object agnosia, knowledge about adequate manipulation of objects that were not recognized may be spared (Grailet *et al.* 1990; Sirigu *et al.* 1991b). Case W.A. was unable to recognize objects visually but performed much better in gesture recognition and imitation tasks (Schwartz *et al.* 1998). In naming tasks, some patients may suffer from selective impairments of the visual or the functional components of the semantic system. For instance, in C.N., a case of optic aphasia, the naming of visually presented static objects was significantly more disturbed than the naming of objects from pantomimes, and noun production was more affected than action verb production (Ferreira *et al.* 1997). Similar cases have been reported in the literature, as well as the inverse pattern of action naming being more severely impaired than object naming (for a review, see Gainotti *et al.* 1995).

Up to now in this section, we have considered that object and gesture recognition resulted from comparison of a visual input to some structural knowledge stored in long-term memory. So, it is assumed that some brain mechanisms are devoted to storing durable characteristics of perceived entities and events, outside the context of actual object use or gesture imitation. In cognitive neuropsychology, however, a further distinction is made between specialized stores for visual recognition and those for semantic memory. Thus, the perceptual or structural knowledge of objects and gestures is assumed to be separate from the more encyclopaedic associative knowledge. For instance, we can see that a toothbrush has a handle and this is a part of the semantic representation of that object. A quite different piece of information is that toothbrushing is generally more appropriate after than before a meal. Yet, some controversies arise about the content of the various memory systems. For instance, how does one answer probe questions such as 'Where do you find toothbrushes, in the kitchen or in the bathroom?' or 'How do you use a toothbrush?' Is it on the basis of actual or imagined visual information or from abstraction of that information in the semantic system? Many discussions about the existence of a unitary *vs.* multiple semantic systems as well as impaired access *vs.* degraded representations stem from that ambiguity. Cases of optic aphasia in which subjects cannot name visually presented objects but can pantomime their use have been interpreted in different ways. One hypothesis is that naming requires deeper semantic processing than do pantomime or actual object use, which can be performed on the basis of visual representations. Another hypothesis is that within a unitary semantic system, objects are characterized by several kinds of features (visual, functional, kinaesthetic, etc.) and that different sets of features are used in naming, matching, sorting, or miming tasks (e.g. Hillis and Caramazza 1995).

The idea that action is represented on multiple levels underlies several recent neuropsychological models of motor disorders. Distinctions are made among perceptual stores for gestures known by vision, more general knowledge of actions, and programmes for practiced movements. Furthermore, parallel access to some of these representations is assumed, allowing the system to bypass local impairments. In particular, actual object use might be spared in patients unable to imitate visually presented gestures. Thus, disorders of gesture production can take various forms, as described in the next section.

Varieties of limb apraxia

Description

Motor control relies on a complex machinery involving specialized cortical areas, basal ganglia, the thalamus, cerebellum, brain stem, and spinal cord. Motor impairments of various kinds may result from injuries to any of these structures. In neuropsychology, special interest is paid to impairments of voluntary action that cannot be explained by primary sensory or motor deficits. These disorders, which are called apraxias, most frequently result from lesions of the parietal or the frontal lobe of the left hemisphere. Assessment of apraxia usually includes three elicitation conditions: verbal command, imitation, and actual object use (Rothi *et al.* 1997b). Various gestures can be compared: meaningful *vs.* meaningless (e.g., 'applaud' *vs.* 'put the palm of the left hand on the right shoulder'), transitive *vs.* intransitive (i.e., involving objects or not; for example, pretending 'playing a guitar' *vs.* 'waving good-bye'), manual *vs.* facial movements (e.g. 'opening a door' *vs.* 'blowing out a candle'), etc. Quality of performance is often assessed on global scales, but there are also attempts to distinguish different error types (substitutions, incorrect spatial and temporal parameters, use of body parts as objects, etc.). Recent technological advances also allow investigators to measure with great precision the spatiotemporal properties of hand movements (Poizner and Soechting 1992; Poizner *et al.* 1995, 1998). More particularly, apraxic patients were found to be unable to specify the movement characteristics (plane, amplitude, speed, etc.) or to coordinate the movement of multiple limb segments.

As actual object use is generally less severely impaired than pantomime or imitation, apraxia has sometimes been considered an artefact of clinical assessment outside the natural context of action. This opinion has recently been criticized (Cubelli and Della Sala 1996; Schwartz and Buxbaum 1997). For instance, when observed during mealtime, apraxic patients were found to produce more action errors than control subjects (e.g., mis-selection or misuse of tools) and to organize the meal in a less ordered way (Foundas *et al.* 1995a). These errors cannot be fully explained by a weakness of the right limb. Kinematic analyses show that when the non-preferred left hand is used, apraxic subjects still differ from normal control subjects with regard to several spatiotemporal characteristics of the movements, regardless of whether tools and objects are present (Clark *et al.* 1994).

Apraxia may affect manual and facial movements, yet it is still unclear whether limb and oral (or buccofacial) apraxia result from the breakdown of a single control mechanism (Square-Storer *et al.* 1990). In a study of 15 patients suffering from left hemisphere damage, both facial and manual movements were impaired in eight cases and dissociations were found in six other cases; one subject had normal scores in the two tasks (Raade *et al.* 1991). This result suggests that facial and manual movements depend on separate systems, as one may expect, considering that some factors, such as use of visual feedback and organization of movements in external space, are solely relevant for limb praxis. However, in that study, only single movements were assessed. As Kimura (1993) assumes that 'the system responsible for controlling multiple oral and manual movements must lie outside the single-oral movement system' (p.74), her hypothesis cannot be ruled out from the findings of Raade *et al.* (1991).

Cognitive models

Since Liepmann in 1900 and 1905 (see Rothi and Heilman 1996), several investigators have attempted to identify various forms of apraxia through information processing models. The intuition of Liepmann was that motor impairments might result from breakdowns on different levels. Disruption of so-called 'movement formulae' on a central level affects the selection of the movement before its execution. These formulae are transformed into actual muscular activity through so-called 'innervatory patterns' which involve more anterior cerebral regions. Thus, brain lesions may affect the conception of the movement (ideational apraxia), its realization (motor apraxia), or the pathway from ideas to motor centres (ideomotor apraxia). Liepmann's conception is akin to the contemporary notions of motor planning and motor preparation. Recent models, like those of Roy and Hall (1992) or Rothi *et al.* (1997a), are more precise about these central representations of action and they distinguish among several kinds of knowledge (see Figs 1.2 and 1.3).

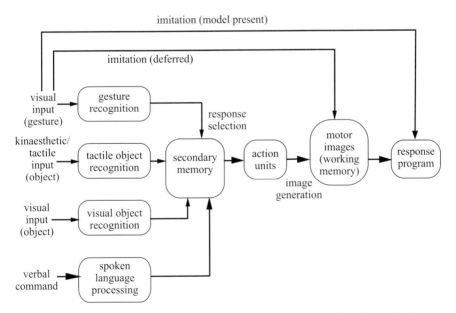

Fig. 1.2 An information processing model (redrawn from Roy and Hall 1992) showing parallel activation of motor programmes from visual models (imitation) and from instructions to pantomime (bold arrows).

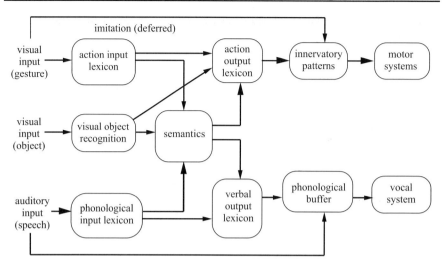

Fig. 1.3 An information processing model of gesture and spoken word production from input presented in different modalities (redrawn from Rothi *et al.* 1997a).

The model of Roy and Hall (1992) is mainly aimed at accounting for dissociations of performance in pantomime and imitation tasks (see also Roy and Square 1994). The first difference between these tasks is the modality of input. Pantomimes are elicited either by verbal command or by actual objects (e.g., 'show me how to use a hammer'), whereas imitation requires visual analysis of the information given by the examiner. Some specific impairments may be due to defective processing of input, such as in cases of auditory comprehension deficits. Furthermore, these tasks also require different memory processes. Pantomime involves the activation in semantic memory of knowledge of an object's function in order to select a particular response and to generate a mental image of its form. This selection stage is bypassed in imitation tasks in which the visual input may directly activate the motor programme in the production subsystem, and the response can be programmed with limited knowledge of object use. However, if imitation is delayed (i.e., if the model is absent during execution), the response has to be stored in a working memory subsystem. Thus, some apraxic subjects can imitate despite inadequate pantomime just as anomic patients can repeat words that they cannot find when presented with a picture. Conversely, in the case of impaired visual analysis of gestures, pantomime may be preserved and imitation defective. If the production subsystem is affected, the two tasks are disrupted but gesture recognition may remain intact. Working memory impairments will disrupt the delayed imitation of movement sequences but not the copying of them while they are being modelled. On the group level, performance inversely related to working memory demands. Delayed imitation was more impaired than reproduction of a motor sequence shown in photographs, and imitation of sequences was more impaired than imitation of single movements (Roy *et al.* 1993).

In a similar model, proposed by Rothi *et al.* (1997a), only isolated gestures are considered. Five layers are distinguished by analogy with the architecture of models previously developed in the domain of lexical processing (Fig. 1.3):

1. Visual or auditory input is analysed through primary sensory systems.

2. This information activates recognition units in modality-specific perceptual stores: phonological input lexicon, object recognition system, input action lexicon, etc.

3. In the semantic system, functional and encyclopaedic knowledge can be accessed from these various modalities.

4. Modality-specific output components are conceived: a phonological output lexicon and an action output lexicon.

5. Manual and speech movements are assembled within short-term stores.

Some of these steps can be bypassed. Direct connections are assumed between sensory analysis and short-term stores, in the auditory–oral and in the visual–manual modalities, respectively. These ways are used for repetition of meaningless syllables or imitation of meaningless movements. Repetition or imitation without comprehension is also possible through direct links between input and output lexicons. Finally, another direct connection is assumed between the object recognition system and the action output lexicon, allowing for activation of practiced motor schema without intervention of the semantic system.

A comparison of these models shows several similarities. Several kinds of input to the system are distinguished: verbal command, objects, and gestures. Multiple mental representations of gestures are assumed. Pantomime from spoken instruction requires semantic processing, whereas imitation can be performed without comprehension. The main difference between the two conceptions lies in the assumption of an input and an output action lexicon made by Rothi *et al.* (1997a) but not by Roy and Hall (1992). These components would be necessary to explain the better imitation of meaningful than of meaningless actions; but the evidence for this is inconclusive (e.g., Alexander *et al.* 1992; Schnider *et al.* 1997). Rothi *et al.* (1997a) also suppose that the output action lexicon can be directly activated by visual object recognition. However, this aspect of the model does not take into consideration the distinction made between two visual systems for recognition and action (see the preceding sections on 'Pointing to, grasping, and handling objects' and on 'Gesture imitation and comprehension'). Finally, the mechanism allowing for the imitation, without comprehension, of visually presented gestures can also be interpreted in a different way. The exploration of the so-called 'direct route' led Goldenberg (1995, 1996) to assume a mediation of visuomotor transformations by a general representation of the body schema. As a group, apraxic patients were found to be highly disturbed in a task in which they had to reproduce meaningless movement on a life-sized mannequin. Unexpectedly, the matching between visual input and output was not facilitated in that condition, resulting in similar performance to tasks in which the subjects cannot see their hands. Thus, it is concluded that impaired imitation was not solely due to difficulties in translating visuospatial coordinates of gestures into egocentric references, and that the route between visual analysis of gesture and motor execution was not as direct as previously assumed.

Notwithstanding these points of disagreement, the cognitive models are supported in other respects by several single-case studies (for a review, see *Neurocase* 1995). For instance, the patient G.W. showed severe impairments in the spatio-temporal organization of movements, but no problem in gesture comprehension, tool selection, or answering general questions about tool functions (Rapcsak *et al.* 1995). However, G.W. also failed in imagining actions in order to answer questions such as 'If you are using a handsaw, which joint moves more: shoulder or wrist?' (Ochipa *et al.* 1997). Thus, the conceptual system for action is assumed to be intact and dissociable from a production system underlying actual and imagined movement. Conversely, in cases of so-called 'conceptual apraxia', impairments are observed in tasks requiring minimal movement, such as matching a hammer and a nail (Ochipa *et al.* 1992). Investigators claiming that limb apraxia is a unitary syndrome and that dissociations are artefacts of severity effects (some tasks may be more difficult than others) have not assessed knowledge of action through conditions that do not require movement execution (e.g. Belanger *et al.* 1996).

Dissociation between conceptual knowledge and actual object use was also found in naturalistic action (Buxbaum *et al.* 1997). In D.M., a case of semantic dementia, performance was severely impaired in a range of verbal and nonverbal tasks assessing the representation of tool meaning: object naming, answering a question such as 'Are scissors used on cloth or stone?', or deciding whether a drill is to be associated with a screw or a nail. However, D.M. was able to pantomime the use of objects and he had no problem functioning in daily life. In contrast, the semantic memory of patient H.B. was intact but the organization of action was severely disturbed in tasks requiring multiple actions, such as preparing toast or a cup of instant coffee. These observations suggest that semantic memory is neither sufficient nor necessary for object use in daily life routines, which are thus performed through a 'nonsemantic route'. This proposal is akin to a previous distinction made between 'knowing that' and 'knowing how', or between a declarative and a procedural memory.

To sum up, studies on the breakdown of action contribute to cognitive neuropsychologists' attempt to isolate the different components of complex processes such as object recognition, tool use, or sentence production. Previously unitary syndromes fractionate into more specific impairments. General terms such as 'limb apraxia' or 'agrammatism' are used, at best, as abbreviated labels for large classes of various disorders in the domain of action control and sentence processing, respectively. In this context, can we conceive the existence of a single control mechanism for speech and gestures?

Speech and gestures

Speech and communicative gestures are both impaired by left-hemisphere lesions, and controversies have arisen about the possible common bases of these disorders. These discussions rely on different arguments depending on the kind of gestures considered. In the preceding sections of this chapter, we have mainly considered the actual use of objects (reaching, handling) or reference to concrete objects (pointing, pantomime). Because of the emancipation of social communicative gestures from physical action, another class of gestures must also be considered: speech-related gestures. These two categories of communicative movements and their relationships to aphasias deserve separate treatments.

Aphasias and apraxias

The issue of the relationships between disorders of language and autonomous gestures can be addressed in different ways, on the group or the individual level.

In group studies, subjects sampled on the basis of a broad criterion (e.g., left vs. right hemisphere lesions) are submitted to a battery of tests assessing complex functions: language, pantomime recognition, pantomime production, etc. Significant correlations are found among these tests. Statistical techniques such as multiple regression analysis and structural equation modelling allow the investigators to evaluate the proportion of variance in performance that is explained by the intervention of a general factor (Wang and Goodglass 1992; Duffy *et al.* 1994).Yet several interpretation problems remain in the identification of this general factor. First, as both meaningful and meaningless oral and manual movements are impaired in cases of left-hemisphere lesions, Kimura (1993) argued that the problem was not in symbol processing but in the selection of movements. Such an explanation, however, cannot account for the significant associations between gesture imitation and comprehension. The inclusion of auditory and visual comprehension tasks in the study of Wang and Goodglass (1992) led the investigators to call the general factor 'symbolic'. Second, there is a long tradition in aphasiology of distinguishing between lower-level impairments in performing speech gestures (a disorder called apraxia of speech, phonetic disintegration, or anarthria) and higher-level impairments in assembling the phonological word forms. Kinematic and acoustic analyses show qualitative differences in the speech movements of apraxic and aphasic patients (McNeil and Kent 1990; Seddoh *et al.* 1996). Likewise, a distinction is generally made between an impaired ability to assemble a phonological structure in both naming and repetition tasks, and impaired lexical access with spared repetition. More generally, the idea that performance in name and sentence production can be disturbed on different levels is not clearly incorporated in unitary models of aphasia and apraxia which do not consider the varieties of aphasic disorders (for a comprehensive treatment of that complex issue, see Caplan 1992). Third, as associations between impairments of language and praxis may be due to the contiguity of brain regions subserving specific processes, rather than to the intervention of a unitary mechanism, the general factor could simply be the size of the lesion. Finally, even if there is a significant correlation between aphasia and apraxia, some very severe aphasic patients do not suffer from apraxia and the inverse pattern of apraxia without aphasia has also been identified. Among the ten apraxic non-aphasic subjects of the series of patients examined by Papagno *et al.* (1993), seven had a lesion localized in subcortical structures only. It is thus suggested that dissociations can be explained by the anatomical substrates of speech and gesture processing.

In single-case studies, attention is focused on these exceptions. The general assumption is that even a small number of dissociations is sufficient to rule out the hypothesis of a unitary mechanism underlying language and praxis. Admittedly, single-case studies have to face the general methodological problem of controlling for artefacts of task demands. Cases of aphasia without apraxia are much more frequent in clinical populations than the reverse, and aphasic–apraxic patients can still be trained to use communicative gestures when speech therapy has failed (Coelho and Duffy 1990; Cubelli *et al.* 1991). This might indicate that gesture processing is less difficult than speech processing or that its representation in the brain is more diffuse, with a larger contribution of the right hemisphere (Rapcsak *et al.* 1993). Thus, it is necessary to demonstrate double dissociations with the same tasks used with different patients. Unfortunately, neuropsychological instruments are generally created for specific purposes and they lack standardization. We have many careful descriptions of aphasia and apraxia but almost no single-case studies in which both praxis and language are assessed in detail. Nonetheless, available information suggests that gesture production or comprehension may be selectively disturbed in the absence of aphasia (e.g., Rapcsak *et al.* 1995; Rothi *et al.* 1986). In this context, it is also interesting to find cases of selective impairments within the same manual modality (see Chapter 2). For instance W.L., a case studied by Corina *et al.* (1992), suffered from aphasia in American Sign Language as a consequence of a large frontotemporoparietal lesion in the left hemisphere. Sign production was impaired in naming and repetition tasks, as was sign comprehension in matching tasks and in response to commands. However, in conversations and confrontation naming tasks, the patient frequently used spontaneous pantomimes instead of well-formed signs. In formal assessment of gesture processing, pantomime production and comprehension were significantly better preserved than sign production and comprehension. Furthermore, the imitation of sequences of meaningless movements, which according to Kimura (1993) is generally more sensitive to apraxia than pantomime, was within normal range. This dissociation does not favour the hypothesis of a unitary mechanism for linguistic and nonlinguistic gestures, even if the reverse dissociation, limb apraxia without sign language aphasia, would be still more prejudicial to the conception of signing disorders as a consequence of apraxia.

Speech-related gestures

According to McNeill (1992, p.342), it is crucial to distinguish gesticulation that accompanies speech from autonomous communicative gestures impaired in cases of limb apraxia. Aphasia and apraxia may dissociate, whereas in cases of aphasia, coverbal gestures and speech would be impaired in parallel. Unfortunately, we have almost no information about the spontaneous gesticulation of apraxic subjects during conversations with which to demonstrate a double dissociation (but see Borod *et al.* 1989; Foundas *et al.* 1995b). With regard to the change of gesticulation in cases of aphasia, various views have been expressed. Investigators differ from each other both in their way of defining aphasia subtypes and in their conceptions of the relationships between gestures and speech.

McNeill (1992; see also McNeill *et al.* 1990) relies on a classic but now controversial distinction made between anterior (nonfluent) and posterior (fluent) aphasia. The speech of anterior aphasics is typically effortful, grammatical words are lacking, and information is conveyed in a telegraphic style. The posterior aphasics considered in McNeill's group produced a kind of jargon, using non-words or sentences devoid of coherence. Subjects were observed while retelling a cartoon story. This allowed the experimenter to guess the meaning of the gestures independently of the quality of the speech. On the basis of gesture form and meaning, a distinction is made between simple punctuating movements lacking content, called 'beats', and imagistic movements including several changes of direction, called 'iconic gestures'. Significant differences were found between the two subgroups of aphasics in their use of these two kinds of gesture. Anterior aphasics had gestures of greater amplitude than those of normal control subjects and their iconic to beat ratio was also superior. The gestures of posterior aphasics were more similar to those of normal subjects, with a large number of beat gestures. In both subgroups, gestures were used to compensate for speech production difficulties. Anterior aphasics performed iconic gestures to express in a holistic way the mental images they could not represent in sentences. In posterior aphasics, too many verbal forms were competing for output and contact with imagery was loosened, but beat gestures were performed for various discourse functions.

There are some problems with such a conception. First, on a theoretical level, it is difficult to reconcile the idea that aphasic patients can use gestures to compensate for language impairments with the notion of a unitary system underlying speech and gestures. Similarly, distinction among various forms of aphasia implies that language processing involves several components that may be selectively impaired. If agrammatism is defined as a loss of function words, it cannot have an analogue in coverbal gesticulation, which does not contain grammatical morphemes (one of the major differences between gesticulation and sign languages concerns the morphosyntactic features: see Goldin-Meadow *et al.* 1996). In fact, there are more than two kinds of aphasia and it is not easy to relate the distinction made between fluent and nonfluent aphasics to current models of speech production (Feyereisen *et al.* 1991). Second, on an empirical level, no clear relation between the use of content words and the production of iconic gestures was found when more heterogeneous samples of aphasic patients were considered with various kinds of fluent and nonfluent subjects (e.g., Lott and Goodglass 1996; for a review of previous studies, see Feyereisen and de Lannoy 1991, Chapter 6). Inconsistencies of results concerning the iconic to beat ratio may also result from variance in discourse production conditions (picture description, story recall, and conversation).

Hadar and co-workers compare gesture production in three groups of patients (Hadar and Yadlin-Gedassy 1994; Hadar *et al.* 1998b). Conceptual, semantic, and phonological aphasic patients are distinguished on the basis of an information processing model in which word production results from the completion of successive stages: the activation of defining features of the referent in a preverbal representation of the message, the selection of a unit in a semantic lexicon, and the generation of the word form in a phonological lexicon (Hadar and Butterworth 1997). All patients had defective naming scores but, in addition, conceptual aphasics were impaired in picture semantic processing tasks whereas phonological aphasics were impaired in repetition tasks. In these studies, attention was focused on so-called 'ideational gestures' (i.e., movements with more than one change of direction), and subsequently classed into four categories: iconic, deictic, conventional, and indefinite. The proportion of iconic gestures was found to be lower and that of indefinite gestures was found to be higher in aphasics suffering from conceptual impairments than in the two other subgroups. The rate of ideational gesture production was also higher in these two subgroups than in control subjects. These results are compatible with the conception of a prelinguistic origin of ideational gestures, during the stage of message construction. Impairment at this level affects the production of words and gestures, whereas impairments at later stages allow the subjects to compensate for word finding difficulties by increased production of iconic gestures. Less convincing is the claim made by Hadar and co-workers that the production of iconic gestures may directly facilitate lexical access. An increased rate of ideational gestures in some aphasics as compared with control subjects can be explained by the influence of the message level on the gesture production system or by a release from the competition with the speech production system (Feyereisen 1997).

Further evidence for the relative autonomy of gesture and speech production was found in studies on normal and pathological ageing. A comparison of the performance of younger (ages 18–24) and older (ages 62–80) female subjects describing three-dimensional objects showed an age-related decline in the use of representational gestures. The groups did not differ in the use of non-representational gesture nor in the quality of verbal descriptions as assessed by external judges (Cohen and Borsoi 1996). Further studies are needed to examine the cognitive correlates of this change in gesture quality, in particular with regards to the capacity to generate mental images. In the longitudinal study of a case of progressive aphasia by Béland and Ska (1992), the patient was requested to describe complex activities such as preparing a sandwich. Pictures of tools and objects were presented in order to alleviate memory demands. From the onset of the observations, the frequency of nouns and verbs decreased, as did the number of descriptive gestures, which were replaced by an increasing number of pointing gestures. Qualitative changes also occurred in the relations of gestures to speech content. At the beginning of the illness, the majority of descriptive gestures accompanied meaningful discourse. Progressively, they were performed along with stereotyped utterances, onomatopoeias, or in silence. Partial compensation for speech impairments was thus possible, but pointing gestures were used to replace nouns more often than pantomimes were used as substitutes for verbs.

The seminal work of McNeill (1992) suggested a contribution of visuospatial cognition to the production of gestures. Gestural communication relies on several uses of space. McNeill and Pedelty (1995) made distinctions among a concrete (or physical) space in which the iconic gestures take place, a referential space (performance of the same movement in the same location in order to represent anaphorically some referent), and a structural space showing the organization of the discourse (as in the expression 'on the one hand, on the other hand'). In that context, renewed attention was given to the effects of right-hemisphere damage on the production of gestures during discourse. As a group, the gestures of patients suffering from right-hemisphere lesions were not found to be different from those of normal subjects (Blonder *et al.* 1995). However, we do not know the proportion of these patients in which visuospatial processing, emotional expression, prosody, or discourse comprehension was impaired. A more fruitful research strategy was used by Hadar *et al.* (1998a) who selected four subjects suffering from left-limb paralysis. In a mental rotation task, this group had a mean score significantly inferior to that of matched control subjects. Gestures were recorded during the description of complex pictures. The rate of production of ideational gestures tended to be lower in right-hemisphere patients than in control subjects; but more significantly, they performed iconic gestures in a lower proportion and deictic gestures in a higher proportion. To my knowledge, this study was the first one to support empirically the hypothesis that visual imagery contributes to the production of iconic gestures.

Conclusions

The aim of the present chapter was to introduce the reader to the variety of disorders in language and gesture processing that may result from brain damage. Some data on brain imaging in normal subjects were also considered. Due to space limitations, the abundant literature on the cerebral bases of linguistic functions was not analysed in detail. The focus was limited to a discussion of the hypothesis of common mechanisms for the control of speech and manual movements. In short, current neuropsychological investigations do not support the notion of a single system for linguistic communication and manual activity. First, I have presented studies on control of action showing that manual activity depends on several specialized subsystems for the visual guidance of pointing, reaching, and manipulating movements. This 'dorsal' system is separate from a 'ventral' system used in object and gesture recognition. Thus, the production of a gesture involves multiple representations of its location in space, its shape, and its function, rather than a single visuomotor image. Second, movements performed from memory and movements performed from vision were found to rely on different mechanisms. This idea underlies most cognitive models of limb apraxia, which assume separate components for input and output processing of gestures. This fractionation of neurological syndromes into more specific impairments occurred in parallel in the domains of language and action. It does not favour the hypothesis of a common cerebral basis for speech and gestures, although a breakdown of a particular function, the generation of mental images of motor action for instance, may affect verbal and nonverbal tasks in similar ways.

The present review has not covered the whole domain of the neuropsychology of communicative movements, and several issues were neglected. Among other social functions, I have not considered the use of gaze for referential purpose. In fact, very few studies have analysed the cerebral mechanisms underlying this behaviour, except in the context of infantile autism (Baron-Cohen and Ring 1994; Leekam *et al.* 1997). The use of facial movements in the communication of actual or simulated emotional states was not discussed either. The right hemisphere probably plays a greater role in this area than in manual communication (see, e.g., Blonder *et al.* 1993, 1995). However, very little information has been gathered on the influence of affective meaning on the control of hand and face movement, on the relationship between oral and limb apraxia when emotional gestures have to be performed on request, or on the distinctive characteristics of spontaneous and posed displays (for reviews, see Borod 1993; Gainotti *et al.* 1993; Matsumoto and Lee 1993; Borod *et al.* 1997). Finally, studies on developmental disorders of action were also disregarded (Dewey 1995). Nonetheless, I hope that the framework used to study manual expression can stimulate research on other forms of communication, as it was stimulated by previous research on lexical and visual processes. Cognitive neuropsychology has the ambition of discovering the architecture of each of the several information processing systems that are implemented in the brain.

References

Alexander, M. P., Baker, E., Naesser, M. A., Kaplan, E., and Palumbo, C. (1992). Neuropsychological and neuroanatomical dimensions of ideomotor apraxia. *Brain*, **115**, 87–107.

Baron-Cohen, S. and Ring, H. (1994). A model of the mindreading system: neuropsychological and neurobiological perspectives. In *Children's early understanding of mind: origins and development* (ed. C. Lewis and P. Mitchell), pp. 183–207. Lawrence Erlbaum, Hove.

Béland, R. and Ska, B. (1992). Interaction between verbal and gestural language in progressive aphasia: a longitudinal case study. *Brain and Language*, **43**, 355–85.

Belanger, S. A., Duffy, R. J., and Coelho, C. A. (1996). The assessment of limb apraxia: an investigation of task effects and their cause. *Brain and Cognition*, **32**, 384–404.

Bell, B. D. (1994). Pantomime recognition impairment in aphasia: an analysis of error types. *Brain and Language*, **47**, 269–78.

Blonder, L. X., Burns, A. F., Bowers, D., Moore, R. W., and Heilman, K. M. (1993). Right hemisphere facial expressivity during natural conversation. *Brain and Cognition*, **21**, 44–56.

Blonder, L. X., Burns, A. F., Bowers, D., Moore, R. W., and Heilman, K. M. (1995). Spontaneous gestures following right hemisphere infarct. *Neuropsychologia*, **33**, 203–13.

Borod, J. C. (1993). Cerebral mechanisms underlying facial, prosodic, and lexical emotional expression: a review of neuropsychological studies and methodological issues. *Neuropsychology*, **7**, 445–63.

Borod, J. C., Fitzpatrick, P. M., Helm-Estabrooks, N., and Goodglass, H. (1989). The relationship between limb apraxia and the spontaneous use of communicative gesture in aphasia. *Brain and Cognition*, **10**, 121–31.

Borod, J. C., Haywood, C. S., and Koff, E. (1997). Neuropsychological aspects of facial asymmetry during emotional expression: a review of the normal adult literature. *Neuropsychology Review*, **7**, 41–60.

Buxbaum, L. J., Schwartz, M. F., and Carew, T. G. (1997). The role of semantic memory in object use. *Cognitive Neuropsychology*, **14**, 219–54.

Caplan, D. (1992). *Language: structure, processing, and disorders*. MIT Press, Cambridge MA.

Clark, M. A., Merians, A. S., Kothari, A., Poizner, H., Macauley, B., Rothi, L. J. G., and Heilman, K. M. (1994). Spatial planning deficits in limb apraxia. *Brain*, **117**, 1093–106.

Coelho, C. A. and Duffy, R. J. (1990). Sign acquisition in two aphasic subjects with limb apraxia. *Aphasiology*, **4**, 1–8.

Cohen, R. L. and Borsoi, D. (1996). The role of gestures in description-communication: a cross-sectional study of aging. *Journal of Nonverbal Behavior*, **20**, 45–63.

Corina, D. P., Poizner, H., Bellugi, U., Feinberg, T., Dowd, D., and O'Grady-Batch, L. (1992). Dissociation between linguistic and nonlinguistic gestural systems: a case for compositionality. *Brain and Language*, **43**, 414–47.

Cubelli, R. and Della Sala, S. (1996). The legacy of automatic/voluntary dissociation in apraxia. *Neurocase*, **2**, 449–54.

Cubelli, R., Trentini, P., and Montagna, C. G. (1991). Reeducation of gestural communication in a case of chronic global aphasia and limb apraxia. *Cognitive Neuropsychology*, **8**, 369–80.

Decety, J. (1996). Do imagined and executed actions share the same neural substrate? *Cognitive Brain Research*, **3**, 87–93.

Decety, J., Grèzes, J., Costes, N., Perani, D., Jeannerod, M., Procyk, E., Grassi, F., and Fazio, F. (1997). Brain activity during observation of actions: influence of action content and subject's strategy. *Brain*, **120**, 1763–77.

Degos, J. D., Bachoud-Levi, A. C., Ergis, A. M., Petrissans, J. L., and Cesaro, P. (1997). Selective inability to point to extrapersonal targets after left posterior parietal lesions: an objectivization disorder? *Neurocase*, **3**, 31–39.

Dewey, D. (1995). What is developmental dyspraxia? *Brain and Cognition*, **29**, 254–74.

Duffy, R. J., Watt, J. H., and Duffy, J. R. (1994). Testing causal theories of pantomimic deficits in aphasia using path analysis. *Aphasiology*, **8**, 361–79.

Faillenot, I., Toni, I., Decety, J., Grégoire, M.-C., and Jeannerod, M. (1997). Visual pathways for object-oriented action and object recognition: functional anatomy with PET. *Cerebral Cortex*, **7**, 77–85.

Ferreira, C. T., Giusiano, B., Ceccaldi, M., and Poncet, M. (1997). Optic aphasia: evidence of the contribution of different neural systems to object and action naming. *Cortex*, **33**, 499–513.

Feyereisen, P. (1991). Brain pathology, lateralization, and non verbal behavior. In *Fundamentals of nonverbal behavior* (ed. R. S. Feldman and B. Rimé), pp. 31–70. Cambridge University Press.

Feyereisen, P. (1997). The competition between gesture and speech production in dual-task paradigms. *Journal of Memory and Language*, **36**, 13–33.

Feyereisen, P. and de Lannoy, J.-D. (1991). *Gestures and speech: psychological investigations*. Cambridge University Press.

Feyereisen, P., Pillon, A., and de Partz, M.-P. (1991). On the measures of fluency in the assessment of spontaneous speech production by aphasic subjects. *Aphasiology*, **5**, 1–21.

Foundas, A. L., Macauley, B. L., Raymer, A. M., Maher, L. M., Heilman, K. M., and Rothi, L. J. G. (1995a). Ecological implications of limb apraxia: evidence from mealtime behavior. *Journal of the International Neuropsychological Society*, **1**, 62–6.

Foundas, A. L., Macauley, B. L., Raymer, A. M., Maher, L. M., Heilman, K. M., and Rothi, L. J. G. (1995b). Gesture laterality in aphasic and apraxic stroke patients. *Brain and Cognition*, **29**, 204–13.

Gainotti, G., Caltagirone, C. and Zoccolotti, P. (1993). Left/right and cortical/subcortical dichotomies in the neuropsychological study of human emotions. *Cognition and Emotion*, **7**, 71–93.

Gainotti, G., Silveri, M. C., Daniele, A., and Giustolisi, L. (1995). Neuroanatomical correlates of category-specific semantic disorders: a critical survey. *Memory*, **3**, 247–64.

Goldenberg, G. (1995). Imitating gestures and manipulating a mannikin—the representation of the human body in ideomotor apraxia. *Neuropsychologia*, **33**, 63–72.

Goldenberg, G. (1996). Defective imitation of gestures in patients with damage in the left or right hemispheres. *Journal of Neurology, Neurosurgery, and Psychiatry*, **61**, 176–80.

Goldenberg, G. and Hagmann, S. (1997). The meaning of meaningless gestures: a study of visuo-imitative apraxia. *Neuropsychologia*, **35**, 333–41.

Goldin-Meadow, S., McNeill, D., and Singleton, J. (1996). Silence is liberating: removing the handcuffs on grammatical expression in the manual modality. *Psychological Review*, **103**, 34–55.

Goodale, M. A. (1996). One visual experience, many visual systems. In *Attention and performance*, Vol. XVI: *Information integration in perception and communication* (ed. T. Inui and J. L. McClelland), pp. 369–93. MIT Press, Cambridge, MA.

Goodale, M. A., Jakobson, L. S., and Keillor, J. M. (1994). Differences in the visual control of pantomimed and natural grasping movements. *Neuropsychologia*, **32**, 1159–78.

Grafton, S. T., Arbib, M. A., Fadiga, L., and Rizzolatti, G. (1996). Localization of grasp representations in humans by positron emission tomography 2. Observation compared with imagination. *Experimental Brain Research*, **112**, 103–11.

Grailet, J.-M., Seron, X., Bruyer, R., Coyette, F., and Frederix, M. (1990). Case report of a visual integrative agnosia. *Cognitive Neuropsychology*, **7**, 275–309.

Hadar, U. and Butterworth, B. (1997). Iconic gestures, imagery, and word retrieval in speech. *Semiotica*, **115**, 147–72.

Hadar, U. and Yadlin-Gedassy, S. (1994). Conceptual and lexical aspects of gesture: evidence from aphasia. *Journal of Neurolinguistics*, **8**, 57–65.

Hadar, U., Burstein, A., Krauss, R., and Soroker, A. (1998a). Ideational gestures and speech in brain-damaged subjects. *Language and Cognitive Processes*, **13**, 59–76.

Hadar, U., Wenkert-Olenik, D., Krauss, R., and Soroker, N. (1998b). Gesture and the processing of speech: neuropsychological evidence. *Brain and Language*, **62**, 107–26.

Hillis, A. E. and Caramazza, A. (1995). Cognitive and neural mechanisms underlying visual and semantic processing: implications from 'optic aphasia'. *Journal of Cognitive Neuroscience*, 7, 457–78.

Jeannerod, M. (1994). The representing brain: neural correlates of motor intention. *Behavioral and Brain Sciences*, 17, 187–245.

Jeannerod, M. (1997). *The cognitive neuroscience of action*. Blackwell, Oxford.

Jeannerod, M., Decety, J., and Michel, F. (1994). Impairment of grasping movements following a bilateral posterior parietal lesion. *Neuropsychologia*, 32, 369–80.

Kimura, D. (1993). *Neuromotor mechanisms in human communication*. Oxford University Press, New York.

Leekam, S., Baron-Cohen, S., Perrett, D., Milders, M., and Brown, S. (1997). Eye-direction detection: a dissociation between geometric and joint attention skills in autism. *British Journal of Developmental Psychology*, 15, 77–95.

Lieberman, P. (1991). Speech and brain evolution. *Behavioral and Brain Sciences*, 14, 566–8.

Lieberman, P. (1992). Could an autonomous syntax module have evolved? *Brain and Language*, 43, 768–74.

Lott, P. and Goodglass, H. (1996). Gestural behavior of aphasic patients. *Brain and Language*, 55, 185–7.

Matsumoto, D. and Lee, M. (1993). Consciousness, volition, and the neuropsychology of facial expressions of emotion. *Consciousness and Cognition*, 2, 237–54.

McDonald, S., Tate, R. L., and Rigby, J. (1994). Error types in ideomotor apraxia: a qualitative analysis. *Brain and Cognition*, 25, 250–70.

McNeil, M. R. and Kent, R. D. (1990). Motoric characteristics of adult aphasic and apraxic speakers. In *Advances in Psychology*, Vol. 70: *The cerebral control of speech and limb movements* (ed. G. R. Hammond), pp. 349–86. North-Holland, Amsterdam.

McNeill, D. (1992). *Hand and mind: what gestures reveal about thought*. University of Chicago Press.

McNeill, D. and Pedelty, L.L. (1995). Right brain and gesture. In *Language, gesture, and space* (ed. K. Emmorey and J. Reilly), pp. 63–85. Lawrence Erlbaum, Hillsdale, NJ.

McNeill, D., Levy, E. T., and Pedelty, L. L. (1990). Speech and gesture. In *Advances in Psychology*, Vol. 70: *The cerebral control of speech and limb movements* (ed. G. R. Hammond), pp. 203–56. North-Holland, Amsterdam.

Milner, A. D. and Goodale, M. A. (1995). *The visual brain in action*. Oxford University Press, New York.

Motomura, N. and Yamadori, A. (1994). A case of ideational apraxia with impairment of object use and preservation of object pantomime. *Cortex*, 30, 167–70.

Neurocase (1995). Cognitive studies of apraxia. *Neurocase*, 1, 19–24.

Ochipa, C., Rothi, L. J. G., and Heilman, K. M. (1992). Conceptual apraxia in Alzheimer's disease. *Brain*, 115, 1061–71.

Ochipa, C., Rothi, L. J. G., and Heilman, K. M. (1994). Conduction apraxia. *Journal of Neurology, Neurosurgery, and Psychiatry*, 57, 1241–4.

Ochipa, C., Rapcsak, S. Z., Maher, L. M., Rothi, L. J. G., Bowers, D., and Heilman, K. M. (1997). Selective deficit of praxis imagery in ideomotor apraxia. *Neurology*, 49, 474–80.

Papagno, C., Della Sala, S., and Basso, A. (1993). Ideomotor apraxia without aphasia and aphasia without apraxia: the anatomical support for a double dissociation. *Journal of Neurology, Neurosurgery, and Psychiatry*, 56, 286–9.

Poizner, H. and Soechting, J. F. (1992). New strategies for studying higher level motor disorders. In *Cognitive neuropsychology in clinical practice* (ed. D. Margolin), pp. 435–64. Oxford University Press, New York.

Poizner, H., Clark, M. A., Merians, A. S., Macauley, B., Rothi, L. J. G., and Heilman, K. M. (1995). Joint coordination deficits in limb apraxia. *Brain*, **118**, 227–42.

Poizner, H., Clark, M. A., Merians, A. S., Macauley, B., Rothi, L. J. G., and Heilman, K. M. (1998). Left hemispheric specialization for learned, skilled, and purposeful action. *Neuropsychology*, **12**, 163–82.

Raade, A. S., Rothi, L. J. G., and Heilman, K. M. (1991). The relationship between buccolingual and limb apraxia. *Brain and Cognition*, **16**, 130–46.

Rapcsak, S. Z., Ochipa, C., Beeson, P. M., and Rubens, A.B. (1993). Praxis and the right hemisphere. *Brain and Cognition*, **23**, 181–202.

Rapcsak, S. Z., Ochipa, C., Anderson, K. C., and Poizner, H. (1995). Progressive ideomotor apraxia: evidence for a selective impairment of the action production system. *Brain and Cognition*, **27**, 213–36.

Rizzolatti, G., Riggio, L., and Sheliga, B. M. (1994). Space and selective attention. In *Attention and performance*, Vol. XV: *Conscious and nonconscious information processing* (ed. C. Umiltà and M. Moscovitch), pp. 231–65. MIT Press, Cambridge, MA.

Rothi, L. J. G. and Heilman, K. M. (1996). Liepmann (1900 and 1905): a definition of apraxia and a model of praxis. In *Classic cases in neuropsychology* (ed. C. Code, C. W. Wallesch, Y. Joanette, and A.R. Lecours), pp. 111–22. Psychology Press, Hove.

Rothi, L. J. G., Mack, L., and Heilman, K. M. (1986). Pantomime agnosia. *Journal of Neurology, Neurosurgergy, and Psychiatry*, **49**, 451–4.

Rothi, L. J. G., Ochipa, C., and Heilman, K. M. (1997a). A cognitive neuropsychological model of limb praxis and apraxia. In *Apraxia: the neuropsychology of action* (ed. L. J. G. Rothi and K. M. Heilman), pp. 29–49. Psychology Press, Hove.

Rothi, L. J. G., Raymer, A. M., and Heilman, K. M. (1997b). Limb praxis assessment. In *Apraxia: the neuropsychology of action* (ed. L. J. G. Rothi and K. M. Heilman), pp. 61–73. Psychology Press, Hove.

Roy, E. A. and Hall, C. (1992). Limb apraxia: a process approach. In *Advances in Psychology*, Vol. 85: *Vision and motor control* (ed. L. Proteau and D. Elliott), pp. 261–82. North-Holland, Amsterdam.

Roy, E. A. and Square, P. A. (1994). Neuropsychology of movement sequencing disorders and apraxia. In *Neuropsychology* (ed. D. W. Zaidel), pp. 183–218. Academic Press, San Diego, CA.

Roy, E. A., Brown, L., Winchester, T., Square, P., Hall, C., and Black, S. (1993). Memory processes and gestural performance in apraxia. *Applied Physical Activity Quarterly*, **10**, 293–311.

Schnider, A., Hanlon, R. E., Alexander, D. N., and Benson, D. F. (1997). Ideomotor apraxia: behavioral dimensions and neuroanatomical basis. *Brain and Language*, **58**, 125–36.

Schwartz, M. F. and Buxbaum, L. J. (1997). Naturalistic action. In *Apraxia: the neuropsychology of action* (ed. L. J. G. Rothi and K. M. Heilman), pp. 269–89. Psychology Press, Hove.

Schwartz, R. L., Barrett, A. M., Crucian, G. P., and Heilman, K. M. (1998). Dissociation of gesture and object recognition. *Neurology*, **50**, 1186–8.

Seddoh, S. A., Robin, D. A., Sim, H. S., Hageman, C., Moon, J. B., and Folkins, J. W. (1996). Speech timing in apraxia of speech versus conduction aphasia. *Journal of Speech and Hearing Research*, **39**, 590–603.

Sirigu, A., Grafman, J., Bressler, K., and Sunderland, T. (1991a). Multiple representations contribute to body knowledge processing: evidence from a case of autotopagnosia. *Brain*, **114**, 629–42.

Sirigu, A., Duhamel, J. R., and Poncet, M. (1991b). The role of sensorimotor experience in object recognition: a case of multimodal agnosia. *Brain*, **114**, 2555–73.

Sirigu, A., Cohen, L., Duhamel, J. R., Pillon, B., Dubois, B., and Agid, Y. (1995). A selective impairment of hand posture for object utilization in apraxia. *Cortex*, **31**, 41–55.

Square-Storer, P. A., Roy, E. A., and Hogg, S. C. (1990). The dissociation of aphasia from apraxia of speech, ideomotor limb, and buccofacial apraxia. In *Advances in Psychology*, Vol. 70: *The cerebral control of speech and limb movements* (ed. G. R. Hammond), pp. 451–76. North-Holland, Amsterdam.

Stein, J. F. (1991). Space and parietal association areas. In *Brain and space* (ed. J. Paillard), pp. 185–222. Oxford University Press, New York.

Wang, L. and Goodglass, H. (1992). Pantomime, praxis, and aphasia. *Brain and Language*, **42**, 402–18.

CHAPTER 2

Neural disorders of language and movement: evidence from American Sign Language

David P. Corina
University of Washington

Introduction

As with spoken languages, sign languages can be described and analysed in terms of linguistic categories such as those developed in the subfields of phonology, morphology, and syntax (Klima and Bellugi 1979; Liddell 1980; Wilbur 1980; Lillo-Martin 1991; Corina and Sandler 1993). Insights from the analysis of sign language structure provide a new framework for studying the neurological systems underlying language, motor, and visual systems. This chapter provides an overview of three neurological disorders affecting sign language use and serves to illustrate how knowledge of the structure of sign languages can be instrumental in cultivating a more thorough understanding of the neurological basis of language and motor systems. Investigations of sign language aphasia serve to underscore the importance of left-hemisphere structures for signed languages. Studies of signers with Parkinson's disease provide novel insight into the extrapyramidal motor system's role in the execution of the complex sequential movements which comprise American Sign Language (ASL). Finally, a discussion of apraxic disorders helps to frame the differences between complex linguistic gestural systems such as ASL and limb control in the service of pantomime and object use.

Aphasia

Aphasia refers to a range of impairments in the use of language that is caused by injury or damage in the perisylvian region of the left hemisphere (Fig. 2.1). There is now overwhelming evidence that right-handed deaf signers, like hearing persons, exhibit language disturbances when critical left-hemisphere areas are damaged. In contrast, when the right hemisphere is damaged, resulting impairments are visuospatial in nature (Poizner *et al.* 1987; for recent reviews see Corina

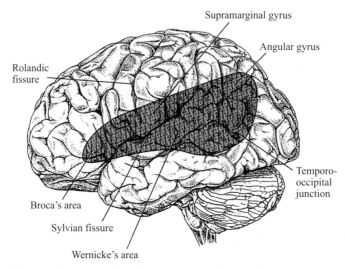

Supramarginal gyrus

Angular gyrus

Rolandic
fissure

Temporo-
occipital
junction

Broca's area

Sylvian fissure

Wernicke's area

Fig. 2.1 Left hemisphere perisylvian language areas. (Reproduced with permission from Beaumont, J. G., Kenealy, P. M., and Rogers, M. J. C. (eds) (1996). *The Blackwell Dictionary of Neuropsychology*, Blackwell, Oxford.)

1998a,b). Taken together, these findings show that deaf signers evidence complementary specialization for language and non-language skills, suggesting that development of hemispheric specialization is not dependent upon exposure to oral/aural language. However, there is growing awareness that the specializations of the cerebral hemispheres probably cut across higher cognitive faculties in both deaf and hearing individuals (Just *et al.* 1996; Neville *et al.* 1998). This is to be expected as we refine our understanding of the functional systems involved in complex cognitive behaviours like language, memory, and attention.

In users of spoken languages, language production impairment is associated with left-hemisphere anterior lesions, notably Broca's area. Execution of speech movements, for example, involves the cortical zone encompassing the lower posterior portion of the left frontal lobe (Goodglass 1993). Left-frontal anterior regions are also implicated in impairment of sign language production. Damage to this region in life-long signers results in effortful and dysfluent production, reducing signing to single-sign utterances in some cases (see, for example, case G.D. in Poizner *et al.* 1987). In addition, cortical stimulation of this region has been shown to affect motor output of signing, even though this region is proximal to sites subserving speech-motor control (Corina *et al.*, 1988c). In hearing individuals, language comprehension deficits are associated with left-hemisphere posterior lesions, especially posterior temporal lesions, for example Wernicke's area. Similar patterns have been observed in users of signed languages. Signers W.L. and K.L., for example, who had damage to posterior temporal structures, evidenced marked comprehension deficits such as failing to follow signed commands, and showed poor performance on a test of single sign recognition (Poizner *et al.* 1987; Corina *et al.* 1992). However, anatomical considerations suggest that language comprehension deficits in the deaf may result from lesions more posterior than those observed in users of spoken language. Additionally, as discussed below, highly specific deficits have been observed following right hemisphere damage (for discussion see Corina 1998b). In sum, evidence from lesion studies of deaf signers indicates a left-hemisphere dominance for sign language processing, and global patterns of comprehension and production deficits following posterior and anterior damage, respectively.

Sign language breakdown following left-hemisphere damage is not haphazard, but affects independently-motivated linguistic categories. This observation provides support for viewing aphasia as a unique and specific cognitive deficit rather than as a subtype of a more general motor or symbolic deficit. The most thorough evidence comes from studies of sign language production deficits following left-hemisphere damage. We focus here on the description of phonemic paraphasias and errors of lexical and inflectional morphology observed in several deaf signers with left-hemisphere lesions.

Phonemic parapahsia

Paraphasia refers to the production of unintended syllables, words, or phrases during the effort to speak. Spoken language phonemic paraphasias arise from the substitution or omission of sublexical phonological components (Blumstein 1973). In ASL, sublexical structure refers to the formational elements that comprise a sign form: handshape, location, movement, and orientation. In signed languages, paraphasic errors involve substitutions within these parameters. Moreover, as in spoken languages, phonological paraphasias in sign aphasia do not compromise the syllabic integrity of a word; that is, we observe substitutions of movements rather than omissions, as the latter would violate syllable well-formedness in ASL (Brentari 1993). For example, the sign ENJOY, which requires a circular movement of the hand, was articulated with an incorrect up-and-down movement by one aphasic signer, K.L. This error suggests a substitution in the formational parameter of movement (Poizner *et al.* 1987). While selectional errors could occur among any of the four sublexical parameters, the most frequently reported errors are those affecting the handshape parameter. Corina *et al.* (1992) describe in some detail the errors produced by signer W.L., errors which almost entirely involved handshape specifications. In these errors, W.L. often substituted an incorrect handshape for the sign while maintaining the location and movement of the intended sign (Fig. 2.2). The complexity of these substitutions is illustrated in Fig. 2.3, which shows a handshape paraphasia for the sign SISTER. This sign is normally articulated with an 'L' handshape, but in W.L.'s paraphasia we observe the substitution of an 'F' handshape. While on the surface these forms appear quite different, independent linguistic analysis has argued that in fact the surface forms 'L' and 'F' differ by a single feature specification of the selected fingers (the

Correct

Error

FINE (5 handshape)

*FINE (Y handshape)

SCREWDRIVER
(H handshape)

*SCREWDRIVER
(A• handshape)

WHITE
(5 to fO handshapes)

*WHITE
(fO to 5 handshapes)

Fig. 2.2 Paraphasic sign language errors involving the parameter of handshape. The left panels illustrate the correct forms of three ASL signs, FINE (top), SCREWDRIVER (centre), and WHITE (bottom). The right panels illustrate corresponding paraphasic forms. Copyright Ursula Bellugi, The Salk Institute, San Diego, CA.

index finger and thumb) in the underlying representation (Corina 1993). Based on a linguistic analysis of these types of errors, Corina *et al.* (1992) have argued that these substitutions are phonemic in nature, rather than simply phonetic misarticulations. These phonemic handshape errors differ in kind from the phonetic misarticulations observed in Parkinson's disease (see below).

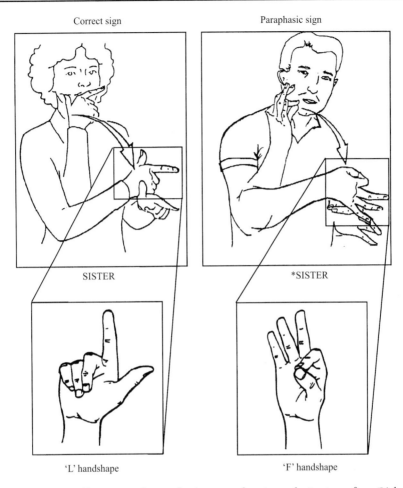

Fig. 2.3 Linguistically-motivated paraphasic error showing substitution of an 'L' hand-shape for an 'F' handshape in the sign SISTER. Even though the surface forms of these handshapes appear quite distinct, they are very similar in underlying phonemic representation.

The preponderance of handshape errors in signing aphasics is quite interesting. One of the most striking asymmetries in spoken language phonemic paraphasias is that errors overwhelmingly favour consonant distortions. Linguistic analyses of ASL have suggested that handshape specifications (and perhaps static articulatory locations) may be more consonantal in nature, whereas movement components of ASL may be analogous to vowels (Perlmutter 1993; Brentari 1993; Corina and Sandler 1993). At present, the vulnerability of consonants relative to vowels across languages and language modalities is not well understood.

Morphological vulnerability

A common error pattern in spoken language aphasia is the substitution and omission of words and parts of words (for example, the sentence 'The boy is walking' may be reduced to 'He walk'). The meaning-bearing units of languages (which may be an entire word, e.g. 'boy,' or a portion of a word, e.g. '-ing') are referred to as morphemes. Because languages differ in the degree to which they use morphology to mark obligatory grammatical distinctions (e.g., case and gender, subject and object agreement, etc.), patterns of impairment may be more striking in some languages than in others (Bates *et al.* 1991). ASL is a highly inflected language; for example, morphosyntactic agreement distinguishing grammatical subject and object requires directional movement trajectories in certain classes of ASL verbs. In the absence of grammatical movement trajectories, a verb sign will be produced in an uninflected 'citation' form. Poizner and colleagues (1987) describe vulnerability of ASL morphology in a number of patients. Patient G.D. consistently omitted required inflectional morphemes in her spontaneous sign-ing, and instead produced uninflected citation forms of the verbs. Patient P.D. produced both omissions in inflectional morphology and inconsistent verb agree-ment substitutions. That is, P.D. failed to maintain consistent verb movement trajectories to spatial locations, as is required by ASL syntax and discourse conventions. G.D. had a large left-hemisphere lesion that involved most of the convexity of the left frontal lobe, including Broca's area. P.D. had a subcortical lesion in the left hemisphere, with anterior focus deep to Broca's area and pos-terior extension into the white matter in the left parietal lobe. The general pattern of omissions versus substitutions in signers G.D. and P.D., respectively, is con-sistent with profiles of agrammatic and paragrammatic impairment reported for users of spoken language.

Facial expressions serve a dual function in ASL: they convey both affective and linguistic information. Separate classes of facial expressions participate in these two distinct functions (Baker and Padden 1978; Baker-Shenk 1983; Corina 1989; Reilly *et al.* 1990; Reilly and Bellugi 1996). The use of facial morphology following left-hemisphere lesion has recently been investigated. Differential impairment of these two classes of facial expressions, linguistic and affective, has been reported (Kegl and Poizner 1991; Corina *et al.*, in press). For example, left-hemisphere-damaged signer G.D showed considerable reduction in facial expressions used for linguistic purposes, but maintained exuberant affective facial expressions. S.M., a right-hemisphere-damaged signer who was not aphasic for sign language, showed the reverse pattern—preserved linguistic facial expressions and a paucity of affective expressions. In summary, production of sign language morphology, in its many guises, is vulnerable following left-hemisphere damage in deaf signers.

Semantic impairments in sign production have also been reported following left-hemisphere damage. Signer W.L., in the course of a naming test, produced semantic–phonological blends. For example, W.L. signed TREE as a semantic blend of the formationally similar signs GREEN and TREE. This type of semantic impairment has been observed in a cortical stimulation mapping procedure in a deaf signer. Under stimulation of supramarginal gyrus, subject S.T. signed HORSE when asked to name the picture of a cow, signed SLEEP when shown a picture of a bed, and signed FARM when shown a picture of a pig (Corina *et al.*, 1998c). All of these incorrect signs share considerable phonological overlap with their intended semantic targets.

Taken together, these results demonstrate that language production abilities in deaf signers break down in linguistically significant ways. Paraphasic errors result in phonemic, morphological, and semantic impairments. These findings provide evidence that language impairments following stroke in deaf signers are aphasic in nature and do not reflect general problems in symbolic conceptualization or motor behaviour.

Right-hemisphere contributions

Typically, right-hemisphere-damaged signers are reported as having well-preserved language skills. However, more recent studies suggest that this story may be changing. Right-hemisphere damage in signers may, as is the case in hearing persons, disrupt the meta-control of language use and result in disruptions of discourse abilities (Brownell *et al.* 1990; Kaplan *et al.* 1990; Rehak *et al.* 1992). Analysis of language use in right-hemisphere-lesioned subjects J.H. (Corina *et al.* 1996) and D.N. (Poizner and Kegl 1992; Emmorey *et al.* 1995; Emmorey 1996) reveals contrasting disruptions. In everyday signing and in picture description tasks, J.H. showed occasional non-sequiturs and abnormal attention to details, which are characteristic of the discourse of hearing patients with right-hemisphere lesions (Delis *et al.* 1983). Subject D.N. showed a different pattern of discourse disruption; although D.N. was successful at spatial indexing within a given sentence, several researchers noted that she was inconsistent across sentences. That is, she did not consistently use the same index point from sentence to sentence. In order to salvage intelligibility, D.N used a compensatory strategy in which she restated the noun phrase in each sentence, resulting in an overly repetitive discourse style. The cases of J.H. and D.N. suggest that right-hemisphere lesions in signers can differentially disrupt discourse content (as in the case of J.H.) and discourse cohesion (as in the case of D.N.). Lesion site differs significantly in these two patients; J.H.'s stroke involved central portions of the frontal, parietal, and temporal lobes, while D.N.'s lesion was predominantly medial and involved the upper part of the occipital lobe and superior parietal lobule. Whether similar lesions in hearing individuals would result in differential discourse patterns awaits further study.

There is new evidence that right-hemisphere structures may play a crucial role in the production and comprehension of ASL classifiers. ASL classifiers contain morphologically complex forms that convey salient visual properties of the objects they signify. In the classifier system, classifier handshapes (handshapes that designate semantic classes of objects, analogous to classifiers in spoken languages) are combined with movement morphemes to designate complex location and motion predicates involving one or more objects (Supalla 1986). This system of classifiers is unique in its conflation of language and visuospatial properties. In tests requiring classifier descriptions, D.N. showed problems in the depiction of movement direction, object relations, and object orientation. In cases in which two-hand articulations were required, D.N. displayed great hesitancy and often made multiple attempts at getting the two hands to represent correctly the spatial relationship of the objects. Importantly, D.N. showed no motor weakness which would account for these errors. Another common error was the simplification of classifier handshapes. In classifier descriptions requiring precise orientation of an object, and especially in multiple object relations, D.N. often used unmarked 'generic' object classifiers. Her performance suggests that she was aware of the correct classifier handshape (she could use these occasionally), but she had developed a strategy of substitution to avoid the spatial demands imposed by the system of ASL classifiers.

Disturbances in syntactic processing in ASL have been attested after left-hemisphere damage. More surprising, perhaps, is the finding that some signers with right-hemisphere damage also exhibited problems. Two of the right-hemisphere-damaged subjects, S.M. and G.G., tested by Poizner *et al.* (1987), showed performance well below controls on two tests of spatial syntax. Indeed, as pointed out in Poizner *et al.* (1987), 'Right lesioned signers do not show comprehension deficits in any linguistic test, other than that of spatialized syntax.' Poizner and colleagues speculated that the perceptual processing involved in the comprehension of spatialized syntax involves both left and right hemispheres; certain critical areas of both hemispheres must be relatively intact for accurate performance. The deficits in syntactic comprehension in the right- and left-hemisphere-damaged subjects raise an interesting theoretical question: Should these deficits in comprehension be considered aphasic in nature, or should they be considered secondary impairments arising from a general cognitive deficit in spatial processing? In the cases of impaired discourse production and classifier use, it is reasonable to suppose that right-hemisphere cognitive deficits manifest themselves in aspects of language use. In these cases it seems reasonable to suppose that right-hemisphere damage does not disrupt linguistic representations *per se*, but may impair the execution and processing of certain linguistic structures in sign language, namely those in which spatial information plays a particularly salient role. However, the issues become more complicated when we consider the syntactic aspects of ASL. How are the principles involved in processing referential and locative information different from those central to syntactic processing? Further work is required to tease apart these complicated theoretical questions.

In summary, aphasia studies to date provide ample evidence for the importance of the left hemisphere in mediation of sign language in the deaf. Sign language disturbances following left-hemisphere damage show a linguistically significant breakdown, and there is growing evidence for the role of the right hemisphere in aspects of ASL discourse, classifier use, and syntactic comprehension. Descriptions of sign language structure have been useful in illuminating the nature of aphasia breakdown as well as raising new questions concerning the hemispheric specificity of linguistic processing.

Parkinson's disease

Parkinson's disease is a degenerative disorder of the brain that affects the extra-pyramidal motor system and is mainly characterized by progressive tremor, bradykinesia (slowness of movement), and rigidity. Degeneration of the substantia nigra with subsequent decrease of striatal dopamine is responsible for the motor and cognitive disturbances seen in Parkinson's patients (Litvan 1996). The motor deficits observed in these subjects are not specific to language, but are evidenced across the general domain of motor behaviours. In hearing patients with Parkinson's disease, motor system dysfunction affects the speech articulators. The initial problem in the untreated patient is a failure to control respiration for the purpose of speech, and there follows a forward progression of articulatory symptoms involving the larynx, pharynx, tongue, and, finally, the lips (Critchley 1981). Perceptual features of speech changes include aprosody (i.e., monopitch, mono-loudness, diminished stress contrasts, and rate abnormalities), impairment of articulation (such as imprecise consonants), and vocal quality deviations (such as harsh or breathy voice). Physiological studies show that patients with Parkinson's disease have reduced articulatory displacements relative to normal speakers, which may appear as rigidity, and improper coordination of agonist–antagonist muscle pairs or groups (Gentil *et al.* 1995).

Recently there has been increased interest in research of deaf signers' behaviours under conditions of Parkinson's disease; because sign language provides greater access to articulatory movements, it presents new opportunities for quantifying linguistic movements. Poizner and colleagues have presented several case studies of Parkinsonian signers (Poizner and Kegl 1992, Brentari and Poizner 1994, Brentari *et al.* 1995). These signers show disturbed joint use, flattening of phonological distinctions, and timing disruption (Poizner and Kegl 1992). Signers with Parkinson's disease have been described as signing in a monotonous fashion, with a severely restricted range of temporal rates and tension in signing, two features which normally serve to signal emphasis (Wilbur 1980). Accompanying restrictions in limb movements are deficits in the motility of facial musculature, which further reduce expressivity in signing.

In Parkinsonian signing, generally, the scope of sign movement and precision of articulation are compromised. Poizner and colleagues have described several examples of these changes, including distalization of movements, reductions in contact between sign articulators, and laxing of handshapes. Distalization of movement refers to the displacement of sign movements to joints closer to the extremities. For example, a sign like GIVE contains a path movement away from the signer and is normally articulated by straightening the elbow joint, thus moving the hand away from the body. A distalization of this movement would maintain the joint angle of the elbow and substitute an outward nod of the wrist, also moving the hand away from the signer. The end result is maintained directionality of movement with reduced articulatory demands. However, when this displacement occurs the perceptual saliency of signing suffers.

In addition to anomalies in overall movement and articulation, Parkinsonian signing is often characterized by a reduction in the overall size of articulatory space and loss of articulatory contacts. Under normal circumstances, signs are articulated at body locations ranging from the top of the head to the lower torso, and the hand(s) often make physical contact either at or between specific locations. In Parkinsonian signing, there is often a systematic reduction of sign articulation that results in signs being articulated at the torso (as opposed to distinct, lexcially specified locations). For example, Brentari and Poizner (1994) report their subject J.H. as signing BOY, normally articulated on the forehead, at the torso level. In fact, most of J.H.'s signs were articulated near the waist during free conversation. Figure 2.4 (top panel) illustrates the sign WATER, normally articulated at the chin, articulated in neutral space about the chest. In Parkinsonian signers, physical contacts between the major articulators and body locations may be entirely lost. The lack of contact is consistent with a description of overall smoothing of articulation in signers with Parkinson's disease; maintenance of physical contacts with body locations probably places significant demands on the updating and programming of movement plans used in signing.

The handshapes of signers with Parkinson's disease are often quite lax, and do not maintain the crisp closure or opening of finger postures seen in normal signing (see Fig. 2.4, middle panel). Importantly, the handshapes observed (and indeed all the articulatory distinctions) are approximations of the intended form, and not incorrect substitutions. As illustrated in Fig. 2.4 (lower panel), differences in hand orientation have been shown to migrate towards less-marked orientations about the sagittal plane, and reductions in the magnitude of orientation changes required by some signs have been documented (Brentari and Poizner 1994). These findings are consistent with a general disruption of motor control which leads to phonetic disruptions in signing, rather than higher-level phonemic disruptions that are apparent in aphasic signing.

Timing disruptions

Studying the differences in the timing of handshape transitions in ASL has proven useful in documenting temporal disruption in Parkinsonian signing. In ASL one can make a distinction between word-internal handshape changes and the handshape transitions which occur between two independent signs (see Corina 1993 for discussion). Word-internal handshape changes are observed in single signs like THROW; here, the handshape transitions from a closed fist to a handshape with straight and outstretched index and middle fingers (i.e., the 'H' handshape).

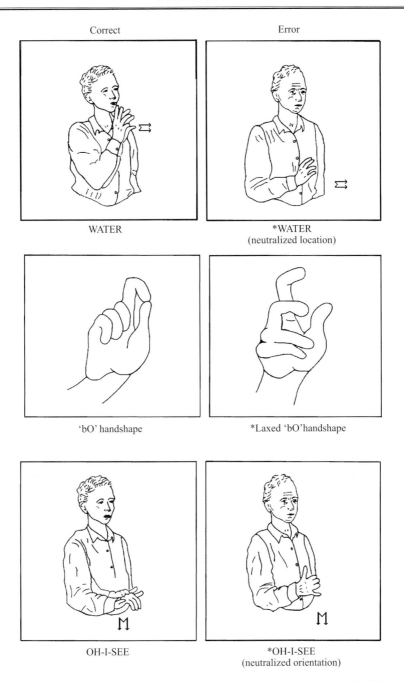

Correct   Error

WATER   *WATER
                                             (neutralized location)

'bO' handshape   *Laxed 'bO' handshape

OH-I-SEE   *OH-I-SEE
                                             (neutralized orientation)

Fig. 2.4 Examples of sign forms under conditions of Parkinson's disease. The left panels illustrate the correct forms. The right panels illustrate phonetic errors. (Adapted from Brentari and Poizner (1994), with permission of author.)

In these cases, the handshape change is coextensive with the duration of the sign as commonly measured. These same two handshapes can be observed in the context of a phrase. For example, in the phrase YEAR NAME, the hand shape for YEAR is the closed fist handshape, and the handshape for NAME is the 'H' handshape. In normal signing, the time required for handshape transitions occurring between words in a phrase is often a subset of the total time required to get into the starting position for executing the next sign. This stands in contrast to word-internal handshape changes, where the duration of the handshape is the total length of the sign's articulation. Parkinsonian signers are more apt to use the entire time between sign transitions to configure their handshapes for the upcoming signs, while normal signers are better able to anticipate and preconfigure the handshapes accordingly.

All Parkinsonian patients typically show hesitation and slowing in the initiation and execution of movements. Sequential movements appear to be particularly difficult and are often accompanied by a progressive fading of motor performance during the execution of a motor sequence. Several studies have documented that the fading of performance in sequential tasks is not just a reflection of some additive function of slowed single movements, but rather is indicative of an impaired ability to switch between the sequential movements (Berardelli *et al.* 1986; Agostino *et al.* 1992). Indeed, slowness in movement execution and slowness in switching are common manifestations of basal ganglia disease (Agostino *et al.* 1996). In one sample of normal ASL signing, switches between one sign and the next exhibit pause durations of approximately 120 ms, while pause durations between linguistic phrases are on the order of 450 ms (Brentari and Poizner 1994). Differences in the temporal duration of pauses occurring between words and between phrases reflect the normal patterning of signed sentences and help demarcate linguistically significant boundaries (Fischer 1975). Poizner and colleagues have shown that the signers with Parkinson's disease tend to execute all signs in a slow and uniform temporal rate. Parkinsonian subjects show similar temporal pauses between words and phrases (unlike normal signing), and this lack of temporal differentiation adds to the perceptual phenomena of monotonous signing. The lack of differentiation may very well reflect disruption of processes involved in the rapid motor shifts which are required for fluent multi-word signing.

In summary, the general movement disorders associated with Parkinson's disease affect sign language abilities and result in phonetic disruption in the articulation of signing. Motor disruption leads to errors involving timing, scope, and precision of articulation features which are common to both Parkinsonian speech and signing. The study of timing relationships in signing provides further evidence that basal ganglia dysfunction affects not only movement execution (e.g., slowing) but also the switching between movements. In addition, the study of complex sign movements which require multiple motor sub-plans for controlling path and handshape movements provides further evidence of compromise. While normal signers decouple temporal relationships between handshapes and arm movements in certain linguistic contexts (for example, during transitional movements), Parkinsonian signers maintain this coupling, even in contexts where this is not required. Whether this behaviour is a further reflection of lack of switching ability, reflects an overall synchronization of motor plans, or is a manifestation of the effect of slowed signing, awaits further study. Taken together, these studies illustrate the benefits of addressing questions of motor control from a perspective of sign language production.

Apraxia

Apraxia is defined as an impairment of the execution of a learned movement in response to a stimulus that would normally elicit the movement (see Chapter 1). Such impairments are subject to the conditions that the afferent and efferent systems involved are intact, and that the difficulty is not due to inattentiveness or lack of cooperation (Geschwind and Damasio 1985). The left inferior parietal lobe has been considered an area responsible for the representation of learned movement. Lesions associated with the left inferior parietal lobe result in an inability to perform and comprehend gestures, whereas damage more anterior to this region may result in production impairment with sparing of pantomime comprehension (Heilman *et al.* 1982; Rothi *et al.* 1991). Apraxia is a multifaceted construct with many subtypes of impairment, and efforts to understand apraxic impairments are hampered by lack of consistent definitions. Apraxic disorders may affect symbolic intransitive movements (such as saluting) as well as everyday movements (like dressing oneself), and may even impede the ability to copy meaningless limb movements. Most researchers acknowledge two main categories of apraxia: ideational apraxia and ideomotor apraxia. In ideational apraxia, the patient is specifically impaired in the ability to recall previously well-established actions, such as those involved in object use. Ideomotor apraxia refers to an inability to imitate an unfamiliar action or series of actions (McCarthy and Warrington 1990).

In assessments of apraxia, subjects are often asked to perform simple movements of the limbs and face, both in response to verbal commands and by imitation, and with objects both present and absent. Because sequential non-linguistic orofacial behaviours are difficult to measure, there is great interest in studying users of sign language to address issues of apraxia. Here again, the availability of linguistic and non-linguistic complex sequential limb movements presents new opportunities for objective quantification and analysis (see, for example, Poizner *et al.* 1998).

In the early reports of sign aphasia it is not uncommon to find statements that various subjects were not apraxic, or that they had intact praxic functions. However, in many of these early studies, correct use of common objects was considered sufficient to label the subjects nonapraxic. More convincing dissociations of sign language impairment with well-preserved ideational praxic abilities (e.g., conventionalized gesture and pantomimed object use) are reported in Sarno *et al.*

(1969), Kimura *et al.* (1976), Chiarello *et al.* (1982), Poizner *et al.* (1987) (cases P.D. and K.L.), Corina *et al.* (1992), and Poizner and Kegl (1992). Subject W.L., for example, had a marked sign language aphasia affecting both production and comprehension of signs (Corina *et al.* 1992). Interestingly, W.L. produced unencumbered pantomime, often involving stretches of multi-sequenced panto-mime to communicate ideas for which a single lexical sign would have sufficed. Moreover, both comprehension and production of pantomime were found to be better preserved than was sign language. In contrast, aphasic subject G.D., who had a large fronto-anterior lesion, showed impaired ability to produce representa-tional intransitive and transitive movements to command, but nevertheless showed normal performance on a pantomime recognition test (Poizner *et al.* 1987). These cases re-emphasize the fact that language impairments following left-hemisphere damage are not attributable to undifferentiated symbolic impair-ments. More importantly, these cases demonstrate that linguistic gesture (e.g., ASL) is not simply an elaborate pantomimic system.

A more controversial issue concerns differential impairment of meaningless manual movements and sign language ability. According to Kimura (1993), the left hemisphere appears to be essential for selecting most types of movement postures. Thus, Kimura treats language production impairments following left-hemisphere damage as secondary to an impairment in sequential movement programming. A diagnostic test developed by Kimura and Archibald (1974) re-quires experimenters to perform a series of meaningless unfamiliar hand and arm movements for immediate reproduction by subjects. Two left-hemisphere-damaged, language-impaired signers showed impairment in imitating complex nonlinguistic movements (Kimura *et al.* 1976; Chiarello *et al.* 1982). These find-ings were taken as support for Kimura's position that signing disorders are mani-festations of movement disorders. Subsequently, two aphasic signing subjects did not show any disruption on an abbreviated version of this test, suggesting a dissociation between linguistic impairment and sequential movement disorders (Poizner *et al.* 1987; Corina *et al.* 1992). The conflicting results raise questions about the validity of the measures used and suggest the need for more careful assessments of sequential motor control in deaf signers.

There are, however, theoretical reasons why we *might* expect a dissociation between sequential movement control and linguistic movement. The emphasis on impairments in the selection of sequentially based movements as an explanation of aphasic impairment misses a crucial distinction of linguistic systems. Languages (both signed and spoken) are not simply extreme cases of highly sequentialized movements. A unique characteristic of human language is that smaller, meaning-less units are built up to form higher-order, complex units. This hierarchical com-position is a crucial element of language structure. Thus, a model of motor production based solely on sequential movement will not successfully account for the complexities of language behaviour. In summary, there is strong evidence that favours a dissociation between ideomotor and ideational movements and signing. Although there is some evidence for dissociations between sequential movement disorders and sign language use, more rigorous testing is required to evaluate conclusively the extent of these dissociations.

Conclusion

In conclusion, the study of sign language has provided new avenues for understanding neurological disorders which affect language and movement. Studies of aphasia provide convincing evidence that left-hemisphere perisylvian areas subserve important functions for both spoken and signed languages. Recent evidence from effects of right-hemisphere damage on aspects of sign function has forced us to reconsider questions concerning the domain specificity of neurocognitive functions underlying language. Data from signers with Parkinson's disease reveal significant articulatory-phonetic problems similar to those observed in users of spoken languages. The ability to quantify external limb movements in these subjects has provided further insights into the role of the extrapyramidal motor system in execution of complex human movements. Finally, studies of apraxia indicate clear dissociations between sign language behaviour and ideational gestural abilities. Future work in this domain will likely reveal further distinctions between the degree of specialization for language and human movement capabilities.

References

Agostino, R., Berardelli, A., Formica, N. S., Accornero, N., and Manfredi, M. (1992). Sequential arm movement in patients with Parkinson's disease, Huntinton's disease and dystonia. *Brain*, 115, 1481–95.

Agostino, R., Sanes, J. H., and Hallett, M. (1996). Motor skill learning in Parkinson's disease. *Journal of the Neurological Sciences*, 139, 218–26.

Baker-Shenk, C. (1983). A micro analysis of the nonmanual components of questions in American Sign Language. Unpublished D.Phil. thesis, University of California, Berkeley.

Baker, C. and Padden, C. (1978). Focusing on the nonmanual components of American Sign Language. In *Understanding language through sign language research* (ed. P. Siple), pp. 27–57. Academic Press, New York.

Bates, E., Wulfeck, B., and MacWhinney, B. (1991). Cross-linguistic studies in aphasia: an overview. *Brain and Language*, 41, 123–48.

Berardelli, A., Accorneo, N., Argenta, M., Meco, G., and Manfredi, M. (1986). Fast complex arm movements in Parkinson's disease. *Journal of Neurology, Neurosurgery and Psychiatry*, 49, 1146–9.

Blumstein, S. E. (1973). *A phonological investigation of aphasic speech*. Mouton, The Hague.

Brentari, D. (1993). Establishing a sonority hierarchy in American Sign Language: the use of simultaneous structure in phonology. *Phonology*, 10, 281–306.

Brentari, D. and Poizner, H. (1994). A phonological analysis of a deaf Parkinsonian signer. *Language and Cognitive Processes*, 9, 69–99.

Brentari, D., Poizner, H., and Kegl, J. (1995). Aphasic and Parkinsonian signing: differences in phonological disruption. *Brain and Language*, 48, 69–105.

Brownell, H. H., Simpson T. L., Bihrle, A. M. and Potter, H. H. (1990). Appreciation of metaphoric alternative word meanings by left and right brain-damaged patients. *Neuropsychologia*, **28**, 375–83.

Chiarello, C., Knight, R., and Mandel, M. (1982). Aphasia in a prelingually deaf woman. *Brain*, **105**, 29–51.

Corina, D. P. (1989). Recognition of affective and noncanonical linguistic facial expressions in hearing and deaf subjects. *Brain and Cognition*, **9**, 227–37.

Corina, D. P. (1993) To branch or not to branch: underspecification in ASL handshape contours. In *Phonetics and phonology: current issues in ASL phonology* (ed. G.R. Coulter), pp. 63–95. Academic Press, San Diego, CA.

Corina, D. P. (1998a). The processing of sign language: evidence from aphasia. In *Handbook of neurolinguistics* (ed. B. Stemmer and H. A. Whitaker), pp. 3133–329. Academic Press, San Diego, CA.

Corina, D. P. (1998b). Aphasia in users of signed language. In *Aphasia in atypical populations* (ed. P. Coppens, Y. Lebrun, and A. Basso), pp. 261–310. Lawrence Erlbaum Assoc., Hillsdale, NJ.

Corina, D. P. and Sandler, W. (1993). On the nature of phonological structure in sign language. *Phonology*, **10**, 165–207.

Corina, D. P., Poizner, H. P., Feinberg, T., Dowd, D., and O'Grady, L. (1992). Dissociation between linguistic and non-linguistic gestural systems: a case for compositionality. *Brain and Language*, **43**, 414–47.

Corina, D. P., Kritchevsky, M., and Bellugi, U. (1996). Visual language processing and unilateral neglect: evidence from American Sign Language. *Cognitive Neuropsychology*, **13**, 321–51.

Corina, D. P., Bellugi U., and Reilly, J. S. (in press). Neuropsychological studies of linguistic and affective facial expressions in deaf signers. *Speech and Language*.

Corina, D. P., McBurney, S. L., Hinshaw, K., Brinkley, J., Lettich, E., and Ojemann, G. A. (1998c). Left hemisphere specialization for American Sign Language: A cortical stimulation study. *Society for Neuroscience Abstracts*, **24**, 19.

Critchley, E. M. (1981). Speech disorders of Parkinsonism: a review. *Journal of Neurology, Neurosurgery and Psychiatry*, **44**, 751–8.

Delis, D. C., Wapner, W., Gardner, H., and Moses, J. A. (1983). The contribution of the right hemisphere to the organization of paragraphs. *Cortex*, **19**, 43–50.

Emmorey, K. (1996). The confluence of space and language in signed languages. In *Language and space* (ed. P. Bloom, M. Peterson, L. Nadel, and M. Garrett), pp. 171–209. MIT Press, Cambridge, MA.

Emmorey, K., Corina, D. P., and Bellugi, U. (1995). Differential processing of topographic and referential functions of space. In *Language, gesture and space* (ed. K. Emmorey and J. Reilly), pp. 43–62. Erlbaum, Hillsdale, NJ.

Fischer, S. (1975). Influences on word order change in American Sign Language. In *Word order and word order change* (ed. C. Li), pp. 3–25. University of Texas Press, Austin, TX.

Gentil, M., Pollak, P., and Perret, J. (1995). Parkinsonian dysarthria, *Revue Neurologique*, **151**, 105–12.

Geschwind, N., and Damasio, A. R. (1985). Apraxia. In *Handbook of clinical neurology*, Vol. 45 (ed. P. J. Vinken and J. A. M. Frederiks), pp. 423–32. Elsevier Science, Amsterdam.

Goodglass, H. (1993). *Understanding aphasia*. Academic Press, San Diego, CA.

Heilman, K. M., Rothi, L. J., and Valenstein, E. (1982). Two forms of ideomotor apraxia. *Neurology*, **32**, 342–6.

Just, M. A, Carpenter. P. A., Keller. T. A., Eddy, W. F., and Thulborn, K. R. (1996). Brain activation modulated by sentence comprehension. *Science*, **274**, 114–6.

Kaplan, J. A., Brownell, H. H., Jacobs, J. R., and Gardner, H. (1990). The effects of right hemisphere damage on the pragmatic interpretation of conversational remarks. *Brain and Language*, **38**, 315–33.

Kegl, J., and Poizner, H. (1991). The interplay between linguistic and spatial processing in a right-lesioned signer. *Journal of Clinical and Experimental Neuropsychology*, **13**, 38–9.

Kimura, D. (1993). *Neuromotor mechanisms in human communication*. Oxford University Press.

Kimura, D. and Archibald, Y. (1974). Motor functions of the left hemisphere. *Brain*, **97**, 337–50.

Kimura, D., Battison, R., and Lubert, B. (1976). Impairment of non-linguistic hand movements in a deaf aphasic. *Brain and Language*, **3**, 566–71.

Klima, E., and Bellugi, U. (1979). *The signs of language*. Harvard University Press, Cambridge, MA.

Liddell, S. K. (1980). *American Sign Language syntax*. Mouton, The Hague.

Lillo-Martin, D. C. (1991). *Universal grammar and American Sign Language: setting the null argument parameters*. Kluwer, Dordrecht.

Litvan, I. (1996). Parkinson's disease. In *The Blackwell dictionary of neuropsychology* (ed. J. G. Beaumont, P. M. Kenealy, and M. J. C. Rogers). Blackwell, Oxford.

McCarthy, R.A. and Warrington, E.K. (1990). *Cognitive neurospychology*. Academic Press, San Diego, CA.

Menn, L. and Obler, L. K. (1990). *Agrammatic aphasia*. Benjamins, Amsterdam.

Neville, H. J., Bavelier, D., Corina. D. P., Rauschecker, J. P., Karni, A. Lalwani, A., Braun, A., Clark, V. P., Jezzard, P., and Turner, R. (1998). Cerebral organization for language in deaf and hearing subjects: biological constraints and effects of experience. *Proceedings of the National Academy of Sciences of the USA*, **90**, 922–9.

Perlmutter, D. (1993). Sonority and syllable structure in American Sign Language. In *Phonetics and phonology* (ed. G. Coulter), pp. 227–59. Academic Press, San Diego, CA.

Poizner, H. and Kegl, J. (1992). Neural basis of language and motor behavior: perspectives from American Sign Language. *Aphasiology*, **6**, 219–56.

Poizner, H., Klima, E. S., and Bellugi, U. (1987). *What the hands reveal about the brain*. MIT Press, Cambridge, MA.

Poizner, H., Merians, A. S., Clark, M. A. Macauley, B., Gonzalez Rothie, L. J., and Heilman, K. M. (1998). Left hemisphere specialization for learned, skilled and purposeful action. *Neuropsychology*, **12**, 163–82.

Rehak, A., Kaplan, J. A., Weylman, S. T., Kelly, B., Brownell, H. H., and Gardner, H. (1992). Story processing in right-hemisphere brain-damaged patients. *Brain and Language*, **42**, 320–36.

Reilly, J. S. and Bellugi, U. (1996). Competition on the face: affect and language in ASL Motherese. *Journal of Child Language*, **23**, 219–39.

Reilly, J. S., McIntire, M., and Bellugi, U. (1990). The acquisition of conditionals in American Sign Language: grammaticized facial expressions. *Applied Psycholinguistics*, **11**, 369–92.

Rothi, L. J. G., Ochipa, C., and Heilman, K. M. (1991). A cognitive neuropsychological model of limb praxis. *Cognitive Neuropsychology*, **8**, 443–58.

Sarno, J., Swisher, L., and Sarno, M. (1969). Aphasia in a congenitally deaf man. *Cortex*, **5**, 398–414.

Supalla, T. (1986). The classifier system in American Sign Language. In *Noun classes and categorization* (ed. C. Craig), pp. 181–214. Benjamins, Amsterdam.

Wilbur, R. (1980). The linguistic descriptions of American Sign Language. In *Recent perspectives on American Sign Language* (ed. H. Lane and F. Grosjean), pp. 7–31. Erlbaum, Hillsdale, NJ.

CHAPTER 3

Emotional and conversational nonverbal signals

Paul Ekman

University of California, San Francisco

Introduction

In this chapter I revise and expand formulations which distinguished among a number of different types of body movements and facial expressions (Ekman and Friesen 1969). Some of the terminology and most of the conceptual distinctions have been preserved, but refinements and expansions have benefited from empirical findings and theoretical developments. The crucial issue remains to distinguish among quite different activities, which are shown in facial and/or bodily movement, but which have quite different functions, origins, and coding.

Emblems

Emblems are the only true 'body language', in that these movements have a set of precise meanings, which are understood by all members of a culture or subculture. I borrowed the term 'emblem' from Efron (1968), the pioneer in studying cultural differences in body movements. Emblems are socially learned and thus, like language, culturally variable. A message may have an emblem in one culture, and no emblem in another cultural setting, or the same movement pattern may have quite different meanings in different cultural settings.

There are, however, multicultural emblems, which may occur for quite different reasons. First, and most obvious, some emblems from one culture may be adopted by members of another culture who have observed them. The 'finger' emblem in common use in North America is well known by intercultural contact, and sometimes used in other cultures. Such contact may be direct or through mass media. Darwin (1872 [1998]) proposed quite a different mechanism to explain his observation that the shrug, which denotes helplessness, while not universal, is quite widespread. It is a movement, he said, which is antithetical to the movement patterns used to denote the capability to attack. If a culture were to develop an emblem for helplessness, then, from Darwin's reasoning, it would likely be this antithetical movement. Eibl-Eibesfeldt (1970) has claimed that the eyebrow flash, used to denote a greeting, is universal. I disagree; there are some cultures where it is not in use (e.g. the United States). But it is quite widespread, appearing in many cultures. I explain its frequent occurrence as due to the selection of one element—raising of the eyebrows—of the full display of surprise. If a culture develops an emblem for an initial greeting, and uses the face in addition or in place of the hands, then it is likely that part of a surprise display would be used.

Emblems may repeat a word as it is said, replace a word in a flow of speech, provide a separate comment related to the words spoken, or occur as the sole reply. Emblems may be iconic, i.e. the movements look in some way like the message they are signifying, or arbitrarily coded. Emblems most often involve the hands, but some are performed using the shoulders, changes in head positioning, or facial movements.

Emblems are typically performed in a 'presentation position': directly in front of the performer, between the waist and the head. They usually have a staccato or punctuated appearance, with a sudden beginning and ending. The performer is as aware of using an emblem as he or she is of the words being spoken.

An exception is the 'emblematic fragment'. This is the gestural equivalent of a slip of the tongue. Emblematic fragments occur outside of the presentation position, and only part of the full emblem is performed, in a non-punctuated fashion. The onset and offset may be gradual rather than abrupt, and the performer usually is unaware of making the movements. Like verbal slips, emblematic fragments may reveal repressed information, or deliberately suppressed information (Ekman 1992a).

Emblems can be performed with hand, head, or facial movements. In those cultures we have studied, the majority of the emblems are performed with hand movements. Emblems are of special use when people cannot rely on words (for example because there is too much noise, or because the people are too far apart to hear one another). When used with speech they can either add a second layer to the conversation, or emphasize and make the spoken words more interesting.

Elsewhere (Ekman and Friesen 1972; Johnson *et al.* 1975) we have described the method we have used to survey the repertoire of emblems in different cultural settings. This method has been used in the United States (Johnson *et al.* 1975), Iran (Trupin 1976), Israel (Broide 1977) and Japan and Papua New Guinea (Ekman, unpublished findings). These cultures differed in the sheer number of emblems (from 67 in the USA to over 200 in Israel), and in the types of messages for which there is an emblem.

It is my impression that it is easy to learn foreign emblems—easier than it is to learn foreign words—but I have done no research to support that casual observation.

Although emblems resemble spoken language, they do not appear to have syntax. Sometimes a person will use a string of emblems, in which the sequence denotes the set of messages in the intended order, but such sequences are not common, and no other more complex relationship among emblems themselves has been evident.

Illustrators

We (Ekman and Friesen 1969) coined the term 'illustrators' to refer to movements that illustrate speech. They are intimately related to the speaker's speech on a moment-to-moment basis, usually augmenting what is said, but sometimes contradicting it. Although Efron did not use this term, he described five different types of illustrators, and I preserve his terminology for naming each type, and add two more (numbers 6 and 7 below) to his list:

1. Batons accent or emphasize a particular word or phrase; they 'beat out the tempo of mental locomotion'.
2. Ideographs sketch a path or direction of thought, 'tracing the itinerary of a logical journey'.
3. Deictic movements point to a present object.
4. Kinetographs depict a bodily action.
5. Spatial movements depict a spatial relationship.
6. Pictographs draw a picture of their referent.
7. Rhythmic movements depict the rhythm or pacing of an event.

These illustrators are typically performed with the hands, although the head may be involved, or even the feet. I made these distinctions (Ekman and Friesen 1969, 1972) when I had been studying bodily movement. After another decade of measuring facial muscular movement, I noticed that certain facial movements can be used as batons, and that this category can be subdivided (Ekman 1979). There are facial (as well as bodily) batons that accent a word. These 'baton accents' typically occur at the same time as an increase in loudness. There are also 'baton underliners', which emphasize a phrase. We have found it is nearly impossible to deliberately disconnect the change in loudness and the baton accent. We have not found anyone who, within a phrase, can deliberately increase loudness on one word and place the baton accent on another word, without unintentionally increasing the loudness of the baton-accented word.

Nearly all of the facial batons involve either brow raising or brow lowering, although it is possible to use nearly any facial movement for this purpose. Brow lowering and brow raising are highly visible facial movements, and movements that we have found are very easy to perform, even by young children (Ekman *et al.* 1980b). Although some individuals use raising more than lowering, or vice versa, for most people the facial movement deployed as a baton accent is related to the content of the word being emphasized. With words such as 'easy', 'light', or 'good', a brow raise tends to be used, while brow lowering is used to emphasize words such as 'difficult', 'dark', or 'bad'. If a person tries to use brow lowering to emphasize a word such as 'light' or 'good', the voice sounds strange and the performance seems rough. I offered two non-exclusive explanations for the association of brow lowering and brow raising with negative and positive words:

[B]row lowering which is employed in a variety of negative emotions (fear, sadness, distress, anger) should carry an implication of something negative, whereas brow raising would be more likely to suggest surprise or interest. Alternatively, the role played by these two actions in conversational signals may be selected on the basis of their current biological function: brow raise increasing and brow lowering decreasing visual input. Their role in conversational signals would thus be viewed as analogues to their biological adaptive value. Either possibility could be true.

Ekman (1979), p.201.

In unpublished research with Linda Camras (described in more detail in Ekman 1979) we found that brow lowering and raising is also used in quite different ways in statements which ask a question. If the speaker is going to use a brow movement at all, then it is likely that the brows will be raised if the speaker knows the answer to the question, and lowered if the speaker does not know the answer to the question be asked. One of the editors of this volume (L.M.) noted how this contrasts with the use of brows in signing.[1] (In many sign languages, American Sign Language amongst them, raised brows are part of the signal for yes-no questions; lowered brows are part of the signal for wh-questions. However, raised brows are also part of the signal for rhetorical questions, which is in keeping with our findings for non-signers.) The tone of voice and pitch level will also differ with these two types of questions.

Illustrators are socially learned, presumably when language itself is learned. Efron dramatically demonstrated that immigrant Lithuanian Jews and Sicilians use very different types of illustrators, but these differences were not preserved in their offspring who assimilated into the mainstream New York City culture.

Although individuals differ in both the type and frequency with which they use illustrators, there are also individual variations. Illustrators increase with the speaker's involvement with the process of speaking, and with both positive and negative affect, and decrease with lowered involvement, boredom or fatigue. A decrease in illustrators also occurs when a person is carefully weighing each word before it is spoken. Although this may occur with caution or ambivalence, it also has proven to be a useful indicator of deception (Ekman *et al.* 1976). We have also found that illustrators increased when depressed patients recovered (Ekman and Friesen 1974).

Illustrators help explain what is being said verbally. They also can serve a self-priming function, helping the speaker get going or get through a difficult to explain thought. Illustrators command the listener's attention, and can help hold the floor for the speaker. We have found (Ekman *et al.* 1980a) that the use of illustrators impresses others as a sign of sociability and friendliness. I expect students would retain more information from a lecturer who uses illustrators, but I don't know of research to support that speculation.

Manipulators

Originally we (Ekman and Friesen 1969) called these movements 'adapters', but I now prefer the more descriptive term 'manipulators'. In these movements one part of the body or face manipulates in some fashion – stroking, pressing, scratching, licking, biting, sucking, etc. – another part of the body or face. An object may also be the object of this attention, or used to perform the manipulation.

The frequency with which these movements occur is amazing, once one begins to notice them. Not just in private, but also in public, people usually touch themselves. One of my favorite classroom exercises is to ask the students to put everything down and stop touching themselves. It is hard for them to maintain this for even five minutes!

While some of these manipulators appear to accomplish grooming or cleaning, many of them seem to have no instrumental goal. Perhaps reassurance or comforting is a possibility, but many manipulators seem simply to reflect a nervousness, or habitual activity. Manipulators appear to be performed on the edge of awareness, in that a person if asked what he or she just did can usually can describe the activity, but was not focusing on it as it occurred. Our observations suggest that most people disattend when another person engages in a particularly noticeable, presumably taboo, manipulator such as ear or nose cleaning. The disattending, I believe, also occurs with little awareness.

Individuals differ not only in their favored manipulator but also in the frequency with which they show these behaviors. They often increase with increasing discomfort, although some people show a decrease, and freeze into a tense restrained position when uncomfortable. And, manipulators may increase when people are totally comfortable, with friends, not worrying at all about appearances.

Our research (Ekman *et al.* 1980a; Ekman 1992a) found that others distrust people who show many manipulators; they are commonly interpreted as signs someone is lying. But, in fact, they are not a reliable sign of lying for most people.

Regulators

We coined this term to draw attention

...to actions which maintain and regulate the back-and-forth nature of speaking and listening between two or more interactants. They tell the speaker to continue, repeat, elaborate, hurry up, become more interesting, less salacious, give the other a chance to talk, etc. They tell the listener to pay special attention, to wait just a minute more, to talk, etc.

Ekman and Friesen (1969), p.82

While illustrators and emblems (and emotional expressions, which I describe next) influence and may also be said to regulate the flow of conversation, I use the term 'regulator' to refer to when those or other actions are primarily functioning for just this purpose alone. Schefflen (1963, 1964, 1965) wrote about regulators,

although that is not what he called them, and made many important contributions, such as the role of postural shifts and mirroring. I have not focused much
on regulators, and my observations are limited.

'Listener responses' were first described, I believe, by Dittman (1972). He
focused on a variety of movements that lead the speaker to continue with what he
is saying. These may include head nods, agreement smiles, forward leans, brow
raises in exclamation, and so forth. I called these 'agreement listener responses' to
distinguish them from another set, 'calls for information' (Ekman 1979). The
listener may lower the brow to signal a lack of understanding or puzzlement with
what has been said. A brow raise may indicate disbelief or incredulity.

I described earlier, but did not before name, 'floor holders', i.e., responses made
by the speaker to prevent interruptions. I have seen this done by holding a hand
out, like a traffic policeman, to prevent the listener from entering the conversation
just yet. 'Turn seekers' are the listener's attempts to gain the floor, which may involve such diverse actions as leaning forward, almost rising from a chair, beginning
to make the lip movements for speaking a word, etc.

Emotional expressions

We originally used the term 'affect display', but each of those words carries surplus
meaning that I would rather avoid. 'Affect' implies more than emotion; it encom-
passes a broader range of phenomena, such as moods. 'Display' is no better a word
than 'expression', which I prefer in deference to Darwin. Also, the use of the term
'expression' serves to raise the issue, which has bothered many ethologists, of
whether these movements on the face are communicative actions or expressions.
This is a false and misleading dichotomy. I maintain (Ekman 1997) that emotional
expressions are involuntary signals which provide important information to
others. These expressions have been selected and refined over the course of evolution for their role in social communication. As involuntary signals they may
occur in response to anything that calls forth an emotion, which may include non-
personal events such as a beautiful sunset or thunder, and may be manifest when
the individual is alone. The presence of others enhances expressions, as emotions
themselves evolved primarily to deal with fundamental life tasks involving child
care, mating, dealing with predators and rivals, etc. (Ekman 1992b).

It is reasonable to call these signals 'expressions' because they are part of an
emotion; they are a sign that an emotion is occurring. I have maintained that a
hallmark of an emotion is that it has a signal, in face and/or voice and/or bodily
movement. There is no involuntary signal which informs conspecifics what the
person is thinking; thoughts are private, but emotions are not. Elsewhere (Ekman
1992b) I have described nine characteristics which distinguish emotions from
reflexes, moods, affective traits, and affective disorders. I think it is a reasonable
assumption that any state which shares the characteristics I describe for an emotion
will have a signal. But that is only an assumption, not sacred theory, waiting to be

challenged by evidence of a secret emotion which has all the other characteristics of the signal emotions.

We do not know much about what people actually derive when they see or hear an expression in the course of a conversation, competing with other sources of information, and embedded in one or another context of previous and simultaneous behaviours, and various expectations. From the research that has been done by removing an expression from context and asking people who are not involved in the situation to make judgements, we know that emotional expressions *can* provide information about the antecedent events, and about single emotion terms. I have proposed that emotional expressions also may convey information about: likely next actions, likely thoughts and plans, the internal state of the expresser which may be in terms of a metaphor, or what the observer might be thinking it would be wise to do next (Ekman 1993).

While the emotional expressions are not learned, we do learn what we termed 'display rules', to manage expressions. These rules, which are to some extent individually and culturally variable, specify who can show which emotion to whom and when. Individuals differ in their success in inhibiting, substituting, masking, or magnifying their expressions.

My own evidence and the evidence of many others support Darwin's claim that these expressions are universal to our species, and some of them shared with other species. Social constructionists, cultural relativists, and those focused on the language of emotions still argue with this claim (see Ekman (1998) for my most recent review of the evidence and the challenges to that evidence).

Words are not emotions, but representations of emotion. The fact that a language does not have a word for an emotion does not mean the emotion does not exist for the users of that language, but rather that it has not been labelled with a single word. English speakers can enjoy the suffering of their enemies but they have no single term for it, while Germans have the word *schadenfreude*. Perhaps the mistaken belief that words are emotions, or the most important feature of an emotion, arose because most of the cross-cultural research (but not all, see Ekman 1972) asked people in different cultures to choose a single emotion word for each face they were shown. While this did produce very strong agreement across cultures, it was not perfect, for single words do not translate exactly from one language to another. Another technique, still involving words, was to use a story to convey a social context, and ask people to indicate which face fitted which social context. Again, very high agreement was observed.

The face is one of the primary sites of emotional expressions; the voice is the other. I believe posture, the positioning of the head and body, is also recruited into the signal of some of the emotions. We (Ekman and Friesen 1978) developed a fine-grained measurement technique for comprehensively describing any facial movement in terms of the particular muscular actions produced. The Facial Action Coding System (FACS) can be used to describe any observed facial action, not just those which may be relevant to emotion. We have found that, even in highly emotional circumstances, most of the facial movements are not emotional signals, but facial illustrators, primarily batons. A few hundred people have learned FACS and are using it to study pain, infant development, sign language, psychopathology, and psychotherapy, as well as emotion (see Ekman and Rosenberg 1997 for a representative sample of those studies).

For each emotion there is not just one facial expression but a family of them. The family includes variations related to intensity, efforts to control the expression, and perhaps also the particular form of the emotion. Taking anger as an example, there is evidence about intensity variations, from annoyance to rage, and how to distinguish controlled from uncontrolled anger, but we do not know if there are different expressions for, for example, self-righteous anger as compared with indignant anger.

It is not certain how many universal expressions there are. The evidence from the judgement of facial expressions is strong for anger, fear, disgust, contempt, surprise sadness/distress, and enjoyment. Keltner (1995) suggests there may also be a universal expression for embarrassment. The other emotions can be signalled by a face in an instant, a frozen movement, but embarrassment apparently requires the unfolding of a sequence of facial and bodily movements. I suspect there is also an expression for awe, but no one has described it. (The evidence from the study of the voice (e.g., Banse and Scherer 1996) has to date not identified any other emotions which have a unique cross-cultural signal.)

I have suggested (Ekman 1992b) that there is an 'unhappiness' group of emotions and a 'happiness' group, and that the members of each of these groups share a particular facial expression. Members of the 'unhappiness' group are sadness, the more agitated version of sadness called distress, guilt, shame, discouragement, and disappointment. My claim is that their appearance on the face is not much different, with only minor variations for each of these related states. Perhaps the voice might provide separate signals for these presumed emotions, but research to determine this has not yet been done.

The 'happiness' group includes sensory pleasure, pride in achievement, amusement, relief, and contentment. My claim here is that these all share the same facial expression—some variation on the action of zygomatic major and the outer portion of orbicularis oculi (6 + 12 in FACS terms)—with only minor variations in the timing of the movements and their strength. Perhaps the voice may provide separate signals for each of these happiness emotions, for it certainly seems obvious that amusement does not sound like relief.

Before closing, let me describe 'referential expressions', for these have been a source of confusion among those studying facial expression, and they are interesting in their own right. A referential expression is a facial movement that refers to an emotion that is not felt by the person showing it. The person is referring to the emotion, much as the person could with a word, showing the emotion but in a way that makes it clear that the person is not feeling it now.

The referential expression then must look like the emotional expression but differ from it for two reasons. Firstly, if it resembles the actual emotional expression the observer might fail to recognize that it was not being felt now, and perceive it as an actual emotional expression. The second reason why it must be transformed is to reduce the likelihood that the person making the referential expression will actually begin to experience an emotion. My research with Robert Levenson (Ekman *et al.* 1983; Levenson *et al.* 1990) found that deliberately making the facial movements associated with a universal expression generates the changes in the autonomic nervous system that occur when emotion is generated in more typical ways. In subsequent research we (Ekman and Davidson 1993) found that deliberately making the facial configuration associated with enjoyment generated many of the changes in the central nervous system which occur when enjoyment occurs spontaneously.

The transformations of the actual emotional expression into a referential expression occur in both time and morphology. Typically the referential expression is either much briefer or much longer than the actual emotional expression, and it involves only one set of facial movements, not the complete array of facial movements associated with an emotional expression. Common examples are the horizontal stretching of the lips, typically performed very quickly, to refer to fear, and the raised upper lip, either brief or very long, to refer to disgust.

A *caveat*: only what I have written about emotional expressions and emblems is based on systematic research in non-Western as well as Western cultures. What little research that so far exists on illustrators, manipulators, and regulators has been done exclusively in Western cultures.

Summary

I have offered a taxonomy of bodily and facial movement, taking account of communicative function, how the movement became part of the organism's repertoire, and the relationship between the movement itself and what it signifies. This five-way classification—emblems, illustrators, manipulators, regulators, and emotional expressions—is based on semiotic, ethological, and psychological perspectives on nonverbal signals. Although largely based on my first writing on this topic (Ekman and Friesen 1969), I have been able here to expand and reformulate my views based on findings obtained in the last thirty years.

References

Banse, R. and Scherer, K. R. (1996). Acoustic profiles in vocal emotion expression. *Journal of Personality and Social Psychology*, 70, 614–36.

Broide, N. (1977). Israeli emblems: a study of one category of communicate nonverbal behavior. Unpublished Master's thesis, University of Tel Aviv.

Darwin, C. (1872). *The expression of the emotions in man and animals.* John Murray, London. Reprinted 1998, edited with foreword, commentary and afterword by P. Ekman. Harper-Collins, London and Oxford University Press, New York.

Dittman, A. T. (1972). Developmental factors in conversational behavior. *Journal of Communication*, 22, 404–23.

Efron, D. (1968). *Gesture and environment*. King's Crown, New York.

Eibl-Eibesfeldt, I. (1970). *Ethology, the biology of behavior*. Hold, Rinehart and Winston, New York.

Ekman, P. (1972). Universals and cultural differences in facial expressions of emotion. *Nebraska symposium on motivation, 1971* (ed. J. Cole), pp. 207–83. University of Nebraska Press, Lincoln, NE.

Ekman, P. (1979). About brows: emotional and conversational signals. In *Human ethology*, (ed. M. von Cranach, K. Foppa, W. Lepenies, and D. Ploog), pp. 169–248. Cambridge University Press.

Ekman, P. (1992a). *Telling lies: clues to deceit in the marketplace, marriage, and politics*, 2nd edn. W. W. Norton, New York.

Ekman, P. (1992b). An argument for basic emotions. *Cognition and Emotion*, 6, 169–200.

Ekman, P. (1993). Facial expression of emotion. *American Psychologist*, 48, 384–92.

Ekman, P. (1997). Expression or communication about emotion. In *Uniting psychology and biology: integrative perspectives on human development* (ed. N. Segal, G. E. Weisfeld, and C. C. Weisfeld), pp. 315–38. APA, Washington, DC.

Ekman, P. (1998). Facial expressions. In *The handbook of cognition and emotion* (ed. T. Dalgleish and T. Power), pp. 301–20. John Wiley and Sons, Ltd, Chichester.

Ekman, P. and Davidson, R. J. (1993). Voluntary smiling changes regional brain activity. *Psychological Science*, 4, 342–45.

Ekman, P. and Friesen, W. V. (1969). The repertoire of nonverbal behavior: categories, origins, usage, and coding. *Semiotica*, 1, 49–98.

Ekman, P. and Friesen, W. V. (1972). Hand movements. *Journal of Communication*, 22, 353–74.

Ekman, P. and Friesen, W. V. (1974). Nonverbal behavior and psychopathology. In *The psychology of depression: contemporary theory and research* (ed. R. J. Friedman and M. N. Katz), pp. 203–32. J. Winston, Washington, DC.

Ekman, P. and Friesen, W. V. (1978). *Facial action coding system: a technique for the measurement of facial movement*. Consulting Psychologists Press, Palo Alto, CA.

Ekman, P. and Rosenberg, E. L. (eds) (1997). *What the face reveals: basic and applied studies of spontaneous expression using the facial action coding system (FACS)*. Oxford University Press, New York.

Ekman, P., Friesen, W. V., and Scherer, K. (1976). Body movement and voice pitch in deceptive interaction. *Semiotica*, 16, 23–7.

Ekman, P., Friesen, W. V., O'Sullivan, M., and Scherer, K. (1980a). Relative importance of face, body, and speech in judgments of personality and affect. *Journal of Personality and Social Psychology*, 38, 270–7.

Ekman, P., Roper, G., and Hager, J. C. (1980b). Deliberate facial movement. *Child Development*, 51, 886–91.

Ekman, P., Levenson, R. W., and Friesen, W. V. (1983). Autonomic nervous system activity distinguishes between emotions. *Science*, 221, 1208–10.

Johnson, H. G., Ekman, P., and Friesen, W. B. (1975). Communicative body movements: American emblems. *Semiotica*, 15, 335–53.

Keltner, D. (1995). Signs of appeasement: evidence for the distinct displays of embarrassment, amusement, and shame. *Journal of Personality and Social Psychology*, 68, 441–54.

Levenson, R. W., Ekman, P., and Friesen, W. V. (1990). Voluntary facial action generates emotion-specific autonomic nervous system activity. *Psychophysiology*, 27, 363–84.

Schefflen, A. E. (1963). The significance of posture in communication systems *Psychiatry*, 26, 316–31.

Schefflen, A. E. (1964). Communication and regulation in psychotherapy. *Psychiatry*, 27, 126–36.

Schefflen, A. E. (1965). Quasi-courtship behavior in psychotherapy. *Psychiatry*, 28, 245–57.

Trupin, C. M. (1976). Linguistics and gesture: an application of linguistic theory to the study of emblems. Unpublished doctoral dissertation, University of Michigan.

Note

1. Editor's note: See Emmorey (Chapter 8) for a discussion of facial expressions in ASL.—L.M.

CHAPTER 4

Language from faces: uses of the face in speech and in sign

Ruth Campbell

University College London

*This chapter is dedicated to Harry McGurk and Christian Benoit,
pioneers of audiovisual speech research whose untimely deaths in
Spring 1998 are much mourned.*

Introduction

The human face, with its score or so of muscles and its intricate neural control, is the most visible and best modulated of our human signalling systems. Movements of the eyes, brows, nose, and mouth can be detected at a great distance and from coarse images. The slightest *moue* of disappointment or the smallest flick of the eyes is immediately perceived and correspondingly well controlled by the producer. Facial acts are incorporated into all human behaviours from thinking (upward gaze, lowered brow) to intense muscular effort (puffed face, pursed lips). It has been claimed (Coles 1998) that an inability to move the face, due to bilateral congenital nonfunction of the seventh cranial nerve (Moebius syndrome), can be as disabling to human communication as a sensory loss. These people can speak, because the jaw and tongue are controlled by cranial nerves other than nerve VII, but above the lower lip the face has a mask-like appearance. It has also been suggested (Baron-Cohen 1995) that congenital blindness can hamper the normal development of communicative and representational skills, because the blind child cannot see facial behaviour, especially direction of gaze. Where someone is looking, and the face acts that occur when someone is looking at a scene of interest, can be critical cues to the fact that humans have intentions that lie behind their actions.

The perception of human face acts has traditionally been explored within two fairly circumscribed frameworks: the framework of emotional expression (face acts reflect primary emotions (Darwin 1872, reprinted 1998; Ekman 1989)) and the communicative display framework (face acts accompany, enhance, or control communication (Eibl-Eibesfeldt 1989; Fridlund 1991; Russell and Fernández-Dols 1997)). Clearly both approaches have much to say about face readings and their biological, psychological, and social significance. These approaches, however, are not directly concerned with the way that the face is used in language-based communication, and this chapter takes as its theme the roles that faces can play within language. Here I am not concerned with the production of face acts, such as brow movements accompanying speech, which may be construed, as may some manual gestures, as intrinsic to language production (see Chapter 5), but more with the perception of face acts under specific communicative constraints. This in turn gives rise to interesting questions concerning the boundaries of language perception and of other modes of representation and communication. We have started to explore these experimentally and neurophysiologically, and the aim of this chapter is to describe this work. The work falls into two parts: reading faces for speech and reading faces for nonvocal language—primarily sign languages of the deaf.

Speechreading and audiovisual speech: phonology by eye

While it is generally thought that reading the face for speech is of importance primarily to the deaf and hard of hearing, there is plenty of evidence that its use is pervasive in hearing people. Infants are sensitive to the relation between heard speech and facial gesture, and are discomfited when the 'fit' is wrong (Dodd 1979; Kuhl and Meltzoff 1982, 1984). Hearing people are prone to a powerful audiovisual speech illusion—the McGurk illusion, first described by McGurk and MacDonald (1976), where, when a face seen speaking an utterance such as 'aga' is dubbed to a synchronized voice saying 'aba', 'ada' is what is often 'heard'. This appears to be a phonological illusion, for it, and its many variants, are moderated by parameters that control phonetic status for a particular perceiver (see Green 1998). It is sensitive to different language backgrounds of speaker and perceiver (Sekiyama and Tohkura 1993; Sekiyama *et al.* 1995). In line with this, infants appear to develop 'McGurk sensitivity' to the language in which they are reared by the start of the second half of the first year of life (Burnham and Dodd 1996; Rosenblum *et al.* 1997), much as their auditory speech perception appears to 'tune in' to native language contrasts at around this time (Werker and Tees 1992). Seeing the speaker improves the intelligibility of noisy speech—sometimes to a level equivalent to increasing signal to noise ratio by 15 db: the audiovisual speech advantage (Sumby and Pollack 1954). In part this can be ascribed to complementarity of audible and visible features of speech—many of the phonetic contrasts that are lost in noise (such as place of stop-consonant articulation), are readily seen on the face (Summerfield 1987).

But speechreading goes beyond this for hearing people. We can easily identify, by eye, speech that is well contextualized and highly predictable and, in noise, may not even realize that it is 'unheard'. We have no difficulty identifying photographs of different mouthshapes as particular vowels or classifying a face picture where the tongue is seen touching the teeth as a face saying 'th'. When the form of the face cannot be seen, but the dynamic properties of the face are maintained—as when the facial surface is illuminated by point lights—it can still influence auditory speech perception, generating (albeit reduced) McGurk effects and audiovisual speech advantage (Rosenblum and Saldaña 1996). Moreover, it is not necessary for all the visible information to be located in the mouth region. While lip movements are undoubtedly the most important factor in reading speech from faces (Summerfield 1979), the correlated movements of the cheek and chin are also informative and highly visible, and can, under some conditions, be sufficient to recapture the acoustic properties of the message directly from the changes in vocal cavity shape due to jaw and lip actions (Munhall and Vatikiotis-Bateson 1998). People do not even look concertedly at the lips when speechreading (Vatikiotis-Bateson *et al.* in press).

The face is part of the system from which speech is perceived—just as it is part of the apparatus for producing it. We may choose to ignore this (as in watching dubbed movies), or not feel the need for it (as in listening to the telephone or radio), since the auditory channel can often carry sufficient information for the message to be intelligible, but it would be dangerous to lose sight of it. For example, any theory of speech perception that defines speech primarily in acoustic terms cannot accommodate many of the findings indicated above. For another thing, speech can interact with other face acts in interesting ways. Tartter (1980) suggested that since smiling shortens the vocal tract by retracting the lips, 'smiling speech' should have a typically higher frequency than 'nonsmiling speech'. She also showed that this distinction was perceptible. More recent studies suggest that 'smiling speech' is also more memorable (Johansson and Rönnberg 1996).

How does reading speech from faces relate to other readings of the face?

Speechreading, then, is a natural perceptual process that analyses face actions in phonological terms. How is this achieved? We have been probing this primarily by exploring (silent) speechreading in relation to other processes performed on facial images. The first question we asked was, 'To what extent does speech-reading make use of processes common to the reading of other face acts?'.

One influential model of face processing (Bruce and Young 1986) afforded a useful framework in which to pose this question, for it suggested that accessing face images for speech and for other interpretations of the face, such as facial identity, should be essentially independent. That is, we should not have to process facial identity in order to see what someone is saying. While at one level this is a commonsense prediction (for we can speechread unfamiliar faces), at another level it is not: for instance, it is possible that it is only when identity starts to be processed from the face that speech may start to be analysed. And how might speechreading a face affect other tasks one may perform on the face? Can speechreading interact with (say) decisions about familiarity?

In one set of experiments, pairs of face images were presented for a speeded 'same-different' decision. The images were of familiar or unfamiliar faces making mouthshapes as for saying 'food' and 'feed'. Face familiarity did not affect speed or accuracy of these decisions (Campbell *et al.* 1996). Another set of experiments used individual face images which were seen for a simple decision ('Is the face saying 'food' or 'feed'?'). This decision was not speeded by seeing that face in an earlier trial and was relatively insensitive to whether the face was familiar or not (Campbell and de Haan 1998). However, when the second task was identity judgement ('Is this someone you know?'), prior exposure to that face for a speechreading decision speeded the decision for familiar faces. This confirms the conclusion of Ellis *et al.* (1990), based on similar experiments but with different images of posed facial expressions of emotion, that the only part of the face processing system sensitive to repetition priming is that related to the identification of familiar people. The essence of repetition priming resides in the system that has stored a flexible and powerful representation of the known individual, and this can be activated by watching him speak, or smile—or perform any other face act.

Semi-independence of speechreading and reading faces for other things?

Speechreading a face, then, can affect subsequent identity processing, but our studies found no evidence for a complementary effect of identity (i.e., familiarity of the seen face) on speechreading. However, using a different paradigm, Schweinberger and Soukup (1998) suggest that identity processing does affect speeded face-speech classifications. They examined the effects of task-irrelevant variations on face-image classification. That is, a face image presented to classify for identity may vary in mouthshape, while for classifying lipspeech, changes in identity may be seen. While identity decisions were unaffected by such task-irrelevant variation, speech classification was not. Under these conditions, images of different speakers slowed the speech discrimination task ('Is it an 'ee' or an 'oo'?') when compared with the baseline conditions where identity and speech were correlated or constant across speakers. There is further evidence that the specific identity of a known face can have implications for audiovisual speechreading. Walker *et al.* (1995) showed that McGurk effects produced by dubbing an unfamiliar (other-sex) voice to a personally familiar face were lower than when an unfamiliar face was dubbed in this way. Since Green *et al.* (1991) had shown that, for unfamiliar faces, McGurk effects were similar for other-sex and same-sex face-voice dubbing, these effects of identity processing on speechreading might arise post-perceptually. They could make use of stored identity knowledge about what someone sounds like, once the speaker's face has been identified.

Reports from a quite different research area also suggest that varying the identity of the speaker can be bad for understanding what is said. The identification of spoken items is worse when several speakers, rather than just one, have to be processed (Mullenix *et al.*1989; Pisoni 1993; Nygard *et al.* 1994). Although first demonstrated in auditory speech tasks, these findings extend to visual speech. Visible changes in the number and type of speaker affect memory for and processing of spoken words (Sheffert and Fowler 1995; Saldaña *et al.* 1996).

A further complication is that while seeing multiple speakers may be 'bad for speech' when the measured variable is speech content, it can be 'good for speech' when several heard voices are not spatially separated (i.e., in monaural recordings of several speakers talking at once). Under these conditions, a seen speaker synchronized to one of two heard messages in the monaural stream enables that particular signal to be readily disambiguated. Indeed, Spelke (1979) showed that the ability to use such synchronized audiovisual events to parse the multimodal stream of information occurs early in infancy. One important recent finding (Driver 1996) is that the separation of a two-voice monaural message improves recognition not only of the speaker-synchronized channel, but also of the other acoustic message—but only when the perceiver believes the auditory signals to be spatially separated. By using dummy loudspeakers, Driver was able to generate illusory spatial separation of such monaural inputs.

So it appears that there is relative rather than absolute independence of the visual processes that support speechreading and those that support other face readings, especially identity. While speechreading (or at least classifying facial images for speech) is not measurably more onerous when unfamiliar rather than familiar faces are seen, nevertheless there is a gain to comprehension in seeing one rather than several speakers and identity can sometimes impact on speech analysis. To this extent, these recent studies using reaction time methodologies and unnatural—because stilled—face displays support more traditional findings in the lipreading research that point to familiarity of the speaker as a factor influencing lipreadability (Berger 1972).

Implications for neurological processing

Two simple questions that can be posed are: 'To what extent does speechreading make use of language systems in the brain?' and 'To what extent does it use systems in the brain that analyse faces?' Studies with two brain-lesioned patients at first gave a very simple answer: damage to left medial occipitotemporal regions, which also impaired some reading functions, could impair speechreading but leave all other aspects of face processing intact, while damage to right medial occipitotemporal regions failed to affect speechreading but compromised identity and expression analysis (Campbell *et al.* 1986). This simple right hemisphere–left hemisphere dichotomy, with its strong implication that speechreading dissociates from other face processing abilities, is not absolute. Indeed, one of the lessons of the partial independence of speech and identity processing suggested by the recent experimental findings reviewed above is that we should not expect to find complete separability of these functions in the brain either. Recent brain imaging

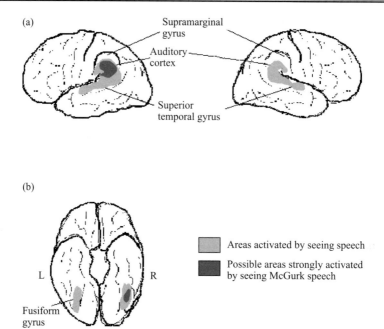

(a)

Supramarginal gyrus

Auditory cortex

Superior temporal gyrus

(b)

L   R

Areas activated by seeing speech

Possible areas strongly activated by seeing McGurk speech

Fusiform gyrus

Fig. 4.1 Diagrammatic view of brain regions implicated in speechreading. (a) Lateral view of the brain. (b) Interior surface of the brain.

studies suggest that some circumscribed regions of the posterior part of the brain, centred on the fusiform gyrus for still images and more anterior structures in the superior temporal sulcus for moving faces (see Fig. 4.1 for these locations), are recruited whether faces are presented for identification or discrimination. These regions are also activated when faces or parts of faces are passively viewed, as when they are distractors in a task that requires the person to detect other types of objects. In most cases, the right-hemisphere sites are more active than those in the left hemisphere (Bentin *et al.* 1996; Kanwisher *et al.* 1997; McCarthy *et al.* 1997; Calvert *et al.* 1997; Puce *et al.* 1998). At this level, where the face is analysed 'as a face' and its parts start to be analysed, we would expect all face readings to depend on intact occipitotemporal function, especially in the right hemisphere.

More specific localization of function can depend on task, suggesting different networks can be recruited. For example, one study (Diesch 1995) suggests that audiovisual fusions are strongest when the image projects to the right hemisphere and the corresponding speech sound is heard by the left hemisphere. But this is true only for syllables of high phonotactic regularity (a fusion produced by hearing 'ba' and seeing 'ga'—perceived as 'da'). When a more complex perception occurs (heard 'ga' and seen 'ba' giving perceived 'bga'), this pattern disappears. Why? We know that primary auditory cortex is activated by any sound stimulus bilaterally, but phonological material activates other parts of the left hemisphere, especially around the supramarginal gyrus (see Fig. 4.1). Phonologically regular material should preferentially cause activation in this area. For phonetically plausible, but phonologically unusual material, activation may be more diffuse and include superior temporal regions—and may even include right-hemisphere sites, as the perceiver tries to fit various associations of mouth actions to the mouth openings s/he sees (e.g. 'Could this be a German speaker?' or 'Perhaps this is someone with a swollen tongue trying to speak?'). We have also suggested that the right hemisphere (especially occipitotemporal regions) can have the edge over the left hemisphere in the perception of faces. But it also has the advantage in the perception of visual movement (see, e.g., Plant and Nakayama 1993) and possibly also in 'first pass' perceptual scans which may be relatively coarse grained (low spatial frequency, high contrast). It therefore makes sense that the most effective way of eliciting a perceptual 'da' from heard 'ba' and seen 'ga' is when the specific advantages of speedy right-hemisphere vision-for-faces and left-hemisphere supramarginal speech processing can interact—as reported by Diesch (1995).

The main point here is that audiovisual speech and silent speechreading do not seem to lateralize to the left hemisphere as cleanly as does heard speech: rather they can afford a means whereby the right hemisphere can contribute to the segmental perception of speech. Left-hemisphere superiority for seen speech can nevertheless be shown under some conditions (e.g., see Campbell *et al.* 1996), and the 'final common path' for the speedy categorical identification of phonological segments requires access to supramarginal gyrus in the left hemisphere—whether input is heard or seen. This also fits with the report by Sams and Levänen (1996) that surface-measured electromagnetic indices of brain activity for the detection of an audiovisual syllable (McGurk), were slightly posterior and superior to those observed for a purely auditory syllable, over auditory cortex.

Deafness and speechreading

So far, this chapter has considered speechreading in people with normal hearing. Among the prelingually deaf, seen speech actions carry different status and make different points. Most people born with profound or severe hearing loss are born to hearing parents. The home environment is therefore a speech environment: even if the child is diagnosed early and the parents learn sign, it is rare for the deaf child to be reared in a sign environment with several native signers as primary or secondary caregivers. Since most deaf children are exposed to seen speech, to what extent can they use this as a first language? While much depends on the degree of hearing loss, within the profound hearing loss range (>90 db at 2 Hz in the better ear) the relationship between hearing loss and speechreading skill tends to break down. Some of the best speechreaders yet tested are profoundly prelingually deaf (Bernstein *et al.* 1998), yet many deaf people with similar levels of hearing loss and similar backgrounds are also poor speechreaders and make preferential use of sign (Dodd and Murphy 1992).

Good speechreading in the deaf predicts later hearing (-aided) phonological abilities, and—again—this is not necessarily related to degree of pre-aided hearing loss. To date, there is little to indicate whether deaf and hearing speechreaders, or good and poor deaf speechreaders, differ in their functional and neurophysiological architecture. There are hints—but no more than that—that deaf people who are good speechreaders may have enhanced low-level visual capacities (e.g. Samar and Sims 1983, 1984). But do they recruit other systems and other brain areas that in hearing people would be 'colonized' by hearing? At this stage we simply do not know. One potentially important point is that the phonology of deaf people and that of hearing people may differ radically in their representational and phenomenal qualities. A phonemic contrast is *any* contrast that distinguishes lexemes at a segmental level. Hearing people tend to 'hear' these. In silently reading a poem, for instance, they report that they 'hear the rhymes in the head'. While deaf people too can be sensitive to these features, they may use a different sensory analogue for representation and experience—whether 'felt', 'seen', 'spoken', or simply 'known'. We will need to take care to keep this point in mind in interpreting both deaf and hearing experiences of seen speech.

Speech-based mouth patterns in other communication systems: mouth pictures

The use of mouth patterns derived from speech is a feature of a number of communication systems, and is used often with deaf people. In cued speech (Cornett 1967), speechreading is augmented by hand gestures that distinguish phonemes with identical lip-patterns. For instance, 'guard' and 'carton' may look very similar when spoken. In cued speech the form of the accompanying hand-sign shows whether the one- or the two-syllable word was uttered and suggests that the manner of articulation of the consonants differs. Hand cues can also disambiguate place of articulation of a consonant when this cannot be seen on the mouth: thus the difference between 'kah' and 'tah', which look very similar, would be indicated by a particular handshape. Recent research shows that early immersion in cued speech by deaf children leads to the development of excellent abstract receptive phonology in these youngsters. That is, their use of verbal short-term memory and their sensitivity to rhyme and homophony in spelling are almost indistinguishable from those of hearing people (Leybaert *et al.* 1998).

Mouth patterns are typically used by hearing speakers, often in an exaggerated way, when using sign-supported speech to communicate with a deaf person. Perhaps this is why mouth patterns can be identified in a number of 'natural' sign languages (i.e. those developed among the native deaf). However, these rarely have the dynamic characteristics of a spoken cognate. Typically the first consonant of the utterance, or the stressed vowel, becomes a face action that accompanies a manual utterance. Often this 'mouth picture' is held or repeated over the duration of the manual sign

Speech-like or possibly speech-derived patterns are not the only mouth actions that are incorporated into sign language. Actions such as showing the tongue between the teeth, or lip frication (like blowing a raspberry), or puffing the cheeks can all be part of the set of sign language features. In both British Sign Language (BSL) and American Sign Language (ASL), for instance, lip frication carries adverbial meaning (Marschark *et al.* 1998; Kyle and Woll 1988).

The face in sign

Mouth actions are by no means the only face acts that are used in sign: brow movement and puffing of the cheeks are used to indicate a range of linguistic features, while direction of gaze and pose and movement of the head are vital in reference—both pragmatically and syntactically. Among the syntactic features that use face and head acts, interrogatives, negation, conditionals, topics, and relative clauses are all evident in ASL (Bellugi and Fisher 1972; Baker and Padden 1978; Liddell 1978, 1980, 1986; see also Chapter 8, this volume), and similar functions seem to apply to other sign languages of the deaf, such as BSL (Kyle and Woll 1988).

Reilly and colleagues (Reilly *et al.* 1990, 1991) have explored the acquisition of sign language (ASL) as a first language with specific attention to how face acts become incorporated into the language. They pointed out that the acquisition of the face component was usually neither early nor easy. Even the acquisition of sign lexemes that make use of universal gestures, such as the smile meaning 'happy', could show a delay in the use of the facial component compared with the manual one. Thus, even where face acts appear to map readily onto communicative or emotional displays outside the language domain, their acquisition *within language* could be a late-mastered feature. Petitto (1987) made a similar point with respect to the acquisition of deictic reference in ASL which makes use of indexical pointing gestures. The forms of error made by such deaf children in the process of mastering sign showed conclusively that the face act and the manual gesture distinctions were carried in the developing language system.

Experimental investigations of question-type on the face: looking for categorical perception

Reilly *et al.* (1991) have also explored the development of the ability to ask questions in a syntactically appropriate way in deaf children having ASL as a first language. In both ASL and BSL (as in most sign languages of the deaf), the syntactic features that indicate different ways of asking questions (question-type) require a specific face act: a 'yes–no' question (e.g., 'It's there, isn't it?') uses a head-up, brows-raised face, while a 'wh' (which?, who?, or what?) question (e.g., 'Where did you leave it?') requires a lowered brow and head forward or cocked at an angle. This distinction is acquired quite late in the development of sign language in the child, but becomes incorporated into sign as a clear and obligatory action, so that if the utterance is made without the face act it is unclear whether a question or statement is intended; the utterance is ungrammatical. We have recently been exploring this contrast experimentally in adult native (deaf) BSL signers, and in hearing people learning sign as a second language (L₂ signers), as well as in hearing non-signers (Campbell *et al.*, 1999). Our starting point was the recent finding that facial expression image-sequences can induce categorical perception in viewers. When shown a computer-morphed sequence in which, for example, a happy face is morphed in equal-sized steps to a sad face, a discontinuity in judgement and perception occurs. The viewer's identification of the morphed image items typically 'flips' in the midrange of the happy to sad series, and this sharp change in identification is accompanied by a sharpening of perceptual discrimination, so that pairs of morphed images are discriminated more efficiently when they straddle the category boundary (Etcoff and McGee 1992; Calder *et al.* 1996; de Gelder *et al.* 1997).

Categorical perception was first demonstrated for contrasts carried in speech and, although it has been shown that it can extend beyond speech to other acoustic contrasts and to animals other than humans (e.g. Cutting and Rosner 1974;

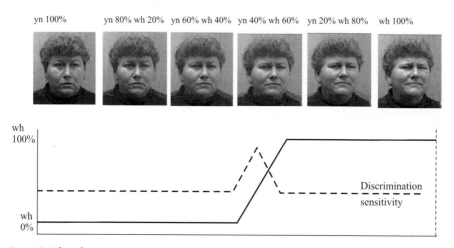

Fig. 4.2 This shows a six-step image morph series for one actor making the two different question-type face acts in BSL (yn = 'yes/no'; wh = 'which?, who? or what?') as endpoint images. The morphing algorithm automatically warps different 'amounts' of each of the endpoint images to make the intermediate images. Idealized categorical perception functions are shown below the image series: the solid line shows a hypothetical predicted categorical sharp change in identification of question type at image 4 (yn, 40%; wh, 60%). This represents the category boundary. The interrupted line shows the corresponding sharpening of discrimination at this point in the series. While the predicted functions were found in deaf subjects for the morph series 'surprised–puzzled', they were not at all pronounced for the question-type series (see text and Campbell *et al.*, 1999).

Kluender *et al.* 1987), nevertheless its ubiquity within speech processing and its sensitivity to language-specific contrasts is well established. Our hypothesis was therefore simple: we predicted that a morphed series of facial images from the posed typical 'yes–no' face to the 'wh' face would be categorically perceived by deaf native signers—but not by other groups. Figure 4.2 shows images from this series for one sign-producer.

In fact we found the opposite. As a group, it was the L_2 signers who showed most evidence of categorical perception for the question-type contrast, while neither deaf native signers nor hearing non-signers generally showed much evidence of it (there were some exceptions within the groups). While we expected (and found) that hearing non-signers were blind to this sign-language-specific feature, it was more surprising that although several deaf people were aware of the distinction and identified it well, this nevertheless failed to 'sharpen' perception in the discrimination task. In a second experiment we showed that all subjects perceived a very similar distinction—that between a surprised and a puzzled face—categorically. So it would seem that L_2 signers are making use of a familiar facial distinction concerned with understanding a facial response (intention) to an event, and 'piggybacking' the linguistic distinction on to that. Why do native deaf signers not do the same? This is a question that we hope to explore further.

Categorical perception for vowel shapes

Perhaps the failure to find categorical perception for a sign-salient contrast on the face could be due to our use of stilled face images? These are, after all, 'unnatural' stimuli. However, a morphed series of vowel shapes, shown to hearing people to identify as 'oo', 'ee', or 'ah', showed marked categorical perception, with enhanced discrimination of image pairs that straddled the perceptual boundaries between the (visual) vowels (Campbell *et al.*, 1997a). The failure to find categorical perception for the question-type contrast probably does not lie in the fact that stilled face images were the stimuli, although it is possible that the perception of still and moving faces may show differences between deaf and hearing people.

Neurophysiology of the face in sign

The fact that the face is used both within sign language and outside of it has provoked some important neuropsychological observations. Corina's (1989) study explored the lateralization of recognition of a number of face-act images in hearing, non-signing adults and deaf adults with sign as a first language. Whereas this task showed a right-hemisphere advantage in hearing subjects, deaf people's lateralization was mixed and sensitive to task-order effects. Corina interprets this result to mean that the face in sign carries linguistic as well as affective significance. In turn, this interpretation suggests that when the face is used within

language, the key representational sites are located in the left hemisphere. This
certainly fits the dissociated facial behaviours that have been observed in some
deaf signers following stroke. Typically left-hemisphere stroke may affect the uses
of the face in language, while sparing other communicative and spontaneous
expressions (Kegl and Poizner 1997). The opposite dissociation characterizes
patients with right-hemisphere lesions (Corina 1998a).

A paradox

This sort of pattern, in which deaf sign-users appear to use similar language-
organizing characteristics of the left hemisphere to those demonstrated in speech-
users, suggests a close analogy between the representational processes that
underpin speech and those that underpin sign. However, it is in this context that
the categorical perception findings—or rather the lack of them for sign-based
distinctions—are paradoxical. The 'typical mode' of left-hemisphere processing—
whether speech or images are the stimuli—is generally component-based and
essentially categorical, while that of the right hemisphere is characterized as con-
figurational, whatever type of material it is processing (e.g. Farah 1988; Kosslyn
1994).

Sign language might therefore be thought to show such componential, categorical characteristics, and this could explain why Corina's deaf subjects showed
reduced right-hemisphere lateralization for facial images that could be construed
within sign. Yet we found that deaf sign-users, with sign as their reported first
language, showed no categorical perception for a sign-based distinction, unlike L_2
sign-users. Perhaps, then, sign acquired as a native language makes more extensive use of processes distributed across both hemispheres than might be supposed
from a study of sign aphasias, where the general picture is that left-hemisphere
lesions lead to language breakdown, right-hemisphere lesions to visuospatial or
other nonlinguistic debility (Poizner *et al.* 1987; Corina 1998a). Indeed, some
recent brain imaging studies support this more distributed model of language
processing in sign (Neville *et al.* 1998), while in the sign-aphasia literature there
are indications that some aspects of sign language may be compromised by right-
hemisphere damage, especially in relation to coherence of signed discourse and
the uses of space in syntactic constructions (Corina 1998b).

From this point of view the statement of Newport (1987, p.478), based on her
attempts to generate categorical perception for manual distinctions in sign, that:
'Language is categorial at the phonetic level even when there is not categorical
perception ... (it) is not relevant to questions of language organisation.' is well
taken. Sign may show different internal processes and modes of organization
(more 'configural', 'spatial') than speech, without compromising its essential segmental, componential linguistic architecture. Face actions will continue to provide
an interesting domain in which to explore this, especially since categorical perception can be readily demonstrated (in deaf signers as in others) for face acts

signalling intention, and since the cortical basis of face processing is relatively well understood.

Conclusions and directions

In this chapter I have not considered how reading the face in language may interact with and separate from other functions, such as reading the face for expression or for age or gender (see Bruce and Young 1998 for a vivid and readable update of these topics). I have focused on two ways in which the face is read in language: in speech and in sign. In both cases, the face contributes in an essential way to the comprehension of the linguistic message. While face-speech and face-sign show some dissociations from other face-readings, both at neurological and at experimental levels, further examination suggests that all face-readings employ a common substrate from which the language module may extract specific information, both functionally (in experimental demonstrations) and neurophysiologically. The extent to which different face-readings may proceed separately and in parallel or, alternatively, in some more interactive fashion is not therefore quite as clear as it seemed only a few years ago, and it seems wiser to explore the extent to which different types of language reading from the face make differential use of specific functional and anatomical resources. Sign may structure language (including face-language) in a way that makes use of rather different processing mechanisms, and also of rather different cortical locales, than does the perception of speech.

The most important aspect of reading language from the face is that it is natural and possible. The movements and poses of the face are grist to the 'language mill' at the contrastive (possibly segmental) level at which one figures out the content of the message. From the ubiquity of the use of the face in sign, and the fact and historical longevity of face-to-face speech, there are likely to be evolutionary advantages in this arrangement.

References

Baker, C. and Padden, C. (1978). Focussing on the nonmanual components of ASL. In *Understanding language through sign language research* (ed. P. Siple), Academic Press, New York.

Baron-Cohen, S. (1995). *Mind-blindness: an essay on the psychology of autism.* MIT Press, Cambridge

Bellugi, U. and Fisher, S. (1972). A comparison of sign language and spoken language: rate and grammatical mechanisms. *Cognition*, **1**, 173–200.

Bentin, S., Allison, T., Puce, A., Perez, E., and McCarthy, G. (1996). Electrophysiological studies of face perception in humans. *Journal of Cognitive Neuroscience*, **8**, 551–65.

Berger, K. W. (1972). *Speechreading principles and methods.* National Educational Press, Baltimore, MD.

Bernstein, L. E., Demorest, M. E., and Tucker, P. E. (1998). What makes a good speech-reader? First you have to find one. In *Hearing by eye II: advances in the psychology of speechreading and audiovisual speech* (ed. R. Campbell, B. Dodd, and D. Burnham), pp. 211–29. Psychology Press, Hove.

Bruce, V. and Young, A. W. (1986). Understanding face recognition. *British Journal of Psychology*, 77, 313–27.

Bruce, V. and Young, A. W. (1998). *In the eye of the beholder.* Oxford University Press.

Burnham, D. and Dodd, B. (1996). Auditory-visual speech perception as a direct process: the McGurk effect in infants and across languages. In *Speechreading by humans and machines* (ed. D. Stork and M. Hennecke), pp. 104–14. Springer-Verlag, Berlin.

Calder, A. J., Young, A. W., Perrett, D. I., Etcoff, N. L., and Rowland, D. (1996). Categorical perception of morphed facial expressions. *Visual Cognition*, 3, 81–117.

Calvert, G., Bullmore, E., Brammer, M., Campbell, R., Woodruff, P., McGuire, P., Williams, S., Iversen, S. D., and David, A. S. (1997). Activation of auditory cortex during silent speechreading. *Science*, 276, 593–6.

Campbell, R. and de Haan, E. H. F. (1998). Repetition priming for face-speech images. *British Journal of Psychology*, 89, 309–23.

Campbell, R., Landis, T., and Regard, M. (1986). Face recognition and lipreading: a neurological dissociation. *Brain*, 109, 509–21.

Campbell, R., de Haan, E. H. F., and de Gelder, B. (1996). The lateralisation of lipreading: a second look. *Neuropsychologia*, 34, 1235–40.

Campbell, R., Benson, P. J., and Wallace, S. B. (1997a). The perception of mouthshape. In *Proceedings of the workshop on audiovisual speech processing* (ed. C. Benoit and R. Campbell), pp. 1–4. ESCOP, Rhodes.

Campbell, R., Zihl, J., Massaro, D. W., Munhall, K., and Cohen, M. M. (1997b). Speech-reading in the akinetopsic patient. *Brain*, 121, 1794–803.

Campbell, R., Woll, B., Benson, P. J., and Wallace, S. B. (1999). Categorical perception of face actions: their role in sign language and in communicative facial displays. *Quarterly Journal of Experimental Psychology*, 52A, 67–95.

Coles, J. (1998). *About face.* MIT Press, Cambridge, MA.

Corina, D. (1989). Affective and noncanonical facial expression in hearing and deaf subjects. *Brain and Cognition*, 9, 227–37.

Corina, D. (1998a). The processing of sign language: evidence from aphasia. In *Handbook of neurolinguistics* (ed. B. Stemmer and H. A. Whitaker), pp. 313–29. Academic Press, New York.

Corina, D. (1998b). Studies of neural processing in deaf signers. *Journal of Deaf Studies and Deaf Education*, 3, 35–48.

Cornett, O. (1967). Cued speech. *American Annals of the Deaf*, 112, 3–13.

Cutting, J. E. and Rosner, B. S. (1974). Categories and boundaries in speech and music. *Perception and Psychophysics*, 16, 564–70.

Darwin, C. (1872). *The expression of the emotions in man and animals.* Originally published by John Murray, London. Reprinted 1998, edited with foreword, commentary and afterword by P. Ekman (Harper-Collins, London).

De Gelder, B., Teunisse, J.-P., and Benson, P. J. (1997). Categorical perception of facial expressions: categories and their internal structure. *Cognition and Emotion*, 11, 1–23.

Diesch, E. (1995). Left and right hemifield advantages of fusions and combinations in audiovisual speech perception. *Quarterly Journal of Experimental Psychology*, 48A, 320–33.

Dodd, B. (1979). Lipreading in infants: attention to speech presented in and out of synchrony. *Cognitive Psychology*, 11, 478–84.

Dodd, B. and Murphy, J. (1992). Visual thoughts. In *Mental lives: case studies in cognition*, (ed. R. Campbell), pp. 48–60. Blackwell, Oxford.

Driver, J. (1996). Enhancement of selective listening by illusory mislocation of speech-sounds due to lipreading. *Nature*, **381**, 66–8.

Eibl-Eibesfeldt, I. (1989). *Human Ethology*. De Gruyter, New York.

Ekman, P. (1989). The argument and evidence about universals in facial expressions of emotion. In *Handbook of social psychophysiology* (ed. H. Wagner and A. Manstead), pp. 143–64. Wiley, Chichester.

Ellis, A. W., Young, A. W., and Flude, B. M. (1990). Repetition priming and face processing: priming occurs in the system that responds to the identity of the face. *Quarterly Journal of Experimental Psychology*, **42A**, 495–513.

Etcoff, N. L. and Magee, J. J. (1992). Categorical perception of facial expressions. *Cognition*, **44**, 227–40.

Farah, M. (1988). Is visual imagery really visual? Overlooked evidence from neuropsychology. *Psychological Review*, **95**, 307–17.

Fridlund, A. J. (1991). Evolution and facial action in reflex, social motive and paralanguage. *Biological Psychology*, **32**, 3–100.

Green, K. (1998). The use of auditory and visual information during phonetic processing: implications for theories of speech perception. In *Hearing by eye II: advances in the psychology of speechreading and audiovisual speech* (ed. R. Campbell, B. Dodd, and D. Burnham), pp. 3–26. Psychology Press, Hove.

Green, K., Kuhl, P. K., Meltzoff, A. N., and Stevens, E. B. (1991). Integrating speech information across talkers, gender and sensory modality: female faces and male voices in the McGurk effect. *Perception and Psychophysics*, **50**, 524–36.

Johansson, K. and Rönnberg, J. (1996). Speech gestures and facial expression in speechreading. *Scandinavian Journal of Psychology*, **37**, 132–9.

Kanwisher, N., McDermott, J., and Chun, M. (1997). The fusiform face area: a module in human extrastriate cortex specialized for face perception. *Journal of Neuroscience*, **11**, 4302–11.

Kegl, J. and Poizner, H. (1997). Crosslinguistic/crossmodal syntactic consequence of left hemisphere damage: evidence from an aphasic signer and his identical twin. *Aphasiology*, **11**, 1–37.

Kluender, K. R., Diehl, R. L., and Killeen, P. R. (1987). Japanese quail can learn phonetic categories. *Science*, **237**, 1195–7.

Kosslyn, S. M. (1994). *Image and brain: the resolution of the imagery debate*. MIT Press, Cambridge, MA.

Kuhl, P. K. and Meltzoff, A. N. (1982). The bimodal perception of speech in infancy. *Science*, **218**, 1138–41.

Kuhl, P. K. and Meltzoff, A. N. (1984). The intermodal representation of speech in infants. *Infant Behavior and Development*, **7**, 361–81.

Kyle, J. G. and Woll, B. (1988). *Sign language: the study of deaf people and their language*. Cambridge University Press, Cambridge.

Leybaert, J., Alegria, J., Hage, C., and Charlier, B. (1998). The effect of exposure to phonetically augmented lipspeech in the prelingual deaf. In *Hearing by eye II: advances in the psychology of speechreading and audiovisual speech* (ed. R. Campbell, B. Dodd, and D. Burnham), pp. 283–302. Psychology Press, Hove.

Liddell, S. (1978). Nonmanual signals and relative clauses in American Sign Language. In *Understanding language through sign language research* (ed. P. Siple), pp. 59–90. Academic Press, New York.

Liddell, S. (1980). *American Sign Language syntax*. Mouton, The Hague.

Liddell, S. (1986). Head thrust in ASL conditional marking. *Sign Language Studies*, **52**, 243–62.

McCarthy, G., Puce, A., Gore, J. C., and Allison, T. (1997). Face-specific processing in the human fusiform gyrus. *Journal of Cognitive Neuroscience*, 9, 605–10.

McGurk, H. and MacDonald, J. (1976). Hearing lips and seeing voices. *Nature*, 264, 746–8.

Marschark, M., LePoutre, D., and Bement, L. (1998). Mouth movement and signed communication. In *Hearing by eye II: advances in the psychology of speechreading and audiovisual speech* (ed. R. Campbell, B. Dodd, and D. Burnham), pp. 245–66. Psychology Press, Hove.

Mullenix, J., Pisoni, D. B., and Martin, C. S. (1989). Some effects of talker variability on spoken word recognition. *Journal of the Acoustical Society of America*, 85, 365–78.

Munhall, K. G. and Vatikiotis-Bateson, E. (1998). The moving face during speech communication. In *Hearing by eye II: advances in the psychology of speechreading and auditory-visual speech* (ed. R. Campbell, B. Dodd, and D. Burnham), pp. 123–39. Psychology Press, Hove.

Neville, H., Bavelier, D., Corina, D., Rauschecker, J., Karni, A., Lalwani, A., Braun, A., Clark, V., Jezzard, P., and Turner, R. (1998). Cerebral organization for language in deaf and hearing subjects; biological constraints and effects of experience. *Proceedings of the National Academy of Sciences of the USA*, 95, 922–9.

Newport, E. L (1987). Task specificity in language learning? Evidence from speech perception and American Sign Language. In *Language acquisition: the state of the art* (ed. E. Wanner and L. Gleitman), pp. 450–86. Cambridge University Press, Cambridge, MA.

Nygard, L. C., Sommers, M. S., and Pisoni, D. B. (1994). Speech perception as a talker-contingent process. *Psychological Science*, 5, 42–6.

Petitto, L. (1987). On the autonomy of language and gesture: evidence from the acquisition of personal pronouns in American Sign Language. *Cognition*, 27, 1–52.

Pisoni, D. B. (1993). Longterm memory in speech perception: some new findings on talker variability, speaking rate and perceptual learning. *Speech Communication*, 13, 109–25.

Plant, G. T. and Nakayama, K. (1993). The characteristics of residual motion perception in the hemifield contralateral to lateral occipital lesions. *Brain*, 116, 1337–53.

Poizner, H., Klima, E. S., and Bellugi, U. (1987). *What the hands reveal about the brain*. MIT Press, Cambridge, MA.

Puce, A., Allison, T., Bentin, S., Gore, J. C., and McCarthy, G. (1998). Temporal cortex activation in humans viewing eye and mouth movements. *Journal of Neuroscience*, 18, 2188–99.

Reilly, J. S., McIntire, M. L., and Bellugi, U. (1990). In *From gesture to language in hearing and deaf children* (ed. V. Volterra and C. J. Erting), pp. 128–45. Springer, Berlin.

Reilly, J. S., McIntire, M. L., and Bellugi, U. (1991). Baby face: a new perspective on universals in language acquisition. In *Theoretical issues in sign language research* (ed. P. Siple and S. D. Fischer), pp. 9–23. University of Chicago Press, Chicago, IL.

Rosenblum, L. D. and Saldaña, H. M. (1996). Visual primitives for audiovisual speech integration. *Journal of Experimental Psychology: Human Perception and Performance*, 22, 318–31.

Rosenblum, L., Schmuckler, M. A., and Johnson, J. A. (1997). The McGurk effect in infants *Perception and Psychophysics*, 59, 347–57.

Russell, J. A. and Fernández-Dols, J. M. (1997). *The Psychology of facial expression*. Cambridge University Press.

Saldaña, H., Nygard, L. C., and Pisoni, D. P. (1996). Episodic encoding of visual speaker attributes and recognition memory for spoken words. In *Speechreading by man and machine* (ed. D. Stork and M. Henneke), pp. 275–83. Springer, Berlin.

Samar, V. J. and Sims, D. C. (1983). Visual evoked correlates of speechreading performance in normal adults: a replication and factor-analytic extension. *Journal of Speech and Hearing Research*, **26**, 2–9.

Samar, V. J. and Sims, D. C. (1984). Visual evoked response components related to speech-reading and spatial skills in hearing and hearing-impaired adults. *Journal of Speech and Hearing Research*, **27**, 162–72.

Sams, M. and Levänen, S. (1996). Where and when are heard and seen speech integrated? MEG studies. In *Speechreading by man and machine* (ed. D. Stork and M. Hennecke), pp. 233–8. Springer, Berlin.

Schweinberger, S. R. and Soukup, G. R. (1998). Modularity in the perception of facial identity emotion and facial speech: asymmetric relationships between different components of face processing. *Journal of Experimental Psychology: Human Perception and Performance*, **24**, 1748–65.

Sekiyama, K. and Tohkura, Y. (1993). Inter-language differences in the influence of visual cues in speech perception. *Journal of Phonetics*, **21**, 427–44.

Sekiyama, K., Braida, L. D., Nishino, K., Hayashi, M., and Tuyo, M. M. (1995). The McGurk effect in Japanese and American perceivers. *Proceedings of the International Congress of Phonetic Sciences*, Stockholm, Vol. 4, pp. 214–17.

Sheffert, S. M. and Fowler, C. A. (1995). The effects of voice and visible speaker change on memory for spoken words. *Journal of Memory and Language*, **34**, 665–85.

Spelke, E. S. (1979). Perceiving bimodally specified events in infancy. *Developmental Psychology*, **15**, 626–36.

Sumby, W. H. and Pollack, I. (1954). Visual contributions to speech intelligibility in noise. *Journal of the Acoustical Society of America*, **26**, 212–15.

Summerfield, A. Q. (1979). Use of visual information for phonetic processing. *Phonetica*, **36**, 314–31.

Summerfield, A. Q. (1987). Some preliminaries to a comprehensive account of audio-visual speech perception. In *Hearing by eye: the psychology of lip-reading* (ed. B. Dodd and R. Campbell), pp. 35–51. Lawrence Erlbaum Associates, Hove.

Tartter, V. (1980). Happy talk: the perceptual and acoustic effects of smiling on speech. *Perception and Psychophysics*, **27**, 24–7.

Vatikiotis-Bateson, E., Eigsti, I.-M, Yano, S., and Munhall, K. G. (in press). Eye movements of perceivers during audiovisual speech perception. *Perception and Psychophysics*.

Walker, S., Bruce, V., and O'Malley, C. (1995). Facial identity and facial speech processing: familiar faces and voices in the McGurk effect. *Perception and Psychophysics*, **57**, 1124–36.

Werker, J. F. and Tees, R. C. (1992). The organization and reorganization of human speech perception. *Annual Reviews of Neuroscience*, **15**, 377–402.

B

The relationships among speech, signs, and gestures

CHAPTER 5

Triangulating the growth point—arriving at consciousness

David McNeill

University of Chicago

The simplest utterance, far from reflecting a constant, rigid
correspondence between sound and meaning, is really a process.
Verbal expressions cannot emerge fully formed, but must develop
gradually.

Vygotsky (1934 [1987]), p.222

Introduction

A tradition in psycholinguistics holds that behind the production of sentences are
mental processes organized in terms of grammatical structure. If someone says,
'and he drops it down the pipe', there is a definite structure. The 'and' is a
discourse conjunction (Schiffrin 1987). Its meaning is that the sentence to come
perpetuates something from the discourse before. The 'he' is a pronoun for an
animate male figure, and is the sentence's subject. 'Drops' or 'drops down' is the
verb, which is the central pivot of the sentence, and the 'it' is a pronoun referring
to an entity presented as inanimate, and is the object of the verb. Finally, 'the pipe'
is the location of the action's result. Combing these constituents we obtain the
meaning that the action of dropping was performed by a definite animate male on
an inanimate entity which as a result went into a pipe. All of this seems straightforward and not a little school-bookish. A psychological model then attempts to
describe the mental processes of the speaker as organized around the respective
constituents—for example, a process of creating a verb phrase ('drops it down'),
another of attaching the location phrase to the verb phrase, and a third of com-
bining the subject and the verb phrase + location to create the whole sentence.
These steps build on more elemental steps of activating lexical items, choosing
pronouns, working out number concord and tense, and so forth. Under the traditional assumption, then, there are subprocesses for the grammatical constituents.
My aim in the following is to undermine this picture and to support Vygotsky's
vision of utterances as unfolding developmental processes instead.

Gestures and growth points

A crucial step is to expand the window of observation, by taking into account speech-synchronized gestures. Gestures are omnipresent, unrehearsed, and near-obligatory partners to speech. They convey meanings (not necessarily the same meanings) linked to spoken utterance and present these linked meanings at the same moment. Among gestures are 'emblems', such as the 'thumbs-up' sign for 'OK'. Emblems are culturally defined, recurrent gestures with standards governing their form-meaning correspondences. While of considerable interest, emblems are not discussed in this chapter (see Kendon 1995 for discussion of emblems used in the vicinity of Naples). We will focus instead on gestures whose form and meaning are instead created 'online' by speakers as they speak, and whose form–meaning pairings are not governed by conventions.

The following is an example of a gesture created 'online'. The gesture in (1) appears unproblematic (see the Appendix on pp. 91–2 for explanation of the notation):

(1) and he grabs a [big oak tree <u>and</u> **bends it** <u>way back</u>]
    The right hand moves forward and upward, taking a grip form as it does. Then during the boldface stroke it appears to grasp and pull back the object.

The gesture conveys a meaning (bending something back), and its execution neatly synchronizes with the spoken constituents of the sentence co-expressively sharing this meaning. Is the gesture the kinesic outcropping of some process that also yields this constituency, a grammatical construction processor supplemented with a 'gesture processor'? Such models of gesture production have been proposed by de Ruiter (in press) and Krauss *et al.* (in press), but examples contradict them.

Consider example (2), which in no way stands out as a speech–gesture performance, but which implies a functional segmentation not that of the constituent structure of the sentence.

(2) and Tweety Bird runs and gets a bowling b[all and <u>drops</u> it do<u>wn</u> the drain]pipe
    The two hands appear to form the top side of a large round object and thrust it down.

The stroke phase, the meaningful movement, coincides with a non-constituent, 'it down'. This pairing could not have been an accident, as we see from the preceding hold. The underlining of 'drops' means that the hands were in position and shaped to make the downward stroke when the verb was uttered, but the stroke was withheld until 'drops' was over. This prestroke hold thus suggests that the verb was actively *excluded* from the gesture. Thus we have a case where gesture and speech formed a combination that did not correspond to a grammatical constituent. There is nothing in the gesture or utterance to set it apart as the product of some kind of exceptional processing step. Speech and gesture are quite ordinary, not different in this respect from the example in (1).

To analyse the processes underlying utterances with gestures, we shall need a unit of analysis that can encompass both the utterance and the gesture. I shall term such units 'growth points' (see McNeill and Duncan, in press). A growth point unit combines imagery and linguistic categorial content. Growth points are inferred from the totality of communicative events with special focus on speech–gesture synchrony and co-expressivity. They are called growth points because

(1) they are theoretical units in which the principles that explain mental change or growth—differentiation, internalization, dialectic, and reorganization—apply to realtime utterance generation;

(2) they are meant to be the initial form of thought out of which a dynamic process of development emerges;

(3) they address the concept that there is a definite starting point for a thought. Mental life is continuous but a given idea can come into being at a certain instant, and the growth point models this discontinuity.

Following Vygotsky (1934 [1987]), growth points will be termed 'minimal psychological units'; that is, the smallest units that retain the essential properties of wholes. The wholes in the present case are meanings presented both as imagery and as linguistic categories. These are combined in growth points and the combination is what we see in the speech–gesture window. Reducing the growth point to its linguistic and gestural components would destroy the whole and with it the possibility of discovering units of psychological processing other than the constituent structures of sentences.

Properties of growth points

Overview

The following generalizations have emerged from extensive cross-linguistic comparisons of speech and its synchronized gestures in several languages, among them English, Spanish, and Mandarin (McNeill and Duncan, in press):

(1) The growth point is a unit of analysis applicable in all languages.

(2) The minimal growth point unit of thinking-for-speaking irreducibly includes imagery and linguistic categorial content. This image-category unit is then 'unpacked' into an utterance with gesture.

(3) The growth point incorporates the context of speaking as a fundamental component.

I shall begin an explanation of the growth point via the third item—the incorporation of context as a fundamental component. This is because context-ualization is fundamental to the formation of the growth point and provides the basis for growth points to map onto structures other than grammatical constituents.

Growth points and differentiation

The growth point is an attempt to think out the implications of speech–gesture synchrony. When words and gesture co-occur, we ask, what does this imply? A growth point is the initial organizing impulse of the utterance, its cognitive starting point viewed microgenetically, and is the core idea of the utterance as it comes into existence. A growth point is meant to be a microgenetic idea unit; that is, a unit on a *diachronic* axis, a unit of mental development over short realtime intervals. To understand the growth point's incorporation of context, it is first necessary to understand its relationship to differentiation. A growth point is the newsworthy content in the immediate context; it is the point of departure from this context and comprises what Vygotsky called a 'psychological predicate' (not necessarily a grammatical predicate).

It is important to note that the context and the psychological predicate are both parts of the growth point. A growth point includes its context. This is possible since differentiation and context are mutually defining; a psychological predicate marks a significant departure in the immediate context *and* implies this context as a background. The term 'context' has a host of meanings (see Duranti and Goodwin 1992), but for my purposes 'context' is the background from which a psychological predicate is differentiated. The speaker shapes the context in a certain way, in order to give significance to the differentiated contrast. Background and contrast are constructed together. The joint product results in the differentiation of a new meaning from a background.

I shall use the terms 'field of oppositions' and 'significant [newsworthy] contrast' to refer to this constructed background and the differentiation of psychological predicates within it.

Analysis of the example

A growth point is theoretically a combination of imagery and language categorial information. It is thus what we see in synchronised speech and gesture. As a theoretical unit, it consists irreducibly of both imagistic and linguistic forms of information at the same time, and this combination of different modalities is the key to its potential for microgenetic change. We accordingly use the gesture context and its synchrony with speech, as noted earlier, to infer the growth point of the utterance. The growth point of (a) is the image of downward movement *plus* the linguistic content of the 'it' (i.e., the bowling ball) and the path particle 'down'. The growth point is both image and linguistic categorial content: an image, as it were, with a foot inside the door of language. Such imagery is important, since it grounds the linguistic categories in a specific visuospatial context. The linguistic categorization is also crucial, since it brings the image into the system of categories of the language, which is both a system of classification and a way of patterning action. The speech and its synchronized gesture are the key to the growth point theoretical unit. The image may also provide the growth point with the property of 'chunking,' a hallmark of expert performance, in this case speech performance (see Chase and Ericsson 1981). A chunk of linguistic output is organized around the presentation of an image.

To apply the concept of differentiation, the significant contrast in example (2) was the downward motion of the bowling ball toward Sylvester, a cat character in a cartoon world. In the field of oppositions, this downward motion was an antagonistic force, countering Sylvester who was clambering up the pipe. This was the core of the speaker's meaning: the bowling ball as an antagonistic force to Sylvester, coming down the pipe against him. Thus, 'it down', the speech segments with the gesture, unlikely though they may seem as a constituent from a syntactic point of view, comprised a psychological predicate—'it' (indexing the bowling ball) and 'down' categorizing the content as an image of an antagonistic force. The main verb, 'drops', on the other hand, as noted earlier, was *excluded* from this growth point. I shall discuss this point in the following section.

Contextual sources of growth points

The idea of an antagonistic force was the contrast embodied in this growth point, because of the particular fields of oppositions that gave it significance. To see this, we need to consider the entire stretch of discourse of which this growth point was a part. A useful way of organizing this analysis is by means of 'catchments'. A catchment is defined as at least two (not necessarily successive) gestures with partially recurring kinesic and spatial features across discourse segments that form a thematic unit (see Kendon 1972). Each gesture in a catchment is simultaneously shaped by its semantic or functional content and its relationship to the catchment or catchments of which it is part.The following 'battle plan' is how Vivian, the speaker of example (2), formulated the episode involving Sylvester and the bowling ball.

Battle plan for Vivian

(3)   he tries going [**up** the insid] [e of the **drainpipe** and]
       1H: RH rises up

→ (4 = 2) Tweety Bird runs and gets a bowling b[all and <u>drops</u> it do<u>wn</u> the
       drain]pipe #
       Symmetrical: 2SHs move down

(5)   [and / **as he's** co<u>ming up</u>]
       Asymmetrical: 2DHs, LH holds, RH up

(6)   [and the **bowling** ball's coming d] [own
       Asymmetrical: 2DHs, RH holds, LH down

(7)   he ssswa<u>llows it</u>]
       Asymmetrical: 2DHs, RH up, LH down

(8)   [# and he comes **out** the bot<u>tom of the drai</u>] [npipe
       1H: LH comes down

(9) and he's **got this** big bowling ball inside h] [im
     Symmetrical: 2SHs

(10) [and **he rolls on down**] [into a bow<u>ling all</u>] [ey
     Symmetrical: 2SHs

(11) and then you **hear a** sstri]ke #
     Symmetrical: 2SHs

This discourse that includes item (2), hereafter item (4), draws from at least three catchments:

C1. The *one-handed* gestures in items (3) and (8). These gestures accompany descriptions of Sylvester's motion, first up the pipe then out of it with the bowling ball inside him. Thus C1 ties together references to Sylvester as a solo force. This one-handed catchment differs from the two-handed catchments, which in turn divide into symmetrical and assymetrical catchments:

C2. Two-handed *symmetrical* gestures in items (4), (9), (10), and (11). These gestures group descriptions where the bowling ball is the antagonist, the dominant force. Sylvester becomes what he eats, a kind of living bowling ball, and the symmetrical gestures accompany the descriptions where the bowling ball asserts this power.

C3. Two-handed *asymmetrical* gestures in items (5), (6), and (7). This catchment groups items in which the bowling ball and Sylvester mutually approach each other in the pipe. Here, in contrast to the symmetrical set, Sylvester and the bowling ball are equals, differing in their direction of motion.

The occurrence of item (4) in the symmetrical catchment shows one of the factors that comprised its field of oppositions at this point—the bowling ball in the role of antagonist. This catchment set the bowling ball apart from its role in C3 where the bowling ball was on a par with Sylvester, and from C1 where it did not figure at all. The significant contrast in C2 was the downward motion of the bowling ball toward Sylvester. Because the gesture embodied this field of oppositions at this point, this downward motion had significance as an antagonistic force.

Sources of 'drops'

The gesture at (4) also contrasted with C1—the one-handed gesture depicting Sylvester as a solo force. This contrast led to the other parts of the utterance in (4) via a partial repetition of the utterance structure of (3). Verbal elements of (3) and (4) appeared in nearly equivalent slots (the match is as close as possible given that (4) is transitive while (3) is intransitive):

(3′) |(Sylvester) | up | in 'he tries going up the inside of the drainpipe'

(4′) |(Tweety) | down | in 'and drops it down the drainpipe'

The thematic opposition in this paradigm is counter-forces—'Tweety-down' versus

'Sylvester-up'. The contrast, in addition to bringing out Tweety and downness, was also the source of 'drops'. This verb expressed Tweety's role in the contrast and shifted the downward force theme to the oppositions about the bowling ball. The feeling we have that the paradigm is slightly ajar is due to the shift from spontaneous to caused motion with 'drops'. This verb however does not alter the counter-forces paradigm but instead transfers the counter-force from Tweety to the bowling ball, as appropriate for the gesture with its downward bowling ball imagery.

One utterance, more than one context

In this way the utterance at (4), though a single grammatical construction, emerged out of two distinct contexts. The contexts were clamped together by the gesture in (4). This gesture put the bowling ball in a field of oppositions in which the significant contrast was what it did (rather than how it was launched), made the nongrammatical pair, 'it down' into a unit, and made a place for the thematic shift of downness from the agent Tweety to the bowling ball via 'drops,' thus providing a rationale for this verb choice.

Unpacking sequences

The unpacking sequence would have begun with the antagonistic forces contrast. This was the core meaning embodied in the gesture. Unpacking then went to the Sylvester counter-forces context in (3) for information on how to unpack (4). The word order ('drops it down') obviously does not correspond to the sequence of generation steps starting from the growth point. That order was something like: 'it down' → 'drops,' etc. (where the arrow signifies the temporal sequence of steps in generating 'drops it down the drain pipe').

According to this explanation, the verb is not the only way to anchor a sentence. In this example the verb was essentially *derived* from the growth point's complex of meanings. In the course of unpacking the growth point, thinking shifted and acquired an agentive cast. In such a case the verb, though uttered first, would have arisen in the sentence generation process after the growth point itself. The dynamics of thinking-for-speaking during unpacking thus highlight the distinction between action by the agent Tweety and the bowling ball, a distinction appropriate in the context at this moment.

Summary of unpacking

Let us summarize the contexts that brought (4) into being:

1. The field of oppositions in which the significance of the downward motion of the bowling ball was that of an antagonistic force—the contrast of (4) with (5): this gave the growth point the core meaning centred on 'it down'. The 'chunk' of

language in (4) was organized around this presentation of the downward image, which in turn was the embodiment of the contextual contrast—this was the underlying source of the utterance.

2. The field of oppositions in which the significance was the counter-forces of 'Sylvester-up' versus 'Tweety-down': this gave a sentence schema that included the words 'drops', 'down', 'drainpipe', and the repetition of the sentence structure with Tweety in the subject slot—this was the source of the grammatical outline.

Understanding that one utterance can clamp together multiple contexts also removes the seeming anachronism of explaining (4) in part via contrasts with utterances yet to come. The speaker, recounting the story from memory, knew that the bowling ball was the ultimate force and also that Sylvester and the bowling ball would first have to approach each other as equals. She structured her narrative around these memories and this was the basis of her contrast at (4). The later sentences themselves were not present; they arose from their own growth points at their own moments of speaking. Nonetheless, the speaker, remembering the cartoon storyline and having the narrative goal of getting Sylvester out of the pipe and into the bowling alley like a living bowling ball, was able to integrate her goal and knowledge of the denouement into the growth points at each stage of her description of the scene.

The moral

Everything said thus far implies that every utterance, even though a self-contained grammatical structure, contains content from outside its own structure. This other content ties the utterance to the discourse, and this occurs at the level of thought. Such a model *incorporates* a context rather than adds it from the outside.

That two contexts could collaborate to form one grammatical structure implies that a sense of grammatical form can enter into utterances in piecemeal and oblique ways that do not follow the patterns of the utterance's formal linguistic description. The single verb phrase 'drops it down' was put together in this piecemeal way. The gesture had the role of clamping together the contexts from which the grammatical unit arose; this may be one reason why gestures occur in the first place: to clamp contexts together into grammatical units.

Implications of Vygotsky's view of words as processes

This analysis of growth points and how they are unpacked implies that the same word or string of words will be different psychologically if they embody different contexts. This is an implication of the Vygotsky insight quoted at the head of the chapter—rather than a fixed form–meaning pair, the 'same' word, if it is a process, can have a different structure in different contexts. An example demonstrating this possibility is the following from two speakers describing the same scene, with the same verb, 'rolls' (discovered by Susan Duncan):

(12) [but it **rolls him out**]
   Hand wiggles (giving manner information).

(13) [and he rolls # **down** <u>the drain</u> spout]
   Hand plunges straight down (giving path information).

In (12), a wiggling-hand gesture synchronized with 'rolls' in the utterance. The inferred growth point consisted of manner content (here shown with gestural 'agitation') categorized as rolling. In (13), the gesture lacked manner and did not synchronize with 'rolls' at all. Instead, the gesture skipped the verb and synchronized with the path particle, 'down', and the ground (Talmy 1985), 'the drain spout' (via a post-stroke hold). The inferred growth point is thus a downward-plunging image that is categorized as down (and drain spout). In other words, even though the same verb occurs, internal organization, gestures, and growth points differ.[2]

We can predict that such differences must occur when the fields of oppositions are different—the growth point and the field being joint constructions by the speaker. This prediction is attested in the contexts of (12) and (13). The speaker of (12) was focusing on the motion of the bowling ball while the speaker of (13) focused on that of Sylvester. The framework of significant oppositions was therefore different and the gesture placements and inferred growth points shifted accordingly.

Context of example (12)
Example (12) was at the end of a series of references to the bowling ball. In this series, the speaker highlighted the ball and what it was doing.

   and he drops a [bowl]ing ball [into <u>the rain spout</u>]
   [and it **goes down**]
   and it * [/] ah*
   you [**can't tell if the bow**<u>ling ball</u> /] [is un* /] [is **und**<u>er Sylvester</u>
   <u>or</u> **ins**ide of him]
   [but it **rolls him out**] (= 12)

Context of example (13)
Example (13) appeared in a series of utterances that began similarly but then shifted to Sylvester and his path. The shift took place before (13) and continued to create a context in which the bowling ball and its manner of motion would have been downplayed while Sylvester's path was the significant new content.

   [the canary] # [**throws***] # [**puts a** # [**bowling**] [ball] #
   into] # [the **drain** <u>spout as the</u>]
   (switch to Sylvester)
   [cat <u>is climbing up</u> /**and**] [it goes <u>into his</u>] [mouth]/
   [and **of course**] # [**into** <u>his</u> stomach] #
   [and he rolls # **down** <u>the drain</u> spout] (= 13)
   [and [**across**] [the **street**] into [the **bowling**] alley #]

Summary of contexts

The formation of a growth point is the highlighting and differentiating what is novel in a field of oppositions. The field defines the significance of the contrast, it establishes what is meaningful in it; the contrast and the field are the growth point. All of this process is meant to be a dynamic system within which new fields are formed and new growth points are differentiated. In such a system, the background of thinking-for-speaking is constantly being updated, and this is possible since it is a creation by the speaker during the course of the discourse.

Growth points and consciousness

I shall attempt to show in this section that growth points are intimately linked to the flow of consciousness. I do not mean that the *process* of symbol formation itself enters consciousness; how we speak and put our thoughts into linguistic form is an example of unconscious processing *par excellence*. But to speak is to think or become conscious of contents in a particular way, and to be conscious of contents in verbal category terms is already a phase of speaking (even if you don't utter a word). Growth points can be viewed as the units of this mode of verbalizable consciousness. They have a dynamic unfolding that is characteristic of consciousness and comprise packages of meanings cross-modally that seem like the contents of consciousness. If the growth point is a unit of this form of consciousness, then visuospatial cognition and gesture enter into consciousness too.[3]

The stream of consciousness

William James, writing a century ago (James 1892 [1961]), was especially interested in the 'stream of consciousness', the conscious stream that flows from object of consciousness to object of consciousness, with the transitions in between being essentially out of consciousness. The key to a growth-point interpretation of the stream of consciousness is the concept of cycles (see McNeill 1992). The unfolding of a growth point begins with the formation of a new growth point which is then unpacked into a structured utterance and gesture that houses the growth point and externalizes its categorial and imagery content. Paradoxically, self-disintegration of the utterance and ideas it contains is a key step in the stream of consciousness. By self-disintegration I mean the rapid disorganization of the preceding growth point, taking place within seconds. The result of this process is to create fragments usable for potential new growth points. The function of self-disintegration is that it creates points of change. It is at such points that the speaker's ideas are likely to be most open to new directions. Self-disintegration leads to a disorganized state in which different images and linguistic forms are simultaneously active but not structured. Without self-disintegration, consciousness could loop endlessly (as perhaps happens in dreams). The stream of consciousness moves from organization to disorganization and on to new organization, and so on indefinitely. It is natural to equate the organization phase with James' objects of consciousness and the disintegration phase with the transitions.

A classic experiment by Jarvella (1971) demonstrates something like self-disintegration in subjects' memory of sentences. Jarvella ingeniously devised pairs of sentences in which identical word strings were organized either as single sentences or as two sentences. The subjects listened to sentences such as the following, presented in a recording:

> **Presentation A:** That he could be intimidated was what *McDonald and his top advisors hoped. This would keep Rarick off the ballot.* (Sentence break seven words before end.)

> **Presentation B:** He and others were labelled as Communists. *McDonald and his top advisors hoped this would keep Rarick off the ballot.* (Sentence break 13 words before end.)

In presentation A the common word string belonged to two sentences while in presentation B it was contained in a single sentence. The unity of the sentence was crucial. Subjects tried to recall verbatim as many words as they could (immediate recall method) and words in the single sentence version were recalled better. More subjects remembered 'hoped', for example, when it was in the middle of 'McDonald and his top advisors hoped this would keep Rarick off the ballot' (presentation B) than when it was the last word of 'That he could be intimidated was what McDonald and his top advisors hoped' (presentation A), even though the number of words back from the test point was the same (namely, eight). Similar differences were found with the other words, 'advisors', 'top', etc. Only for words prior to 'McDonald' was recall the same in presentations A and B. In other words, a kind of amnesia set in at the sentence boundary, and this could mark a point of self-disintegration.

James' 'characters of consciousness'

James emphasized four properties or 'characters' of consciousness:

(1) it is personal;
(2) it is always changing,
(3) our experience of it is continuous, and
(4) 'It is interested in some parts of its object to the exclusion of others, and welcomes or rejects—*chooses* from among them, in a word—all the while' (p.19, italics in original).

The fourth character reminds us of the growth point and its formation through differentiation. The 'choice' of which James spoke is the creation of new significance in a field of oppositions. Analysis of the growth-point cycle shows how the various properties of consciousness mutually support one another. Number (3), consciousness is continuous, number (2), consciousness is always changing, and number (4), consciousness chooses something new, for example, sustain one another. This can be made clear by considering the effects of self-disintegration. Continuous consciousness is punctuated by self-disintegration which thus changes it . To 'choose' is to find something in the fragments of what had came before. Thus self-disintegration entails change and choice. By the same token, continuity and change imply self-disintegration.

How is consciousness felt to be personal, one's own? This property was linked by James to the continuity property when he wrote, 'Thoughts connected as we feel them to be connected are *what we mean* by personal selves' (pp. 20–21). Thus the cyclicity of growth points plays a part in our 'personal selves'. The dynamic character of consciousness explains how consciousness is personal. It is the continual experience of differentiating novel meanings from contexts built up cyclically that is the source of this identity.

James said that the 'fundamental fact' of consciousness it that 'consciousness of some sort goes on'. He said that consciousness would be accurately described if only we could say 'it thinks', the way we can say 'it rains' or 'it blows' (p.19). We cannot say this, so we say that thought goes on. What is the impelling force driving thought in the growth-point version of consciousness?

The formation of a growth point does not take place in a vacuum. A new idea exists within a continuing process of thinking that is partially analysable as a succession of growth points in fields of oppositions. The integration of thought with goals cannot be reduced to purely cognitive operations. It is also dependent on the 'affective-volitional tendency' of which Vygotsky (1934 [1987]) wrote:

Thought is not the last of these planes. It is not born of other thoughts. Thought has its origins in the motivating sphere of consciousness, a sphere that includes our inclinations and needs, our interests and impulses, and our affect and emotion. The affective and volitional tendency stands behind thought. Only here do we find the answer to the final 'why' in the analysis of thinking.

Vygotsky (1934 [1987]) p.282

This affective-volitional tendency is the 'why' of the growth point as well: 'why' the next thing that emerged in the field of oppositions was the image of downward thrusting with the lexical category down attached. This growth point was selected because of a 'volitional' factor, the pursuit of the narrative goal of getting Sylvester out of the drainpipe with the bowling ball inside. Without this factor, we cannot explain why this particular opposition stood out at that moment.

Affect can also have an influence on thinking by changing fields of oppositions and the contrasts regarded as significant within them. Affect can do this without itself being the content of thought (facial expressions seem to be the channel *par excellence* for this content). The influence is indirect, but the growth-point hypothesis shows how affect could function. It works through altering the goals of the speaker and thus the significance of the contrasts, thereby controlling the person's growth points and fields of oppositions. In cartoon narratives, with their narrow affective range, affect is hard to discern, though 'interest value', a mild form of an affective tendency, can be differentiated and does play a role (the speaker of example (4), for example, seems to have been more interested in what the bowling ball was doing, while the one of (18) focused on the cat).

Verbal versus non-verbal consciousness

The treatment of consciousness sketched above is meant for a linguistically engaged individual—the consciousness that arises while a person is producing language. It shows how verbal consciousness is indeed consciousness of one kind, how it is shaped by the character of consciousness, and how it shapes consciousness in return. To produce language is to think and become conscious in a particular way; to be conscious in verbal category terms is already a phase of producing speech (even if you do not produce an overt utterance); and visuospatial cognition and gesture are part of this special mode of consciousness in the growth-point based model. Not all forms of consciousness are verbal, and forms exist in which we seem to be aware of the world directly, without symbolic mediation. *Qualia*, subjective qualities of our conscious experiences of the world (or some part of it), do not require symbols. For non-experts, music and other aesthetic experiences may be non-symbolic (the experience itself, I mean). The linkage of consciousness to symbolic mediation nevertheless is a uniquely human kind of consciousness— consciousness entangled with symbols, and this is what our treatment of consciousness is meant to explain. Whether animals or silicon chips can be said to have *qualia* is part of philosophical debate. The impregnation of the world with symbols is not part of that debate, although it is James' question concerning the stream of consciousness.

Non-relevance to the 'causal powers' debate

A philosophical debate has developed in recent years about the nature of con- sciousness (see Chalmers 1996; see also Searle's (1997a) review of Chalmers, Chalmers' (1997) reply, and a further reply by Searle (1997b); the debate also rages in a new scholarly series, *Journal of Consciousness Studies*). The issues debated, however, have a different focus from that which we find in James. The issues in the philosophical debate are the causal powers that give rise to conscious experience and whether brain-matter is necessary for such experiences or whether entities like silicon chips or national populations, given the right functional organization, would have it as well. The growth point doesn't appear to contribute a great deal to this debate. It offers, instead, a psychological treatment of a topic once *de rigueur* for psychologists but now generally ignored (though see Baars 1987, Johnson-Laird 1983, for exceptions in psychology, and Chafe 1994, for linguistics). If in a psychological treatment the questions are, in a sense, less fundamental than those in the philosophical debate, they are important in a scientific sense, for they shed new light on a host of questions in cognitive psychology, including processes involved with language. At the core of the philosophical debate is the actual nature of conscious experience, what kind of thing in the universe of objects, energy, and forces is it? No question seems more fundamental. Yet consciousness—at least the form of which we have direct experience (that is, our own)—is a psychological activity *par excellence* (how it arises from brain activity is another contentious issue in the philosophical debate). The contribution to consciousness theory made here is that the presence of language changes the nature of consciousness; what James, through intro-spection, considered to be the fundamental character of consciousness seems actually to be the consciousness of thinking for speaking in a verbally engaged individual. The flow of consciousness, its segmentation into 'objects', its 'tran-sitions,' its pace, ownership, and drive to novelty are the properties of conscious experience in cycles of growth-point formation. By the same token, language is a special form of consciousness, native to our species, that is uniquely and differentially shaped by linguistic and cultural codes.

Concluding words

According to Vygotsky, utterances are processes. They are not rigid mappings of meanings onto sounds but are growing things developing over time, gradually. The growth-point hypothesis builds on this insight by portraying speaking as a form of microgenesis. Utterances develop organically and out of this process growth points are proposed as the snapshots of the utterance's starting point. A growth point is inferred from speech–gesture synchrony, buttressed by analyses of the context in which the growth point is differentiated, by functional cooperation between the image and a linguistic category as two poles, and from plausible unpacking strategies. Growth points so considered offer a unit in the stream of consciousness that William James described, a century ago.

References

Baars, B. (1987). *A cognitive theory of consciousness*. Cambridge University Press.
Chafe, W. V. (1994). *Discourse, consciousness, and time: The flow and displacement of consciousness experience in speaking and writing*. University of Chicago Press.
Chalmers, D. J. (1996). *The conscious mind: in search of a fundamental theory*. Oxford University Press.
Chalmers, D. J. (1997). Reply to John Searle. *The New York Review of Books*, 15 May 1997, p. 60.
Chase, W. G. and Ericsson, K. A. (1981). Skilled memory. In *Cognitive skills and their acquisition* (ed. J. R. Anderson), pp. 227–49. Erlbaum, Hillsdale, NJ.
De Ruiter, J.-P. (in press). The production of gesture and speech. In *Language and gesture: window into thought and action* (ed. D. McNeill), Cambridge University Press, Cambridge.
Duncan, S. D., McNeill, D., and McCullough, K.-E., (1995). How to transcribe the invisible—and what we see. In *Zeichen für Zeit: Zur Notation und Transkription von Bewegungsabläufen* (special issue of *Kodikas (Code)*) (ed. D. O'Connell, S. Kowal, and R. Posner), **18**, 75–94.

Duranti, A. and Goodwin, C. (1992). *Rethinking context: language as an interactive phenomenon*. Cambridge University Press.

James, W. (1961). *Psychology: the briefer course*. Harper and Row, New York. [First published in 1892.]

Jarvella, R. (1971). Syntactic processing of connected speech. *Journal of Verbal Learning and Verbal Behavior*, **10**, 409–16.

Johnson-Laird, P. (1983) *Mental models. Towards a cognitive science of language, inference, and consciousness*. Harvard University Press, Cambridge, MA.

Kendon, A. (1972). Some relationships between body motion and speech: An analysis of an example. In *Studies in dyadic communication* (ed. A. Siegman and B. Pope), pp. 177–210. Pergamon, Elmsford, NY.

Kendon, A. (1995). Gestures as illocutionary and discourse structure markers in Southern Italian conversation. *Journal of Pragmatics*, **23**, 247–79.

Kita, S. (1990). The temporal relationship between gesture and speech: A study of Japanese-English bilinguals. Unpublished Master's thesis. University of Chicago.

Krauss, R. M., Chen, Y., and Gottesman, R. F. (in press). Lexical gestures and lexical access: a process model. In *Language and gesture: window into thought and action* (ed. D. McNeill), Cambridge University Press, Cambridge.

Levelt, W. (1989). *Speaking*. MIT Press, Cambridge, MA.

McNeill, D. (1992). *Hand and mind: what gestures reveal about thought*. University of Chicago Press.

McNeill, D. and Duncan, S. D. (in press). Growth points in thinking-for-speaking. In *Language and gesture: window into thought and action* (ed. D. McNeill), Cambridge University Press, Cambridge.

Schiffrin, D. (1987). *Discourse markers*. Cambridge University Press.

Searle, J. (1997a). Consciousness and the philosophers. *The New York Review of Books*, 6 March 1997, pp. 43–50.

Searle, J. (1997b). Reply to David Chalmers. *The New York Review of Books*, 15 May 1997, pp. 60–1.

Talmy, L. (1985). Lexicalization patterns: semantic structure in lexical forms. In *Language typology and syntactic description, Vol. III: Grammatical categories and the lexicon* (ed. T. Shopen), pp. 57–149. Cambridge University Press.

Vygotsky, L. S. (1987). *Thought and language* (trans. A. Kozulin). MIT Press, Cambridge, MA. [First published in 1934].

Appendix

Gesture notation

The following chart summarizes the notation conventions employed in the examples cited in this chapter.

Table 5.1 Gesture notation

Notation	Interpretation
[	beginning of preparation
]	end of retraction
Bold	stroke
Underline	pre- or post-stroke hold (Kita 1990)
#	breath pause
/	silent pause
*	self-interruption
Italics	gesture description

Gesture descriptions are abbreviated as follows: LH = left hand, RH = right hand, 1H = one-handed gesture, 2SHs = two-handed gesture with the hands used in parallel ways, 2DHs = two-handed gesture with the hands used in contrasting ways.

Test situation

Most of the examples are from narrations by adult speakers retelling from memory a 7 minute animated colour cartoon that they had just watched. Speakers told the story to listeners of the same gender and approximately the same age who had not seen the cartoon. Neither speakers nor listeners were aware that gestures were of interest. For details of the method and transcription, see McNeill (1992) and Duncan *et al.* (1995).

Notes

1. With slow-motion video and instantaneous sound from stopped-frames, speech and gesture movements can be synchronized with single-field (33 ms) accuracy. This is within the resolving power of the phonetic system for most speech events.
2. This fact would seem impossible to explain with modular information processing models (see Levelt 1989).
3. It is crucial to be clear that the reference of this statement is the contents of consciousness. I do not mean that the gesture is 'consciously' (i.e., intentionally) performed. Intended gestures may also occur, but the gestures emerging from growth points are not restricted to deliberately performed gestures.

CHAPTER 6

The role of speech-related arm/hand gestures in word retrieval

Robert M. Krauss[a] and Uri Hadar[b]

[a]Columbia University; [b]Tel Aviv University

Introduction

The traditional view that gestures play an important role in communication is so widespread and well entrenched that comparatively little research has been done to assess the magnitude of their contribution, or to determine the kinds of information different types of gestures convey. Reviewing such evidence as exists, Kendon has concluded:

> The gestures that people produce when they talk do play a part in communication and they do provide information to co-participants about the semantic content of the utterances, although there clearly is variation about when and how they do so.
>
> Kendon (1994), p.192

However, other researchers, considering the same studies, have concluded that the available evidence is inconclusive, and equally consistent with the view that the gestural contribution to communication is, on the whole, negligible (Feyereisen and deLannoy 1991; Rimé and Schiaratura, 1991; Krauss *et al.* 1995). Below we will examine in some detail the question of whether gestures communicate.

One reason that gestures are so often ascribed a communicative function may be that it is not obvious what other functions they might serve. In fact, over the past half-century several have been suggested. For example, noting that people often gesture when they are having difficulty retrieving elusive words from memory, Dittmann and Llewelyn (1969) have suggested that at least some gestures may be functional in dissipating the tension that accumulates during lexical search. Dittmann and Llewelyn assume that the failure to retrieve a sought-after word is frustrating, and that the tensions generated by such frustration could interfere with the speaker's ability to produce coherent speech; hand movements provide a means of dissipating excess energy and frustration. Although other investigators have noted the co-occurrence of gestures and hesitation pauses (Freedman and Hoffman 1967; Butterworth and Beattie 1978; Christenfeld *et al.* 1991), none have attributed the gestures to tension management. The tension reduction hypothesis has never been tested experimentally, and it is not clear how it could be, but there is little doubt that gesturing and word retrieval failures co-occur (Ragsdale and Silva 1982; Hadar and Butterworth 1997).

A related possibility, that gesturing occurs during hesitation because it plays a direct role in the process of lexical retrieval, has been suggested by a strikingly diverse group of scholars over the last 75 years (DeLaguna 1927; Dobrogaev 1929; Mead 1934; Werner and Kaplan 1963; Freedman and Hoffman 1967; Moscovici 1967). The idea is not a new one, but the details of the process by which gestures might affect lexical access are both grossly underspecified and underconstrained by the available data.

In this chapter, we will first examine, from a conceptual and empirical perspective, the assumption that the primary role of gestures is communicative; we will conclude that their contribution to communication is relatively small. We will then consider evidence bearing on the possibility that gestures play a facilitative role in lexical retrieval, and conclude that there is some support for this idea. Next, we will propose a cognitive architecture that is consistent with the available evidence and accounts both for gesture production and for the facilitative effects of gestures on lexical retrieval. Finally, we will discuss specifications of the general model and, with them, possible linkages between the speech and the gesture systems.

Gesture and communication

Do gestures serve a communicative function? Any answer to this question must implicitly or explicitly assume a definition of communication, but, generally speaking, discussions of gestural communicativeness have avoided addressing some of the thorny conceptual issues that arise in formulating such a definition. Space considerations preclude us from considering them in detail (see Krauss and Fussell 1996 for a more extended discussion), but a few points will serve to outline our argument: People use both symbols and signs to convey information, but the two kinds of signals convey information in importantly different ways. The difference corresponds to the distinction Grice (1957) draws between 'natural' and 'non-natural' meanings. Natural meanings are comprehended by virtue of a causal connection between the sign and what it is understood to mean, while non-natural meanings are comprehended by virtue of an understanding of the conventions that govern symbol use.[1] Although there is hardly anything resembling a consensus on the details of the process, a fair amount is understood about the way linguistic communication is accomplished, and there seems to be general agreement on two points:

1. As regards language use, it is assumed that communication involves exchanges of intended meanings. In order for a linguistic message to be communicative, the speaker must (a) intend the message to create some particular effect (i.e., a belief) in the addressee; and (b) intend that effect to result from the addressee's recognition of the intention. Levinson puts it nicely: '... communication is a complex

kind of intention that is achieved or satisfied just by being recognized' (Levinson 1983, p.18).

2. It is assumed that language use is a *joint* activity in which the parties collaborate to produce shared meanings. From this perspective, a conversation can be viewed as a series of discursively related contributions in which speakers and hearers take pains to ensure that they have similar conceptions of the meaning of each message before they proceed to the next one.

Unlike symbols, signs do not presuppose the intention of creating a particular effect in order to have that effect, and they do not require the addressee to recognize an intention in order for them to convey information. Sperber and Wilson (1986) illustrate the distinction with the example of a woman who has a sore throat and wishes to inform someone of this fact. She could accomplish this by saying 'I have a sore throat', but the information could equally well be conveyed by saying anything, and allowing the listener to infer her condition from her hoarse voice. In the former case, in which the information is conveyed linguistically, the speaker's intention is critical, while in the second, her intention to convey the information is irrelevant.

One way of defining communication is as information that has been conveyed in accordance with the intentionality and joint action criteria, Thus defined, communication would include most instances of language use, the use of such symbolic gestures or emblems as the 'thumbs-up' sign, and certain deictic gestures. It would exclude sign behaviours such as a hoarse voice or blushing, which, although they unquestionably convey information, do so in a different fashion. The question we address is: would it include what Kendon (1994) calls 'the gestures that people produce when they talk',—what McNeill (1992) calls 'representational gestures' and we have called 'lexical gestures'?

Kendon and others (see Schegloff 1984; de Ruiter, in press) contend that it would. They argue that speakers partition the information that constitutes their communicative intentions, choosing to convey some of it verbally in the spoken message, some of it visibly via gesture, facial expression, etc., and some of it in both modalities. Kendon (1980) uses the example of a speaker saying '... with a big cake on it ...' while making a series of circular motions of the forearm with the index finger pointing downward. Kendon would have the speaker *intending* to convey the idea that the cake was both large *and* round, and choosing to convey ROUND gesturally rather than verbally.

Although there is nothing implausible about Kendon's interpretation, it is unclear from his description of the episode that the speaker's behaviour satisfies the intentionality and joint activity criteria. Since it was explicitly included in the utterance, it is reasonable to assume that the idea of the cake being large was part of the speaker's communicative intention, presumably because it was discursively relevant. Can we assume this is also the case about its being round? Such an assumption would need to be justified with other evidence (perhaps from elsewhere in the narrative), but the mere fact that the gesture occurred and is interpretable in context is insufficient to demonstrate that it was communicatively intended.

Something we saw in one of our own experiments suggests how misleading such observations can be. In that experiment subjects learned the definitions of arcane words, and were later videotaped as they tried to recall the definitions. One of the words was 'deasil', which means 'to move in a clockwise direction'. All 14 of the subjects who remembered the word's definition made a rotary movement of the index finger as they defined it. It seems reasonable to regard the gesture as intended to aid the listener. However, for all but one speaker, the rotation was clockwise relative to the speaker; that is to say, from the addressee's perspective, the movement was counterclockwise, and hence misleading.[2] It is instructive to compare the subjects' behaviour in this situation to what speakers do when they formulate spatial descriptions verbally. According to Schober (1993, 1995), speakers formulating referring expressions about locations overwhelmingly formulate them from the perspective of the addressee. The fact that most of the speech-accompanying gestures in our experiment were formulated from the speaker's perspective underscores the danger of assuming that they were intended in the same way in which the elements of an utterance are intended. Clearly, if they were so intended, they were defective from the addressee's perspective.

Overall, empirical evidence for the communicativeness of gestures is at best equivocal. Experimental findings indicate that, on average, lexical gestures convey relatively little information (Feyereisen *et al.* 1988; Krauss *et al.* 1991, experiments 1 and 2), and that the extent to which they influence the semantic interpretation of utterances is negligible (Krauss *et al.* 1991, experiment 5). Moreover, adding a speaker's gestures to his/her voice does not enhance listeners' performance on a referential communication task, in which it is possible to measure how well a message accomplishes its intended purpose (Krauss *et al.* 1995).

Three studies (Graham and Argyle 1975; Rogers 1978; Riseborough 1981) are often cited as providing empirical support for the hypothesis that hand gestures serve a communicative function, at least in highly specific circumstances. All three purport to find small, but statistically reliable, performance increments on tests of information (e.g., reproduction of a figure from a description; answering questions about an object on the basis of a description) for listeners who could see a speaker's gestures, compared with those who could not, suggesting that the gestures enhanced the effectiveness of the communication. However, all three studies suffer from serious methodological problems, and we believe that little can be concluded from them.

Graham and Argyle (1975) asked six speakers to describe abstract line draw-ings to a small audience of listeners who then tried to reproduce them. In half of the trials, the speakers were prevented from gesturing. Listeners reproduced the figures more accurately from descriptions given when speakers were allowed to gesture. However, the design of the experiment does not control for the possibility that speakers who were allowed to gesture produced better *verbal* descriptions of the stimuli, which, in turn, enabled their audiences to reproduce the figures more accurately, quite apart from any information conveyed by the gestures. The Riseborough (1981) study found an effect of gesturing for only one of three stimuli, and it is not clear that the relevant contrast was statistically reliable. Rogers (1978) found that subjects who both viewed and heard videotaped descriptions of novel actions scored better on multiple choice tests of information than did subjects who only heard the audio track. However, the result was found only when a relatively high level of noise (signal-to-noise ratios of −3 and −8 dB) was added to the audio track. With more favorable signal-to-noise ratios (+2 and +7 dB), seeing the speaker had no demonstrable effect on communication. Rogers also did not control adequately for the 'speechreading effect'—the well established finding that seeing a speaker's lips contributes to the intelligibility of speech (Sumby and Pollack 1954; see also Chapter 4, this volume).

More recently, McNeill *et al.* (1994) have found that gestural information that differed from the information conveyed by the accompanying speech tended to be reflected in listeners' later retellings of the narrative, suggesting that speech and gesture information were combined in memory. This study seems to provide a clear demonstration that at least some co-speech gestures can contribute to listeners' comprehension, but it is not without problems. In our experience, speech–gesture mismatches of the kind used by McNeill *et al.* are relatively rare in adult speech; in the study, the mismatches were enacted simulations rather than naturally occurring events. Even if we were to accept these results at face value, the communicative contribution of the overwhelming majority of the non-mismatched gestures that accompany spontaneous speech still remains to be established.

The fact that speakers gesture more often when they can see their addressees than when they cannot (Cohen and Harrison 1972; Cohen, 1977; Rimé, 1982; Bavelas *et al.* 1992; Krauss *et al.* 1995) is sometimes cited as evidence that the gestures are communicatively intended (Cohen and Harrison 1972; Kendon, 1994). Certainly it is weak evidence at best, since speakers do gesture when their listeners cannot see them. Are the gestures speakers make when they are visually inaccessible different from the ones they make when they can be seen? Not much research has been directed to this question; the little we know of suggests that they are not. Krauss *et al.* (in preparation) coded the grammatical types of 12,425 gestural lexical affiliates (i.e., the word or words in the accompanying speech associated with the gesture) from an experiment in which subjects described stimuli to a partner who was either seated face-to-face or in another room. The grammatical categories of gestural lexical affiliates for the two conditions did not differ, suggesting that speakers gestured at the same points in their narratives regardless of whether or not they could be seen by their partners.

De Ruiter (in press) argues that the occurrence of gesturing by speakers who cannot be seen, and findings that gestures have relatively little communicative value, do not reduce the plausibility of the idea that such gestures are communicatively intended.

Gesture may well be intended by the speaker to communicate, and fail to do so in some or even most cases. The fact that people gesture on the telephone is also not necessarily in conflict with the view that gestures are generally intended to be communicative. It is conceivable that people gesture on the telephone because they always gesture when they speak spontaneously—they simply cannot suppress it.

Although the idea that such gestures reflect overlearned habits is not implausible, the contention that they are both communicatively intended *and* largely ineffective runs counter to a modern understanding of how language (and other behaviours) function in communication. De Ruiter's view implicitly conceptualizes participants as 'autonomous information processors' (Brennan 1991). Such a view stands in sharp contrast with what Clark (1996) and his colleagues have called a 'collaborative' model of language use. In this view, communicative exchange is a joint accomplishment of the participants who work together to achieve some set of communicative goals. Communication requires that speakers and hearers endeavour to ensure they have similar conceptions of the meaning of each message before they proceed to the next one. Indeed, from the collaborative perspective, an utterance has no meaning until the participants have ratified it. The idea that some element of a message is communicatively intended, but consistently goes uncomprehended, violates what Clark and Wilkes-Gibbs (1986) have termed the 'principle of mutual responsibility'.

We believe that symbolic (emblematic) gestures, deictic gestures, and the kind of gestural activity that Clark has termed 'demonstrations' are, as a rule, both communicatively intended *and* communicatively effective. The question we raise is whether there is adequate justification for assuming that all or most co-speech gestures are so intended. We believe there is not. No doubt lexical gestures occasionally are intentionally performed, and it seems likely that some do convey information to a visually attentive listener regardless of whether or not they were so intended by the speaker. However, considering, on the one hand, the amount of gesturing that accompanies speech, and, on the other hand, the paucity of the information gestures seem to convey, it seems to us reasonable to ask whether gestures might be serving some other function.

The question of the functions lexical gestures serve has important implications for models of gesture production. If gestures are communicatively intended in the way utterances are, it seems reasonable to suppose that they share some stages of the production process with speech. If they are not, gesture and speech could have different sources. If gestures facilitate lexical retrieval, the speech production system and the gesture production system must interact. If they do not, the two systems could function autonomously.

Gesture and word retrieval

If hand gestures do not serve a communicative function, why would speakers bother to make them? One possibility is that they play a role in speech production. Empirical support for this notion is mixed. In the earliest published study,

Dobrogaev (1929) reported that speakers instructed to curb facial expressions, head movements, and gestural movements of the extremities found it difficult to produce articulate speech, but the experiment appears to have lacked necessary controls. As was common in that era, Dobrogaev's report fails to describe procedural details, and the results are presented in impressionistic, qualitative terms. More recently, Graham and Heywood (1975) analysed the speech of five speakers who were prevented from gesturing as they described abstract line drawings, and concluded that '... elimination of gesture had no particularly marked effects on speech performance' (p.194). On the other hand, Rimé (1982) and Rauscher *et al.* (1996) found that restricting gesturing adversely affects speech fluency. The Rauscher *et al.* study is especially relevant to our hypothesis that gestures facilitate access to lexical memory, because the effects of preventing gesturing on speech were found to be similar to the effects of making word retrieval difficult by other means (e.g., requiring subjects to use rare or unusual words).

More evidence supporting the association of gesture with word retrieval difficulties comes from studies with brain-damaged subjects. It has been known for some time that adults with Broca's aphasia produce more gestures per unit of speech than normal controls (Goldblum 1978), but there have been claims that these gestures were often disrupted in ways that paralleled the speaker's language disorder (McNeill 1992). In a single-case study, Butterworth *et al.* (1981) showed that their aphasic patient tended to gesture prior to a word retrieval failure (either a hesitation or an erroneous production). More recently, Hadar *et al.* (1998b) found that aphasics whose speech problems primarily concerned word retrieval tended to gesture more than both normal controls and other aphasics whose problems were primarily conceptual. About 70% of the gestures of the aphasics with word retrieval difficulties appeared adjacent to a hesitation or erroneous production. At the same time, and contrary to the hypothesis of a gestural deficit, the composition and form of their gestures were normal.

In a very different kind of study, Hanlon *et al.* (1990) showed that aphasic patients' word retrieval in a picture naming task could be improved by training them to perform gestures just prior to their naming attempt.

Lexical, iconic, and metaphoric gestures

In the two sections that follow, we present a model of speech and gesture production in which the latter supports the former. Our model does not attempt to account for all speech-related gestures, only the subset that we previously have called 'lexical' (Hadar 1989; Krauss *et al.* 1995). Lexical gestures are relatively long, broad, and complex arm–hand movements that often incorporate shapes or dynamics related to the content of the accompanying speech (Hadar *et al.* 1998a,b). Other co-speech gestures that typically are short, simple, and repetitive, called 'beats' by McNeill (1992) and 'motor gestures' by Krauss *et al.* (in press), do not seem to be involved in lexical search, and probably link to speech through other systems (Butterworth and Hadar 1989; Hadar 1989). Discussions of terminological and descriptive aspects of gesture can be found in Rimé and Schiaratura (1992) and Krauss *et al.* (in press). Although the nature of gestural taxonomies is not a settled matter, we do not plan to enter this discussion here, but instead to address some issues that specifically concern lexical gestures.

Investigators often partition the movements we are calling lexical gestures into subcategories, although there is little consensus as to what those subcategories should include and exclude. Probably the most widely accepted is the subcategory of 'iconic gestures'—gestures that represent their meanings pictographically in the sense that the gesture's form is related conceptually to the semantic content of the speech it accompanies (Efron 1941 [1972]). However, not all lexical gestures are iconic. The proportion of lexical movements that are iconic is difficult to determine, and probably depends greatly on the conceptual content of the speech and the flexibility of the standards used to determine iconicity. But, however iconicity is determined, many speech-accompanying movements seem to have little obvious formal relationship to the conceptual content of the accompanying speech. What can be said of these gestures? McNeill (1985, 1987, 1992) deals with the problem by drawing a distinction between gestures that are iconic and gestures that are metaphoric:

Metaphoric gestures exhibit images of abstract concepts. In form and manner of execution, metaphoric gestures depict the vehicles of metaphors ... The metaphors are independently motivated on the basis of cultural and linguistic knowledge.

McNeill (1985), p.356

Despite its widespread acceptance, we have reservations about the utility of the iconic/metaphoric distinction. Our own observations lead us to conclude that iconicity is more a matter of degree rather than of kind. While the forms of some lexical gestures do seem to have a direct and transparent relationship to the content of the accompanying speech, for others the relationship is more tenuous, and for still others finding any relationship at all requires a good deal of imagination on the part of the observer. In our view, it makes more sense to think of gestures as being more or less iconic rather than either iconic or metaphoric. Moreover, although it may be possible to judge the iconicity of gestures fairly reliably, the 'meanings' of such gestures are highly uncertain, even when viewing them along with the accompanying speech. In the absence of speech, the meanings of iconic gestures are indeterminate (Feyereisen *et al.* 1988; Krauss *et al.* 1991).

We also find problems with the iconic/metaphoric distinction at the conceptual level. The argument that metaphoric gestures are produced in the same way as linguistic metaphors does not help us understand how they are generated, since our understanding of the processes by which linguistic metaphors are produced and comprehended is incomplete at best (see Glucksberg 1991; Glucksberg, 1993). So identifying such gestures as visual metaphors may be little more than a way of saying that the nature of their iconicity is not obvious.

In what ways might such classifications be useful? The idea that a gesture is iconic provides a principled basis for explaining why it takes the form it does. Calling a gesture metaphoric can be seen as an attempt to accomplish the same thing for gestures that lack a formal relationship to the accompanying speech. However, we do not believe that identifying gestures as metaphoric really accomplishes that goal, and instead will opt for a model formulated at the level of features as a more satisfactory way of accounting for gestural form.

Speech production

In our model, lexical gestures reflect the use that the speech production system makes of the gesture production system for word retrieval purposes. Before describing the gesture production system, we will review our understanding of the process by which speech is generated. Of course, the nature of speech production is not uncontroversial, and a variety of production models have been proposed. Although these models differ in significant ways, for our purposes their differences are less important than their similarities. Most models distinguish three successive stages of processing, which Levelt (1989) refers to as 'conceptualizing', 'formulating', and 'articulating' (Garrett 1984; Dell 1986; Butterworth 1989). The process is illustrated schematically in Fig. 6.1 below, which is based on Levelt (1989). Let us examine the model's stages more closely.

Conceptualizing involves, among other things, drawing upon declarative and procedural knowledge to construct a communicative intention. We believe that many memorial representations, in a variety of representational formats, are activated initially by contextual triggering and structural (cognitive/affective) biases. Then a more active process of 'focusing' reduces the number of activated representations, and forms connections between those remaining (Sperber and Wilson 1986; Levelt 1989). The output of the conceptualizing stage—what Levelt refers to as a preverbal message—can be thought of as a propositional structure containing a set of pragmatic and semantic specifications (Bierwisch and Schreuder 1992).

This preverbal message constitutes the input to the formulating stage, where the message is transformed in two ways. First, a grammatical encoder maps the to-be-lexicalized concept onto an abstract syntactic structure. At the same time the main lexical entries of the message are selected in the form of lemmas, i.e., abstract symbols representing the selected words as semantic–syntactic entities. Lemmas are selected whose semantic features match a subset of the semantic features of the preverbal message. A 'surface structure' is formed by joining the abstract syntactic structure with the lemmas. Then, by accessing word forms stored in lexical memory and constructing an appropriate plan for the utterance's prosody, the phonological encoder transforms this surface structure into a 'phonetic plan' (essentially a set of instructions to the articulatory system) that serves as the input to the articulatory stage. The output of the articulatory stage is

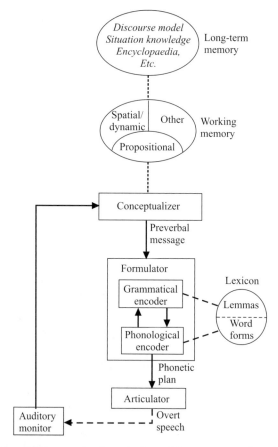

Fig. 6.1 A cognitive architecture for the speech production process (based on Levelt 1989).

overt speech, which is monitored auditorily and used as a source of corrective feedback.

Gesture production

Our model makes several assumptions about mental representation and memory. They are:

(1) Memory employs a number of different formats to represent knowledge, and much of the content of memory is multiply encoded in more than one representational format.

(2) Activation of a concept in one representational format tends to activate related concepts in other formats.

(3) Concepts differ in how adequately (i.e., efficiently, completely, accessibly, etc.) they can be represented in one or another format. The complete mental representation of some concepts may require inputs from more than one representational format.

(4) Some representations in one format can be translated into the representational form of another format (e.g., a verbal description can give rise to visual imagery, and vice versa).

None of these assumptions is particularly controversial, at least at this level of generality.

In our view, gestures originate in the process that precedes conceptualization and construction of the preverbal message. That is to say, we believe their origin *precedes* the formulation of the speaker's communicative intention. Consider Kendon's (1980) aforementioned example of the speaker saying '... with a big cake on it ...' while making a series of circular motions of the forearm with index finger pointing downward. We assume that the articulated word 'cake' derives from a conceptual representation of a particular object in the speaker's long-term memory. The preverbal message outputted by the conceptualizer (and which the grammatical encoder transforms into a linguistic representation) typically incorporates only a subset of the memorial representation's features. From the information Kendon gives us, it seems reasonable to assume that the particular cake the speaker referred to in the example was represented in memory as large and round. Of course, it also had other properties—colour, flavour, texture, and so on—that might have been mentioned but were not, presumably because (unlike the cake's size) they were not relevant to the speaker's goals in the discourse.

Apropos our earlier discussion of communication, a central theoretical question is whether or not the information that the cake was round—i.e., the information contained in the gesture—was part of the speaker's communicative intention. From his discussion, it is clear that Kendon (1980) assumes that it was. Our assumption is that it was not. Below we will consider some of the implications of this assumption.

We follow Levelt in assuming that information transferred from the conceptualizing stage to the formulating stage of the speech processor must be in propositional form. However, the knowledge that is accessed from memory and becomes incorporated into the communicative intention may be multiply encoded in propositional and nonpropositional formats, or even encoded exclusively in nonpropositional formats. In order for nonpropositionally encoded knowledge to be reflected in speech, it must be 'translated' into propositional form.

How do these nonpropositionally represented features come to be reflected gesturally? The model is illustrated in Fig. 6.2. Like the speech production system, the gesture production system has three stages. In the first stage, a 'spatial/dynamic feature selector' takes representations that have been activated in spatial or visual working memory, selects out elementary spatial and dynamic features, and renders them as a set of spatial/dynamic specifications. These specifications

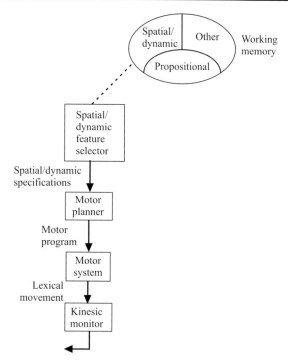

Fig. 6.2 A cognitive architecture for the gesture production system.

are essentially abstract features of movements—velocity, direction, contour, and the like. This set of abstract features serves as input to the 'motor planner', which translates them into a 'motor program'—a set of instructions for executing the lexical gesture. These instructions are then executed by the motor system in the form of a gestural movement. Thus thinking of a particular cake that happened to have been round would activate the spatial feature ROUND, which is translated into a circling motion by the motor planner. A single gesture may reflect one or more spatial/dynamic features. For example, the circling gesture is, at least in principle, capable of representing both shape and circumference. However, some combinations of features may be difficult or impossible to incorporate simultaneously into a single gesture; for example, if both ROUND and THICK were activated features of the remembered cake, the gesture might reflect one or the other, but probably not both.

Once they have been produced, gestures are monitored kinaesthetically in much the same way that the output of the speech production system is monitored auditorily. We will leave the destination of the kinaesthetic monitor's output to be specified later.

It is not difficult to see in general terms how such a system could generate gestures from conceptual content that is concrete and spatial (e.g., *book*, *arc*) or involves movement (e.g., *twist*, *lift*), but gesturing also accompanies talk whose conceptual content is abstract and static. What is the origin of these gestures? In the first place, it is important to know that gesturing is strongly associated with speech having concrete, and especially spatial, content. Speakers describing animated action cartoons were nearly five times more likely to gesture during clauses containing spatial prepositions than they were elsewhere (Rauscher *et al.* 1996). Zhang (reported in Krauss *et al.* in preparation) measured the proportion of time speakers spent gesturing as they defined a variety of common words. Ratings of the 'spatiality' of word concepts accounted for more than half of the variability in the amount of time speakers spent gesturing while defining them.

Although the evidence suggests that gesturing derives primarily from spatial (and, we believe, dynamic) features of concepts, some gesturing accompanies speech that has no apparent spatial or dynamic content. In Zhang's study, subjects gestured more than twice as much when defining 'adjacent' and 'cube' than they did when defining 'thought' and 'devotion'; nevertheless, speakers gestured during about 17% of the time they spent defining the latter two words. Since neither term has explicit spatial or dynamic content, the fact that their definitions were accompanied by gesturing seems inconsistent with our model. In understanding how the model accounts for such gestures, it is important to bear in mind that it assumes gestures to be products of memorial representations rather then of communicative intentions. What we believe to be involved are interconnected systems containing concepts, lemmas, long-term visuospatial representations and motor schemata so arranged that the activation of any concept can result in the activation of a loosely connected motor schema. The outline of such a system has only recently begun to emerge, describing such connections between visuospatial and motor schema mediated by the increasingly popular notion of 'embodiment' (Ballard *et al.* 1997), lemma and visuospatial representations (Bierwisch 1996) and the figurative context of lexical semantics (Gibbs 1997). These ideas, of course, require much more detailed development to connect them to specific gestural phenomena.

Gestural facilitation of speech

Our contention is that lexical gestures facilitate lexical retrieval. The process by which it is proposed this is accomplished is illustrated in Fig. 6.3, in which the gesture production system and the speech production system are connected. We will first describe the general form of the model and then examine some specific issues it raises. In Fig. 6.3, the spatiodynamic information encoded by the gesture is fed via the kinesic monitor to the formulator, where it facilitates lexical retrieval. Facilitation is achieved through cross-modal priming, in which gesturally-represented features of the concept in memory participate in lexical search. Of course, it is possible to specify the site of gestural input more precisely (e.g., the grammatical encoder or the phonological encoder).

Figure 6.3 shows the gesture production system affecting the speech pro-

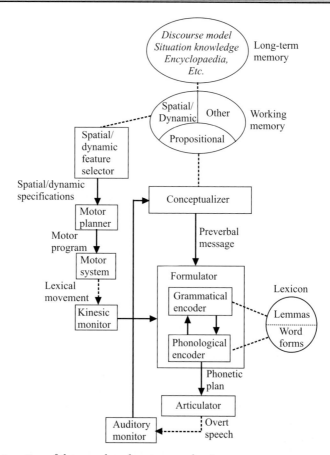

Fig. 6.3 Interaction of the speech and gesture production systems.

duction system. Not shown is a path by which the speech production system provides input to the gesture production system. Some such a link may be necessary to tell the gesture production system when to terminate a gesture.

Further specification of the model

The model illustrated in Fig. 6.3 describes a set of structures and a general process flow. There is considerable empirical support for some aspects of the model, while others are quite speculative. Models of the gesture production system and the process by which it and the speech production system interact must of necessity be speculative because there is relatively little reliable data available to constrain them. Not surprisingly, researchers have made quite different assumptions about the processes involved. In this section we will consider alternative ways of specifying the process of gesture production and gesture–speech interaction, and examine the relevant data.

Gesture origins

In the literature on gesture, the term 'origin' has been used to refer to two different, but related, aspects of the gesture production system. One usage refers to the source of input to the gesture production system; this is the usage we will favour. The other usage of 'origin' refers to the process that triggers or activates the gesture. We will refer to this process as gesture *initiation*, and discuss it, along with gesture termination, in the next section

In Fig. 6.3, the origin of gesture is shown to be the spatial–dynamic representations in working memory that activate the feature selection component of the gesture production system (see Fig. 6.2); in our view, gestures always involve processes that precede the formulation of a communicative intention. Others have made different assumptions. For example, in a model quite similar to ours in other respects, de Ruiter (in press) designates the conceptualizer as the origin of the gesture production system's input. This is consistent with his assumption that lexical gestures are communicatively intended. We have already discussed what we see as problematic with that assumption. Specifying the conceptualizer as the origin of gestures raises the additional problem of how such gestures could aid in lexical access. If the conceptualizer's input to the gesture planner in de Ruiter's model contains the same information as the input to the formulator, it would be difficult to see how gestural information could facilitate lexical retrieval, or why preventing gesturing should make lexical retrieval more difficult.

The idea that lexical gestures have an early origin is consistent with the well-established finding that lexical gestures precede their lexical affiliates temporally (Butterworth and Beattie 1978; Schegloff 1984; Morrel-Samuels and Krauss 1992). Morrel-Samuels and Krauss, for example, examined 60 carefully selected lexical gestures, and found the gesture–speech asynchrony (the time interval between the onset of the lexical gesture and the onset of the lexical affiliate) to range from 0 to 3.75 s, with a mean of 0.99 s and a median of 0.75 s; none of the 60 gestures was initiated after articulation of the lexical affiliate had begun. The durations of the gestures ranged from 0.54 s to 7.71 s (mean = 2.49 s), and only three of the 60 terminated before articulation of the lexical affiliate had been initiated. The product–moment correlation between gestural duration and asynchrony is +0.71.

The idea that lexical gestures originate in short-term memory contrasts with the position taken by McNeill (1992), who argued for multiple links between the speech and the gesture systems, consistent with a connectionist cognitive architecture. We find that such an architecture contributes little to explicating the relationship of gesture and speech because it is insufficiently constrained and, therefore, does not produce sufficiently specific predictions.

Employing more modular architectures, Butterworth and Beattie (1978),

Butterworth and Hadar (1989), and Hadar and Butterworth (1997) have argued in favour of multiple gestural origins, one in short-term memory and the other later in the speech production process. Their argument hinges upon a distinction between iconic gesture and gestures that are indefinite, in the sense that they cannot be affiliated with a specific lexical item. They hypothesize that indefinite gestures originate in short-term memory, while iconic gestures are directly activated by lexical processes. However, the available data do not support this idea. By the logic of their argument, iconic gestures should tend to start during hesitation pauses, while indefinite gestures should not. By the same argument, the gesture–speech asynchrony (i.e., the interval between the initiation of the gesture and the articulation of the lexical affiliate) should be smaller for iconic gestures that start during hesitation pauses than it is for iconic gestures that do not start during hesitation pauses. In neither case is the available evidence supportive (Hadar *et al.* 1998a,b). The Butterworth and Hadar argument brings into focus the important issues of gesture initiation and termination, which we address in the next section.

The initiation and termination of gestures

What causes a speaker to gesture? Krauss *et al.* (1995, in press) assume that the early conceptual processes that produce the input to the conceptualizer routinely implicate non-propositional representations. Some of these derive from spatial or dynamic properties of the processed concepts, and this particular subset of non-propositional representations is linked with the gesture production system: its activation activates the spatial/dynamic features selector. On this account, whenever a spatial representation is activated, a gesture is triggered. Krauss *et al.* (1995, in press) present two kinds of evidence in support of their model: First, speech with spatial content is considerably more likely to be accompanied by gestures than speech with other kinds of content, although this was not found in a study by Hadar and Krauss (in press). Second, preventing speakers from gesturing selectively impairs speech with spatial content (Rauscher *et al.* 1996). Although the latter finding has not yet been independently replicated, the account as a whole seems plausible and consistent with the available data. However, it certainly is possible that the subset of representations linked up with gesture production is not specifically spatial, but visual, as McNeill (1992) suggests, or visuospatial, as Hadar *et al.* (1998a) suggest.

Krauss *et al.* (1995, in press) explain the tendency of gestures to be associated with hesitations by assuming that lexical selection switches off the gesture production system. On this account, if the set of features that activated the gesture is realized in lexical selection, the gesture production process is aborted. Consequently, many gestures are activated but not executed; difficulties encountered in lexical selection may simply allows sufficient time for the gesture to reach execution. Alternatively, a gesture simply may be terminated when a new gesture is initiated.

Butterworth and Hadar have proposed a more complex dual mechanism for gesture initiation in which some gestures are activated directly from short-term memory, while others are initiated by failures of lexical retrieval (Butterworth and Hadar 1989; Hadar and Butterworth 1997). They contend that such failures often initiate a re-run of lexical selection, and that during such re-runs, the formulator attempts to gather more cues for lexical selection by activating non-propositional representations related to the sought-for lexical entry. These non-propositional representations, in turn, activate a gesture. We accept this possibility, but stress that the available evidence suggests that in these cases the loop of the re-run must be 'deep' enough to activate early representations, and it is these early representations which activate the gesture. We also note that the lexical loop may, at best, apply only to those gestures that are associated with hesitations. On our count, these amount to about 70% of gestures in aphasic patients with primarily lexical retrieval problems, but in healthy subjects they amount to about 30% of lexical gestures (Hadar *et al.* 1998b). A different kind of mechanism must be hypothesized to account for gestures that are not associated with hesitation.

The input from gesture to speech

In order to affect lexical retrieval, gesture-related information must enter the speech system. There are a number of possible entry points. Figure 6.3 shows the output of the kinesic monitor feeding into the formulator. This is the simplest inference from the hypothesis of lexical facilitation: gesture-related information acts as input to lexical selection either in the form of additional cues (Hadar and Butterworth 1997) or in the form of cross-modal priming (Krauss *et al.* in press).

Hadar and Butterworth (1997) have suggested that gestural information might be input to the conceptualizer. On this account, gesture-related information would contribute to the construction of the speaker's communicative intention and affect lexical retrieval only indirectly. The available evidence, although far from definitive, is not supportive of this view. Rauscher *et al.* (1996) found that preventing speakers from gesturing increased the relative frequency of non-juncture pauses in their speech. Unlike juncture pauses, which can result from a variety of causes (including conceptualizing), nonjuncture pauses seem mainly to reflect problems in lexical retrieval (see Krauss *et al.* 1996 for a discussion). Hence, the fact that preventing gestures selectively affects hesitations is consistent with the proposition that gestures are involved with lexical retrieval. However, the subjects' task in this study (describing the plots of animated action cartoons) may have made minimal conceptual demands. What Rauscher *et al.* found was that making lexical retrieval more difficult increased the impact of preventing gesturing; similarly, varying the conceptual complexity of the speaker's task might reveal that what we are calling lexical gestures also function at the conceptual level. Research by Goldin-Meadow *et al.* (1993) and observations by McNeill (1992) seem to indicate that gesturing is associated with conceptual activity, but the role they play is far from clear.

Within the formulator, gesture-related information could serve as an input to either the grammatical encoder or the phonological encoder, or to both. Lexical retrieval proceeds in two separate stages—lemma selection and word-form selection—and problems at either stage could result in the kinds of dysfluencies observed by Rauscher *et al.* It is reasonable to assume that gesture-related information enters the speech system at the point at which facilitation occurs, so examining facilitation effects may help us decide this issue. Unfortunately, the empirical evidence is contradictory.

Some findings support the idea of semantic facilitation, suggesting entry via the lemma system. For example, aphasic patients who have problems naming objects tend to produce more lexical gestures if their difficulties involve retrieval of the lemma rather than retrieval of the word form (Hadar *et al.* 1998b). Also, native speakers of Hebrew with good facility in English produced more lexical gestures accompanying self-generated descriptions in both English and Hebrew than they did while translating from Hebrew to English or from English to Hebrew (Teitelman 1997). If one assumes that hesitation in a second language derives from problems in accessing word forms (Kroll and Stewart 1994), then the dearth of gestures contraindicates phonological retrieval as the beneficiary of gesture. However, the same study found more lexical gestures accompanying self-generated descriptions in English than in Hebrew, which is consistent with the word-form hypothesis. To complicate matters further, Dushay (1991) found that subjects in a referential communication task gestured less often when describing abstract figures and synthesized sounds in a second language than in their native language. Dushay's subjects, students taking second year Spanish, were considerably less fluent than Teitelman's, and unpublished data collected by Melissa Lau suggests that frequency of gesturing in L_2 may be a function of the speaker's fluency: the more fluent her English–Cantonese bilinguals were in Cantonese, the more frequently they gestured while speaking it. Like Teitelman, Lau's subjects gestured more when speaking spontaneously than they did when translating, either from Cantonese to English or from English to Cantonese. However, unlike Teitelman's subjects, hers gestured more frequently overall when speaking English (L_1) than Cantonese (L_2). At this point, it is not clear what can be concluded about gestural input to the speech production system from the gestural behaviour of bilinguals.

Finally, since there is no systematic relationship between the semantic features that are part of the lemma and the phonological features that make up the word form, if lexical facilitation is achieved through priming, as Krauss *et al.* (1995) suggest, it seems likely that facilitation occurs at the level of lemma selection.

On the other hand, findings from studies using the 'tip of the tongue' paradigm are consistent with the view that gestures facilitate retrieval at the word form rather than the lemma level. It is well accepted that 'tip of the tongue' retrieval failures in normal subjects tend to be phonological rather than semantic (Brown and McNeill 1966; Jones and Langford 1987; Kohn *et al.* 1987; Jones 1989; Brown 1991; Meyer and Bock 1992), and preventing gesturing increases retrieval failures in the 'tip of the tongue' situation (Frick-Horbury and Guttentag, 1998). In the same vein, Broca's aphasics tend to produce very high proportions of lexical gestures (Cicone *et al.* 1979; McNeill 1992), and their ability to name also seems to benefit from intentionally performing a gesture prior to naming (Hanlon *et al.* 1990). However, there is some disagreement on the nature of naming problems in Broca's aphasia. While some researchers (e.g., Brown 1982) consider these patients' difficulties to be similar to 'tip of the tongue' problems, others (e.g., Williams and Canter 1987) argue that their retrieval failures primarily involve verbs, and therefore originate in lemma selection.

In sum, there is considerable evidence to indicate that the gesture production system's output affects the formulator in the speech production system. Certainly it is possible that gesture-related information also affects the conceptualizer, but the evidence for this is largely anecdotal. Within the formulator, gesture-related information could influence either grammatical or phonological encoding, and there is indirect evidence consistent with both possibilities. Although it seems reasonably clear that information from the gesture production system can affect speech production, we are not yet in a position to specify the locus or loci of these effects.

The output from gesture to speech

At what point does the gesture-related information leave the gesture production system and enter the speech system? As before, there are several possibilities, all underconstrained by the available data. Butterworth and Hadar (1989; Hadar and Butterworth 1997) have suggested that the information leaves the gesture production system from its origin, that is, before generating the gesture. In their account, gesturing might be considered an artefact of the activation of the direct origin, the real purpose of which is to re-run the word selection process. They offer no data to support their claim, but rather adduce it as an inference from considerations of conceptual processing. In their view, gesture acts only to maintain activation of the non-propositional representation long enough for the word selection process to develop. The actual production of gesture, then, can contribute to facilitation, but does so indirectly.

Krauss *et al.* (1995, in press) hold a contrary view—that the gesture must actually be performed for facilitation to occur. In their model, information contained in the gesture, consisting of kinaesthetic and proprioceptive representations, is extracted by the kinesic monitor. It is this information, inputted to the formulator, that facilitates retrieval. They conclude this largely from the finding that limitation of gesturing impairs word retrieval in normal subjects. Note that some impairment can be inferred from the Hadar and Butterworth model as well, but the two accounts differ as to how readily subjects should be able to compensate for gestural immobilization. According to Hadar and Butterworth (1997), but not Krauss *et al.* (1995), compensation should be fairly easy.

Concluding comment

We have described the general outlines of a model for the production of lexical gestures. We also have examined in some detail a number of alternative ways of formulating the model, and considered their strengths and vulnerabilities. One conclusion seems reasonably clear. As things currently stand, there are so few reliable data to constrain theory on gesture production that any processing model must be both tentative and highly speculative. Nevertheless, we do not believe that model building in such circumstances is a waste of time. Models provide a convenient way of systematizing available data. They also compel theorists to make explicit the assumptions that underlie their formulations, thus making it easier to assess in what ways, and to what extent, apparently different theories differ. Finally, and perhaps most importantly, models guide investigators' efforts, and lead them to collect data that will confirm or disconfirm one or another model.

Our account has relied primarily on data from experiments. Experimentation is, of course, a powerful method for generating certain kinds of data, but it also has serious limitations, and Kendon (1994) has remarked on discrepancies between the conclusions reached by investigators who rely on experimental findings and those whose data derive mainly from natural observation. Observational studies have enhanced our understanding of what gestures accomplish, and the recent addition of neuropsychological observations should provide further insight into the gesture production system. The conclusions of careful and seasoned observers certainly deserve to be taken seriously. At the same time, we are uncomfortable with some investigators' excessive reliance upon observers' impressions of gestural form or meaning, especially when the observers are not blind to the content of the accompanying speech. Without the proper controls, such impressions provide a weak foundation for theory and, we believe, are more usefully thought of as a source of hypotheses than as data in their own right.

We have few illusions that we have considered every possible implementation of the model, or that all of the assumptions we have made will ultimately prove to have been justified. Indeed, our own ideas about the process by which lexical gestures are generated have changed considerably over the last several years, and we would be surprised if they did not continue to change as data accumulate. Although many of the data currently available are equivocal, and many more remain to be collected, we believe that the process in which models are produced and data (both experimental and observational) are collected to confirm or disconfirm them will ultimately result in a genuine understanding of how gestures are produced and how they are related to speech.

References

Ballard, D. H., Hayhoe, M. M., Pook, P. K., and Rao, R.P. (1997). Deictic codes for the embodiment of cognition. *Behavioral and Brain Sciences*, **20**, 723–67.

Bavelas, J. B., Chovil, N., Lawrie, D. A., and Wade, A. (1992). Interactive gestures. *Discourse Processes*, 15, 469–89.

Bierwisch, M. (1996) How much space gets into language? In *Language and space* (ed. P. Bloom, M. A. Peterson, L. Nadel, and M. F. Garrett), pp. 31–76. MIT Press, Cambridge, MA.

Bierwisch, M. and Schreuder, R. (1992). From concepts to lexical items. *Cognition*, 42, 23–60.

Brennan, S. E. (1991). Seeking and providing evidence for mutual understanding. Unpublished Ph.D. dissertation, Stanford University.

Brown, A. S. (1991). A review of the tip-of-the-tongue experience. *Psychological Bulletin* 109, 204–23.

Brown, J. W. (1982). Hierarchy and evolution in neurolinguistics. In *Neural models of language processes* (ed. M. A. Arbib, D. Caplan and J. C. Marshall), pp. 447–67. Academic Press, New York.

Brown, R. and McNeill, D. (1966). The 'tip of the tongue' phenomenon. *Journal of Verbal Learning and Verbal Behavior*, 4, 325–37.

Butterworth, B. L. (1989). Lexical access in speech production. In *Lexical representation and process* (ed. W. Marslen-Wilson), pp. 108–35. MIT Press, Cambridge, MA.

Butterworth, B. and Beattie, G. (1978). Gesture and silence as indicators of planning in speech. In *Recent advances in the psychology of language: formal and experimental approaches* (ed. R. N. Campbell and P. T. Smith), pp. 347–60. Plenum, New York.

Butterworth, B. and Hadar, U. (1989). Gesture, speech and computational stages: a reply to McNeill. *Psychological Review*, 96, 168–74.

Butterworth, B., Swallow, J., and Grimston, M. (1981). Gestures and lexical processes in jargon aphasia. In *Jargonaphasia* (ed. J.W. Brown), pp. 113–24. Academic Press, New York.

Chawla, P. and Krauss, R. M. (1994). Gesture and speech in spontaneous and rehearsed narratives. *Journal of Experimental Social Psychology*, 30, 580–601.

Christenfeld, N., Schachter, S., and Bilous, F. (1991). Filled pauses and gestures: it's not coincidence. *Journal of Psycholinguistic Research*, 20, 1–10.

Cicone, M., Wapner, W., Foldi, N., Zurif, E., and Gardner, H. (1979). The relation between gesture and language in aphasic communication. *Brain and Language*, 8, 324–49.

Clark, H. H. (1996). *Using language*. Cambridge University Press.

Clark, H. H. and Wilkes-Gibbs, D. (1986). Referring as a collaborative process. *Cognition*, 22, 1–39.

Cohen, A. A. (1977). The communicative functions of hand illustrators. *Journal of Communication*, 27, 54–63.

Cohen, A. A. and Harrison, R. P. (1972). Intentionality in the use of hand illustrators in face-to-face communication situations. *Journal of Personality and Social Psychology*, 28, 276–9.

DeLaguna, G. (1927). *Speech: its function and development*. Yale University Press, New Haven, CT.

Dell, G. S. (1986). A spreading activation theory of retrieval in language production. *Psychological Review*, 93, 283–321.

de Ruiter, J. P. (in press). The production of gesture and speech. In *Language and gesture: Window into thought and action* (ed. D. McNeill), Cambridge University Press, New York.

Dittmann, A. T. and Llewelyn, L. G. (1969). Body movement and speech rhythm in social conversation. *Journal of Personality and Social Psychology*, 23, 283–92.

Dobrogaev, S. M. (1929). Ucnenie o reflekse v problemakh iazykovedeniia [Observations on reflexes and issues in language study]. *Iazykovedenie i Materializm*, 105–73.

Dushay, R. D. (1991). The association of gestures with speech: a reassessment. Unpublished Ph.D. dissertation, Columbia University.

Efron, D. (1972). *Gesture, race and culture*. Mouton, The Hague. [First published 1941.]

Ekman, P. and Friesen, W. V. (1972). Hand movements. *Journal of Communication*, **22**, 353–74.

Feyereisen, P. and deLannoy, J.-D. (1991). *Gesture and speech: psychological investigations*. Cambridge University Press.

Feyereisen, P., Van de Wiele, M., and Dubois, F. (1988). The meaning of gestures: what can be understood without speech? *Cahiers de Psychologie Cognitive*, **8**, 3–25.

Freedman, N. (1972). The analysis of movement behavior during the clinical interview. In *Studies in dyadic communication* (ed. A. W. Siegman and B. Pope), pp. 153–75. Pergamon, New York.

Freedman, N. and Hoffman, S. (1967). Kinetic behavior in altered clinical states: approach to objective analysis of motor behavior during clinical interviews. *Perceptual and Motor Skills*, **24**, 527–39.

Frick-Horbury, D. and Guttentag, R. E. (1998). The effects of restricting hand gesture production on lexical retrieval and free recall. *American Journal of Psychology*.

Garrett, M. F. (1984). The organization of processing structure for language production: Applications to aphasic speech. In *Biological perspectives on language* (ed. D. Caplan, A. R. Lecours and A. Smith), pp. 172–93, MIT Press, Cambridge, MA.

Gibbs, R.W. (1997). How language reflects the embodied nature of creative cognition. In *Creative thought: an investigation of conceptual structures and processes* (ed. T. B. Ward, S. M. Smith, and J. Vaid), pp. 351–73. APA Publications, Washington, DC.

Glucksberg, S. (1991). Beyond literal meanings: the psychology of allusion. *Psychological Science*, **2**, 146–52.

Glucksberg, S. and Keysar, B. (1993). How metaphors work. In *Metaphor and thought*, 2nd edn (ed. A. Ortony), pp. 401–24. Cambridge University Press.

Goldblum, M. C. (1978). Les troubles des gestes d'accompagnement du langage au cours des lesions corticales uniliaterales. In *Du controle moteur a l'organisation du geste* (ed. H. Hecaen and M. Jeannerod), pp. 383–95. Masson, Paris.

Goldin-Meadow, S. and Mylander, C. (1984). Gestural communication in deaf children: the effects and noneffects of parental input on early language development. *Monographs of the Society for Research in Child Development*, **49**: 3, No. 207, 1–120.

Graham, J. A. and Argyle, M. (1975). A cross-cultural study of the communication of extra-verbal meaning by gestures. *International Journal of Psychology*, **10**, 57–67.

Graham, J. A. and Heywood, S. (1975). The effects of elimination of hand gestures and of verbal codability on speech performance. *European Journal of Social Psychology*, **5**, 185–95.

Grice, H. P. (1957). Meaning. *Philosophical Review*, **64**, 377–88.

Hadar, U. (1989). Two types of gesture and their role in speech production. *Journal of Language and Social Psychology*, **8**, 221–8.

Hadar, U. and Butterworth, B. (1997). Iconic gestures, imagery and word retrieval in speech. *Semiotica*, **115**, 147–72.

Hadar, U. and Krauss, R. M. (in press). Iconic gestures: the grammatical categories of lexical affiliates. *Journal of Neurolinguistics*.

Hadar, U., Burstein, A., Krauss, R. M., and Soroker, N. (1998a). Ideational gestures and speech: a neurolinguistic investigation. *Language and Cognitive Processes*, **13**, 59–76.

Hadar, U., Wenkert-Olenik, D., Krauss, R. M. and Soroker, N. (1998b). Gesture and the processing of speech: neuropsychological evidence. *Brain and Language*, **62**, 107–26.

Hanlon, R. E., Brown, J. W., and Gerstman, L. J. (1990) Enhancement of naming in non-fluent aphasia through gesture. *Brain and Language*, **38**, 298–314.

Jones, G. V. (1989). Back to Woodworth: role of interlopers in the tip-of-the-tongue phenomenon. *Memory and Cognition*, **17**, 69–76.

Jones, G. V. and Langford, S. (1987). Phonological blocking in the tip of the tongue state. *Cognition*, **26**, 115–22.

Kendon, A. (1980). Gesticulation and speech: two aspects of the process of utterance. In *Relationship of verbal and nonverbal communication* (ed. M. R. Key), pp. 207–27. Mouton, The Hague.

Kendon, A. (1983). Gesture and speech: how they interact. In *Nonverbal interaction* (ed. J. M. Weimann and R. P. Harrison), pp. 13–45. Sage, Beverly Hills, CA.

Kendon, A. (1994). Do gestures communicate?: a review. *Research on Language and Social Interaction*, **27**, 175–200.

Kohn, S. E., Wingfield, A., Menn, L., Goodglass, H., Gleason J. B., and Hyde, M. R. (1987). Lexical retrieval: the tip-of-the-tongue phenomenon. *Applied Psycholinguistics*, **8**, 245–66.

Krauss, R. M. and Fussell, S. R. (1996). Social psychological models of interpersonal communication. In *Social psychology: a handbook of basic principles* (ed. E. T. Higgins and A. Kruglanski), pp. 655–701. Guilford, New York.

Krauss, R. M., Morrel-Samuels, P., and Colasante, C. (1991). Do conversational hand gestures communicate? *Journal of Personality and Social Psychology*, **61**, 743–54.

Krauss, R. M., Dushay, R. A., Chen, Y., and Rauscher, F. (1995). The communicative value of conversational hand gestures. *Journal of Experimental Social Psychology*, **31**, 533–52.

Krauss, R. M., Chen, Y., and Chawla, P. (1996). Nonverbal behavior and nonverbal communication: What do conversational hand gestures tell us? In *Advances in experimental social psychology* (ed. M. Zanna), pp. 389–450. Academic Press, San Diego, CA.

Krauss, R. M., Chen, Y., and Gottesman, R. F. (in press). Lexical gestures and lexical access: a process model. In *Language and gesture: window into thought and action* (ed. D. McNeill). Cambridge University Press, New York.

Krauss, R. M., Gottesman, R. F., Zhang, F. F., and Chen, Y. (in preparation). What are speakers saying when they gesture? Grammatical and conceptual properties of gestural lexical affiliates.

Kroll, J. F., and Stewart, E. (1994). Category interference in translation and picture naming: evidence for asymmetric connection between bilingual memory representation. *Journal of Memory and Language*, **33**, 149–74

Levelt, W. J. M. (1989). *Speaking: from intention to articulation*. MIT Press, Cambridge, MA.

Levinson, S. C. (1983). *Pragmatics*. Cambridge University Press.

McClave, E. (1994). Gestural beats: The rhythm hypothesis. *Journal of Psycholinguistic Research*, **23**, 45–66.

McNeill, D. (1985). So you think gestures are nonverbal? *Psychological Review*, **92**, 350–71.

McNeill, D. (1987). *Psycholinguistics: a new approach*. Harper and Row, New York.

McNeill, D. (1992). *Hand and mind: what gestures reveal about thought*. University of Chicago Press, Chicago, IL.

McNeill, D., Cassell, J., and McCollough, K.-E. (1994). Communicative effects of speech-mismatched gestures. *Language and Social Interaction*, **27**, 223–37.

Mead, G. H. (1934). *Mind, self and society*. University of Chicago Press, Chicago, IL.

Meyer, A. S. and Bock, K. (1992). The tip-of-the-tongue phenomenon: blocking or partial activation? *Memory and Cognition*, **20**, 715–26.

Morrel-Samuels, P. and Krauss, R. M. (1992). Word familiarity predicts temporal asynchrony of hand gestures and speech. *Journal of Experimental Psychology: Learning, Memory and Cognition*, **18**, 615–23.

Moscovici, S. (1967). Communication processes and the properties of language. In *Advances in experimental social psychology* (ed. L. Berkowitz), pp. 226–70. Academic Press, New York.

Ragsdale, J. D. and Silvia, C. F. (1982) Distribution of hesitation kinesic phenomena in spontaneous speech. *Language and Speech*, **25**, 185–90.

Rauscher, F. B., Krauss, R. M., and Chen, Y. (1996). Gesture, speech and lexical access: the role of lexical movements in speech production. *Psychological Science,* **7**, 226–31.

Rimé, B. (1982). The elimination of visible behaviour from social interactions: effects on verbal, nonverbal and interpersonal behaviour. *European Journal of Social Psychology*, **12**, 113–29.

Rimé, B. and Schiaratura, L. (1991). Gesture and speech. In *Fundamentals of nonverbal behavior* (ed. R. S. Feldman and B. Rimé), pp. 239–84. Cambridge University Press.

Riseborough, M. G. (1981). Physiographic gestures as decoding facilitators: three experiments exploring a neglected facet of communication. *Journal of Nonverbal Behavior*, **5**, 172–83.

Rogers, W. T. (1978). The contribution of kinesic illustrators toward the comprehension of verbal behaviors within utterances. *Human Communication Research*, **5**, 54–62.

Schegloff, E. (1984). On some gestures' relation to speech. In *Structures of social action* (ed. J. M. Atkinson and J. Heritage), pp. 28–52. Cambridge University Press.

Schober, M. F. (1993). Spatial perspective-taking in conversation. *Cognition*, **47**, 1–24.

Schober, M. F. (1995). Speakers, addressees, and frames of reference: whose effort is minimized in conversations about locations? *Discourse Processes*, **20**, 219–47.

Sperber, D. and Wilson, D. (1986) *Relevance: communication and cognition.* Harvard University Press, Cambridge, MA.

Sumby, W. H. and Pollack, I. (1954). Visual contribution to speech intelligibility in noise. *Journal of the Acoustical Society of America*, **26**, 212–15.

Teitelman, A. (1997). Coverbal gesture in spontaneous speech and simultaneous translation from first to second, and from second to first, language. Unpublished MA thesis, Tel Aviv University.

Werner, H. and Kaplan, B. (1963). *Symbol formation.* Wiley, New York.

Williams, S. and Canter, G. (1987). Action naming performance in four syndromes of aphasia. *Brain and Language*, **32**, 124–36.

Notes

1. We are using the term 'sign' in the traditional semiotic sense—i.e., a display that is causally related to its significance or meaning. Another quite different sense of 'sign' (as in 'sign language') is reflected in the way the term is used in this book's title and elsewhere.
2. We are grateful to Stephen Krieger and Lisa Son for sharing this observation with us, and to Lauren Michelle Walsh, who coded the gestures.

CHAPTER 7

The development of gesture with and without speech in hearing and deaf children

Susan Goldin-Meadow

University of Chicago

Introduction

Gesture—the spontaneous movements of the hands that accompany speech—offers a window into the mind of the speaker. Unlike speech, which assumes a linear and segmented form, gesture conveys information globally and imagistically, exploiting the analogue potential that the manual modality provides (McNeill 1992). Because gesture and speech draw on different representational resources, they can at times express different types of information. As a result, gesture can provide an alternative, perhaps easier, route for the expression of certain ideas—a route that young children just beginning the language learning process may be able to exploit.

The first goal of this chapter is to explore the forms and functions that gesture assumes in the early stages of language learning. We shall find that gesture plays a complementary role with respect to the speech it accompanies, and that it begins to form an integrated system with speech at early stages in language development.

The second goal is to explore gesture's fate when children are unable to learn a spoken language; as when, for example, a child is profoundly deaf. If a deaf child is born to deaf, signing parents, that child will learn sign language as naturally and effortlessly as hearing children learn spoken language (Newport and Meier 1985). But 90% of deaf children are born not to deaf parents, but to hearing parents. These children typically are not exposed to sign language unless their parents make a conscious effort to do so. Some parents choose instead to educate their deaf children orally, training them to make full use of their residual hearing in conjunction with visual and kinaesthetic cues to speech. Oral programmes do not offer instruction in sign language and, in many cases, actively discourage use of the manual modality for communication. Unfortunately, even with intensive oral training, the acquisition of spoken language is extremely difficult for most children with a profound hearing loss (Meadow 1968; Conrad 1979; Mayberry 1992). These children, in a sense, are left only with gesture.

The question then is—what happens to gesture when it is not part of an integrated system with speech but is itself forced to take over the communicative burdens typically assumed by speech (or sign)? Does it retain its global and imagistic form despite its new functions, or does it alter its form to become more linear and segmented, and thus more language-like?

I begin by reviewing the forms and functions that gesture serves in hearing children learning spoken language from their hearing parents. I then contrast gesture when it shares the communicative functions with speech in hearing children, with gesture when it must assume the full burden of communication in deaf children who are incapable of learning speech and are not exposed to a conventional sign language.

The development of gesture with speech in hearing children

Gesture is an early form of communication

At a time in their development when children are limited in what they can say, there is another avenue of expression open to them, one that can extend the range of ideas they are able to express. In addition to speaking, the child can also gesture (Bates 1976; Bates *et al.* 1979; Petitto 1988).

Children typically begin to gesture at around 10 months. They first use deictics, gestures whose referential meaning is given entirely by the context and not by their form. For example, a child may hold up an object to draw an adult's attention to it or, later in development, point at the object. In addition to deictic gestures, slightly older children also produce the conventional gestures common in their cultures, for example, nods and side-to-side headshakes. Finally, children produce iconic gestures, although the number tends to be quite small and variable across children (Acredolo and Goodwyn 1988). Unlike deictics, the form of an iconic gesture captures aspects of its intended referent and thus its meaning is less dependent on context. For example, a child might open and close her mouth to represent a fish, or flap her hands to represent a bird (Iverson *et al.* 1994). Children do not begin to produce metaphoric gestures until relatively late in development (McNeill 1992).

For many young children, gesture is the predominant form of communication at the start. Capirci *et al.* (1998) found that, in a group of 12 children learning Italian, six used gesture as often as, or even more often than, words at 16 months. At 20 months, this number dropped to two. Strikingly, even children acquiring sign language produce gestures in their earliest stages of language learning, typically exhibiting all three of the early types of gestures (deictic, conventional, and iconic). Capirci *et al.* (1998) also observed a hearing child learning both a spoken and a signed language. They attributed a sign (as opposed to a gesture) to the child when the forms the child produced resembled the forms used by adult signers, rather than the forms used by the monolingual child gesturers in the study. At 16 months, but not at 20, the child produced more gestures than either words or signs.

Interestingly, children very rarely combine their gestures with other gestures and, if they do so at all, the phase tends to be short-lived (Goldin-Meadow and Morford 1985). Children do, however, frequently combine their gestures with words and produce these word-plus-gesture combinations well before they combine words with words. Children's earliest gesture–speech combinations contain gestures that convey information redundant with the information conveyed in speech; for example, pointing at an object while naming it (de Laguna 1927; Guillaume 1927; Leopold 1949; Greenfield and Smith 1976). The onset of these gesture–speech combinations marks the beginning of gesture–speech integration in the young child's communications, an accomplishment to which we now turn.

Gesture becomes integrated with speech during the one-word period

The proportion of a child's communications that contains gesture remains constant throughout the single-word period. What changes over this time period is the relationship gesture holds to speech (Butcher and Goldin-Meadow 1998).

At the beginning of the one-word period, three properties characterize children's gestures:

(1) Gesture is frequently produced alone, that is, without any vocalizations at all, either meaningless sounds or meaningful words.

(2) On the rare occasions when gesture is produced with a vocalization, it is combined only with meaningless sounds and not with words; this omission is striking given that the child is able to produce meaningful words without gesture during this period.

(3) The few gesture-plus-meaningless sound combinations that the child produces are not timed in an adult fashion; that is, the sound does not occur on the stroke or the peak of the gesture (cf. Kendon 1980; McNeill 1992).

During the one-word period, two notable changes take place in the relationship between gesture and speech (Butcher and Goldin-Meadow 1998). First, gesture-alone communications decrease and, in their place, the child begins to produce gesture-plus-meaningful-word combinations for the first time. Gesture and speech thus begin to have a coherent semantic relationship with one another. Second, gesture becomes synchronized with speech, not only with the meaningful words that comprise the novel combinations but also, importantly, with the old combinations that contain meaningless sounds. Thus, gesture and speech begin to have a synchronous temporal relationship with one another. These two properties—semantic coherence and temporal synchrony—characterize the integrated gesture–speech system found in adults (McNeill 1992) and appear to have their origins during the one-word period.

The relationship between gesture and speech predicts early language

The onset of gesture–speech integration sets the stage for a new type of gesture–speech combination—combinations in which gesture conveys information that is different from the information conveyed in speech. For example, a child can gesture at an object while describing the action to be done on the object in speech (pointing to an apple and saying, 'give'), or gesture at an object while describing the owner of that object in speech (pointing at a toy and saying, 'mine') (Greenfield and Smith 1976; Masur 1982, 1983; Goldin-Meadow and Morford 1985; Zinober and Martlew 1985; Morford and Goldin-Meadow 1992). This type of gesture–speech combination allows a child to express two elements of a proposition (one in gesture and one in speech) at a time when the child is not yet able to express those elements within a single spoken utterance. Children begin to produce this type of combination in which gesture conveys different information from speech (e.g., pointing at a box and saying 'open') at the same time as, or later than—but, importantly, not before—they begin to produce combinations in which gesture and speech convey the same information (e.g., pointing at a box and saying 'box') (Goldin-Meadow and Butcher 1998). Combinations in which gesture and speech convey different information are first produced *after* gesture and speech begin to work together semantically and temporally. These combinations thus appear to be a product of an integrated gesture–speech system (rather than a product of two systems functioning independently of one another).

In turn, combinations in which gesture and speech convey different information predict the onset of two-word combinations. Goldin-Meadow and Butcher (1998) found in six children learning English as their first language that the correlation between the age of onset of this type of gesture–speech combination and the age of onset of two-word combinations was high ($r_s = 0.90$) and reliable ($p < 0.05$). The children who were first to produce combinations in which gesture and speech conveyed different information were also first to produce two-word combinations. In this regard, it is worth noting that the correlation between gesture–speech combinations and two-word speech is specific to combinations in which gesture and speech conveyed *different* information—the correlation between the age of onset of combinations in which gesture and speech conveyed the *same* information and the age of onset of two-word combinations was low and unreliable ($r_s = 0.46$, not statistically significant).

Thus, once gesture and speech become integrated, the child is able to use the two modalities to complement one another within a single communicative act. Moreover, the ability to use gesture and speech to convey different semantic elements of a proposition is a harbinger of the child's next step—producing two elements within a single spoken utterance (see also Capirci *et al.* 1998; Goodwyn and Acredolo 1998).

Gesture continues to play a role in communication over development

The findings described thus far suggest that gesture and speech become part of a unified system some time during the one-word period of language development. Over time, children become proficient users of their spoken language. At the same time, rather than dropping out of children's communicative repertoires, gesture itself continues to develop and play an important role in communication. Older children frequently use hand gestures as they speak (Jancovic *et al.* 1975), gesturing, for example, when asked to narrate a story (McNeill 1992) or when asked to explain their reasoning on a series of problems (Church and Goldin-Meadow 1986).

As in the earliest stages of language learning, gesture can convey the same information as the speech it accompanies. Consider, for example, a six-year-old child asked whether the amount of water has changed when poured from a tall, thin glass into a short, wide dish. The child might say, 'It's different because the glass is tall and the dish is short,' while gesturing with his hands to indicate, first, the height of the water level in the glass and then the height in the dish. This child has referred to the same dimension, height, in both his speech and gesture.

However, children can also use their gestures to convey information that is not conveyed in speech. Consider a child responding to the same question who also says, 'It's different because the glass is tall and the dish is short.' But this child's gestures are different—she shapes her hands first to mirror the width of the glass and then the width of the dish. The child has, in effect, referred to the two dimensions relevant to eventually solving the problem correctly—height, in speech, and width, in gesture.

Responses in which gesture conveys information that is different from the information conveyed in the accompanying speech are called 'gesture–speech mismatches' (Church and Goldin-Meadow 1986). Mismatches are not unique to school-aged children, nor to water puzzle tasks. Indeed, by this definition, a young child's utterance 'give' produced along with a pointing gesture at a desired object constitutes a gesture–speech mismatch. Communications in which gesture conveys different information from speech have been found in a variety of tasks and over a large age range: 18 month old infants going through their vocabulary spurt (Gershkoff-Stowe and Smith 1991); preschoolers learning to count (Graham 1994) and reasoning about a board game (Evans and Rubin 1979); elementary school children reasoning about conservation problems (Church and Goldin-Meadow 1986) and mathematics problems (Perry *et al.* 1988); middle-schoolers reasoning about seasonal change (Crowder and Newman 1993); children and adults reasoning about moral dilemmas (Church *et al.* 1995); adolescents reasoning about tasks involving Piagetian bending rods (Stone *et al.* 1991); and adults reasoning about gears (Perry and Elder 1996) and problems involving constant change (Alibali *et al.* 1995). Moreover, communications in which gesture and speech convey different information can be quite frequent within an individual. At certain points in their acquisition of a task, children have been found to produce gesture–speech mismatches in over half of their explanations of that task (Church and Goldin-Meadow 1986; Perry *et al.* 1988)

As in the earliest stages of language development, gesture and speech adhere to the principles of gesture–speech integration described by McNeill (1992; see also Chapter 5, this volume) even when the two modalities convey different information. Consider again a child asked to explain why she thinks an amount of water has changed after it has been poured. The child says the amount is different because 'the glass is tall' while indicating the width of the glass in her gestures. Although this child is indeed expressing two different pieces of information in gesture and speech, she is nevertheless describing the same object in the two modalities. Moreover, the timing of the gesture–speech mismatch also reflects an integrated system. The child produces the width gesture as she says 'tall', thus synchronously expressing her two perspectives on the glass.

Further evidence that gesture–speech mismatches reflect an integrated system comes from the fact that, as in the transition from one- to two-word speech, the relationship between gesture and speech is a harbinger of the child's next step. Children who produce many gesture–speech mismatches when explaining their solutions to a task appear to be in a transitional state with respect to that task. They are far more likely to profit from instruction and make progress in the task than children who produce few mismatches (Church and Goldin-Meadow 1986; Perry *et al.* 1988). If gesture and speech were independent of one another, their 'mismatch' would be a random event and, as a result, should have no cognitive consequence whatsoever. The fact that mismatch is a reliable index of a child's transitional status suggests that the two modalities are, in fact, *not* independent of one another (Goldin-Meadow *et al.* 1993).

Thus, gesture continues to accompany speech throughout childhood (and adulthood), forming a complementary system across the two modalities. At all ages, gesture provides another medium through which ideas can be conveyed, a medium that is analogue in nature. It is, in addition, a medium that is not codified and therefore not constrained by rules and standards of form, as is speech.

The development of gesture without speech in deaf children

I now explore what happens to gesture when it is the only form of symbolic communication available to a child. Deaf children whose hearing losses are so severe that they cannot acquire spoken language even with intensive oral training, and whose hearing parents have not exposed them to a model of a conventional sign language, cannot develop a conventional language. They do, however, have gesture at their disposal. What does the development of gesture look like in these deaf children?

Gesture takes on a language-like form at many levels

The gestures that such a deaf person uses to communicate, typically with the hearing members in the household, are called 'home sign'. Home sign has been described in places as far from one another as Belgium, Japan, Nicaragua, and the Rennell Islands (Morford 1996a). The most striking property of home sign is that it resembles conventional sign language (and spoken language) in terms of structure—categorical units organized according to rules (or at least probabilistic tendencies) at several levels—rather than spontaneous gesture which is based on an analogue format. I review these levels below, beginning with the lexical level.

Lexicon

Home sign, like the spontaneous gestures that accompany speech, contains at least two types of gestures: pointing or deictic gestures, and iconic gestures based, for the most part, on pantomime (Tervoort 1961; Kuschel 1973; Kendon 1980; Goldin-Meadow and Mylander 1984). Pointing gestures refer to entities that are typically referred to by nouns in conventional languages (e.g., objects, people, places). Iconic gestures refer to predicates, either actions (e.g., a jabbing motion at the mouth used to refer to 'eat') or attributes (e.g., thumb and index finger forming a circle and held in the air used to refer to the 'round' shape of a penny). However, iconic gestures can also refer to entities (e.g., a jabbing motion at the mouth used to refer to an edible object, such as a grape, or the thumb–finger circle used to refer to the penny itself). While hearing children produce a small number of different types of iconic gestures, deaf home signers produce a large and varied set. Moreover, unlike the spontaneous gestures of hearing speakers whose forms vary with the changing context (McNeill 1992), iconic gestures used in home sign assume forms that are stable across uses and time (Goldin-Meadow *et al.* 1994).

Many home sign systems make a distinction between gestures used as nouns and those used as verbs (Macleod 1973; DeVilliers *et al.* 1993). For example, Goldin-Meadow *et al.* (1994) found that, at the earliest stages of development, one home signer used pointing gestures to fulfil noun-like functions and iconic gestures to fulfil verb-like functions. At the next stage, this child began to use some iconic gestures for noun-like functions but continued to distinguish between nouns and verbs by keeping the sets distinct—one set of iconic gestures was used in noun-like ways, and a completely different set was used in verb-like ways. Finally, the child began using a single iconic form in both noun-like and verb-like contexts, but he again distinguished between the two in two complementary ways:

(1) Syntactically. When used as a noun, the gesture tended to precede pointing, but when used as a verb, the same gesture followed pointing.
(2) Morphologically. When used as a noun, the gesture tended to be abbreviated in form and produced in neutral space. When used as a verb, the same gesture was produced in full form and was displaced towards objects in the room.

Thus, the child's strategy for distinguishing nouns from verbs changed over time, becoming more and more complex. There was, however, from the start, a distinction established between lexical items used to refer to objects, people and places, and those used to refer to actions and attributes.

Semantics

Young home signers combine their lexical items into gesture sentences conveying propositional information that is comparable to the information conveyed by hearing children in their early two-word combinations. Deictic pointing gestures are combined with other pointing gestures (e.g., pointing at a grape and then at himself, to indicate that he had eaten the grape) and with iconic gestures (e.g., pointing at a tower and making the iconic gesture HIT, a request that mother hit the tower and topple it (iconic gestures are displayed in capital letters)).

Each of these sentences contains two elements of a single proposition. Although at this point in their development the children are limited to two gestures per sentence, they appear to know something about the larger argument structures underlying those two-element sentences. At various times, they produce sentences containing gestures for each of the appropriate arguments that a given predicate allows, for example 'baby drink', 'drink juice'; or 'mommy give', 'give juice', 'give me' (Feldman *et al.* 1978). Indeed, for children at the two-gesture stage, the rate at which a semantic element (like 'juice') is put into gestures depends on the argument structure underlying the sentence. A gesture for 'juice' is more likely to appear in a two-gesture sentence with a two-argument structure (*x* drinks *y*) than in a two-gesture sentence with a three-argument structure (*x* gives *y* to *z*), presumably because there is more 'competition' for one of the two slots in the surface form of a sentence conveying a three-argument proposition than in a sentence conveying a two-argument proposition. Patterns of this sort suggest that, at some level, the child knows how many arguments there ought to be in each frame (Goldin-Meadow 1985).

The children are also able to combine two iconic gestures within a single sentence. These combinations involve the concatenation of two propositions (Goldin-Meadow and Mylander 1984). For example, the child produces a BUILD-UP gesture followed by a HIT gesture to request the mother to build the tower (proposition 1) so that he can then hit it (proposition 2). The beginning and end of a gesture sentence are decided on motoric criteria. Thus, in this example, the child does not pause or relax his hands between BUILD-UP and HIT; the two gestures are consequently considered to constitute a single sentence. Devices that permit concatenation of two or more propositions within a single sentence reflect generativity, a property that characterizes all natural language systems.

Syntax and morphology

The gesture sentences that deaf home signers produce have syntactic structure in two senses. First, certain types of semantic elements (e.g., the object of an action) are likely to be gestured while others are likely to be omitted (e.g., the agent of an action). Thus, the sentences adhere to deletion regularities (Feldman *et al.* 1978). Second, the gestures that are produced appear in particular orders. In an analysis of the home sign system of a man living in England, Macleod (1973) found that the home signer typically placed agents, patients, sources, and goals before actions and states. Child (Goldin-Meadow and Feldman 1977; Goldin-Meadow and Mylander 1984) and adolescent (Emmorey *et al.* 1994; Morford 1996b) home signers demonstrate a similar pattern, with the exception that one child in the Goldin-Meadow studies produced transitive agents (but not intransitive ones) and recipients after their actions. These simple 'rules' predict which semantic elements are likely to be gestured and where in the gesture sentence those elements are likely to be produced. In this sense, they constitute syntactic structures.

In addition to structure at the sentence level, young home signers' gestures also have structure at the word level, that is, morphological structure. Each gesture stem is composed of a handshape component (e.g., an 'O' handshape representing the roundness of a penny) and a motion component (e.g., a short arc motion representing a putting-down action). The meaning of the stem as a whole is determined by the meanings of each of these parts ('put-down-round'; Goldin-Meadow *et al.* 1995). As mentioned above, another example of morphological structure is found in the within-gesture variations that mark a gesture as either a noun or a verb. For example, the gesture stem PUT-DOWN-ROUND can either be used as a noun to mean 'penny', or as a verb to mean 'put-down (round)'. When used as a noun, the gesture is likely to be abbreviated and produced in neutral space; when used as a verb, it is likely to be produced in full form and oriented toward the penny itself (Goldin-Meadow *et al.* 1994).

Pragmatics

Young home signers do not invent structural complexity to serve a single function. Rather, they use their gestures for a large number of the functions typically served by language—to manipulate the world around them and to convey information about current, past, and future events. For example, to describe a visit to Santa Claus, one deaf child first pointed at himself, indicated Santa via a LAUGH gesture and a MOUSTACHE gesture, pointed at his own knee to indicate that he sat on Santa's lap, produced a FIRETRUCK gesture to indicate that he requested this toy from Santa, produced an EAT gesture to indicate that he ate a pretzel, and then finished off the sequence with a palm hand arcing away from his body (his way of marking past events) and a final point at himself (Morford and Goldin-Meadow 1997). In addition to the major function of communicating with others, young home signers sometimes use gesture when no one is paying attention, as though 'talking' to themselves (Goldin-Meadow 1993). Finally, the children also use gesture to refer to their own gestures, and to comment on (and indeed criticize) the gestures of others (Singleton *et al.* 1993).

The child's language-like forms are not found in the mother's gestures

Interestingly, the structure found at the lexical, semantic, syntactic, and morphological levels in young home signers' gesture systems *cannot* be traced back to the spontaneous gestures that their hearing parents produce when talking to them. Hearing mothers do use pointing and iconic gestures with their deaf children, not surprisingly since these are the types of gestures that typically accompany talk. However, the particular gestures that the mother uses overlap very little with her child's (Goldin-Meadow and Mylander 1984), suggesting that she has a different lexicon from her child. Moreover, the mother's iconic gestures vary in form far more than her child's—in this sense, the mother can hardly be said to have a lexicon at all. In addition, the mother infrequently uses iconic gestures as nouns while, at later stages, the child does so half of the time (Goldin-Meadow *et al.* 1994).

Hearing mothers rarely combine their gestures into strings, preferring instead to produce their gestures one at a time—again, not surprisingly since this is the typical way gestures are produced when they accompany talk (McNeill 1992). As a result, in terms of semantic structure, the mothers rarely explicitly express in gesture two semantic elements within a single proposition. Moreover, they rarely produce complex gesture sentences containing two or more propositions (Goldin-Meadow and Mylander 1984).

When hearing mothers do produce gesture sentences, either they follow no consistent gesture order whatsoever or they follow a different order from their deaf children (Goldin-Meadow and Mylander 1983). The mothers thus have no syntactic structure to their gestures. In terms of morphological structure, the hearing mother's gestures do not conform to the handshape and motion morphemes found in her child's gestures (Goldin-Meadow *et al.* 1995), nor does she use morphological markings to distinguish between nouns and verbs (Goldin-Meadow *et al.* 1994).

Finally, the hearing mother does not use her gestures for all of the pragmatic functions that the child does. For example, she rarely uses her gestures to refer to the non-present, either displaced objects (Butcher *et al.* 1991) or events displaced in time and space (Morford and Goldin-Meadow 1997).

The children's gesture systems thus appear to be generated in large part by the children themselves. Even the lack of a model does not prevent the human child from communicating with self and other, in the here-and-now and about the non-present, using the segmented and combinatorial representational format that is the hallmark of human language.

The child's invented gesture system affects later language learning

Children who use home sign throughout childhood at some point typically enter a community where they are exposed to a conventional sign language. If home sign is represented as language in the minds of these individuals, then we might expect to see some effects of these home sign systems on the way in which the conventional sign language is acquired (Morford 1998).

To observe *lexical* transfer from home sign, Morford (1998) studied two profoundly deaf children who had developed home sign systems to communicate with their hearing families. She found that, after two years of exposure to American Sign Language (ASL), the children had replaced many of their pointing gestures with ASL nouns in a storytelling task. The ease of transfer from home sign points to ASL nouns suggests that these pointing gestures had indeed served a nominal function in the children's home sign systems. However, the children produced very few ASL verbs in the story, preferring their home sign verbs instead. Morford argues that home sign verbs and ASL verbs have different syntactic frames. ASL predicates mark person, number, and aspect morphologically, while home sign verbs encode semantic elements of the predicates such as path and instrument information. Thus, transfer from home sign to ASL verbs is relatively difficult, requiring more work, and apparently more time, than transfer to ASL nouns.

To observe *morphological* transfer, Morford and her colleagues (Morford *et al.* 1995) gave one of the children in Goldin-Meadow's original sample a test of ASL morphology at age 23. This individual's first intense exposure to ASL was relatively late in life, coming after high school when he attended a college programme for deaf students which brought him for the first time into contact with many other deaf people. Like most deaf individuals who learn ASL after adolescence (Newport 1990), this late-learner made many errors on the morphological test. The interesting point, however, is that his errors on the ASL morphology test were not random and could be predicted, in part, from the home sign system he had developed as a young child. He was most successful in learning those ASL morphemes that were similar in meaning to his home sign morphemes, whether or not they were the same in form. Thus, form appeared to have little effect on his acquisition of ASL morphology—whether the ASL morphemes looked like the home sign morphemes did not affect how easily they were learned. Meaning, however, had considerable influence: ASL morphemes with the same meanings as his home sign morphemes were acquired much more easily than ASL morphemes with different meanings, demonstrating once again the impact home sign appears to have on later learning of ASL.

Finally, to observe *syntactic* transfer, Morford (1996b) assessed how two home signers marked the subject and object of a sentence when recounting a story in a wordless picture book. After two years of exposure to ASL, the children rarely used spatial inflections on verbs that required them. Importantly, spatial inflection was not a device found in their home sign systems. In contrast, both individuals did use gesture order to mark subjects and objects in their sentences, and gesture order *was* used for this purpose in their home sign systems. Presumably, the two were attentive to sign order in ASL because it had been an important cue to syntactic structure in home sign. Interestingly, when learning ASL, which is predominantly a subject–verb–object (SVO) language, they transferred only the generalized rule that sign order expresses relations among semantic elements, and not the specific object–subject–verb (OSV) order found in their home sign systems.

Taken together, these findings not only validate using linguistic categories and rules to describe home sign, but they also demonstrate that early home sign systems are relevant to the language learning that children do when exposed to a conventional system relatively late in life.

The deaf child's gestures look different from the hearing child's

Deaf children developing home sign systems mould gesture into a language-like form. Why don't the gestures that hearing children use also assume this language-like form? Occasionally, they do. For example, a hearing child who is delayed in word-learning may rely on the manual modality for communication and produce a relatively large number of iconic gestures (Goodwyn and Acredolo 1998). However, the gestures used by hearing children never become elaborated into a system. Indeed, hearing children rarely combine their gestures into strings. Like hearing adults (McNeill 1992), hearing children tend to produce gestures one by one, each accompanying a separate clause.

Gesture and speech become integrated into a single system very early in development. As a result, once hearing children begin to learn a spoken system, they are no longer 'free' to have their gestures assume a linear and segmented form. The children's gestures are already part of a complementary system in which speech assumes the segmented and combinatorial aspects of communication, and gesture assumes the imagistic and analogue aspects. Gesture must play by the rules of that system and cannot assume the forms that are reserved for speech.

The constraints of an integrated gesture–speech system are so powerful that they even prevent the deaf children's hearing parents from producing gestures that are segmented and combinatorial in form. One might think that after years of interacting with their gesturing deaf children, the hearing mothers would alter the form of their own gestures, bringing them more in line with their children's. But they do not. Like the gestures of all speakers, the mothers' gestures must 'fit' with the speech that they accompany. Their gestures therefore cannot assume a segmented and combinatorial form. We have previously suggested (Goldin-Meadow *et al.* 1996) that it is only when gesture must assume the full burden of communication that it can take on the segmented and combinatorial forms that are typically the province of speech. Indeed, it is very likely that if the hearing mothers were to stop talking to their children (an unacceptable option given that their goal is to teach their children how to speak), their gestures would begin to assume the language-like forms found in their children's gestures (see Dufour 1992 and Goldin-Meadow *et al.* 1996 for experimental support for this conjecture).

Conclusion

To summarize, what may be most impressive about gesture is its adaptability. Hearing children learning spoken language use gesture early in development. Their gestures are, almost from the start, integrated with the speech they accompany and, as a result, imagistic and analogue in form. Thus, gesture can assume a holistic and imagistic representational format, one that 'fills in' gaps left by the categorical and analytical speech code.

On the other hand, deaf children, unable to learn spoken language and not exposed to a model of conventional sign language, also use gesture early in development. They fashion it into a language-like system with discrete and categorical forms. Thus, gesture can also assume the segmented and combinatorial representational format that is characteristic of human language.

In brief, gesture's flexibility allows it to assume an analogue and mimetic form when it accompanies speech, and a discrete form when it must fulfill the functions of language on its own. Ironically, it may be this very flexibility that has made language the province of speech. While gesture can assume either an analogue or a discrete form, speech is better suited to only one of these forms—the discrete. By default then the discrete and segmented aspect of language falls naturally to speech (Goldin-Meadow and McNeill, 1999).

References

Acredolo, L. P. and Goodwyn, S. W. (1988). Symbolic gesturing in normal infants. *Child Development*, 59, 450–66.

Alibali, M. W., Bassok, M., Olseth, K., Syc, S., and Goldin-Meadow, S. (1995). Gesture reveals mental models of discrete and continuous change. In *Proceedings of the seventeenth annual conference of the Cognitive Science Society* (ed. J. D. Moore and J. F. Lehman), pp. 391–6. Erlbaum, Hillsdale, NJ.

Bates, E. (1976). *Language and context*. Academic Press, New York.

Bates, E., Benigni, L., Bretherton, I., Camaioni, L., and Volterra, V. (1979). *The emergence of symbols: cognition and communication in infancy*. Academic Press, New York.

Butcher, C. and Goldin-Meadow, S. (1998). Gesture and the transition from one- to two-word speech: when hand and mouth come together. In *Language and gesture: window into thought and action*, (ed. D. McNeill), Cambridge University Press.

Butcher, C., Mylander, C., and Goldin-Meadow, S. (1991). Displaced communication in a self-styled gesture system: pointing at the non-present. *Cognitive Development*, 6, 315–42.

Capirci, O., Montanari, S., and Volterra, V. (1998). Gestures, signs, and words in early language development. In *The nature and functions of gesture in children's communications* (ed. J. M. Iverson and S. Goldin-Meadow), pp. 45–60. *New Directions for Child Development* series, no. 79. Jossey-Bass, San Francisco, CA.

Church, R. B. and Goldin-Meadow, S. (1986). The mismatch between gesture and speech as an index of transitional knowledge. *Cognition*, 23, 43–71.

Church, R. B., Schonert-Reichl, K., Goodman, N., Kelly, S. D., and Ayman-Nolley, S. (1995). The role of gesture and speech communication as reflections of cognitive understanding. *Journal of Contemporary Legal Issues*, 6, 123–54.

Conrad, R. (1979). *The deaf child*. Harper and Row, New York.

Crowder, E. M. and Newman, D. (1993). Telling what they know: the role of gesture and language in children's science explanations. *Pragmatics and Cognition*, 1, 341–76.

de Laguna, G. (1927). *Speech: its function and development*. Indiana University Press, Bloomington, IN.

DeVilliers, J., Bibeau, L., Ramos, E., and Gatty, J. (1993). Gestural communication in oral deaf mother–child pairs: language with a helping hand? *Applied Psycholinguistics*, 14, 319–47.

Dufour, R. (1992). The use of gestures for communicative purposes: can gestures become grammatical? Unpublished doctoral dissertation, University of Illinois, Urbana-Champaign, IL.

Emmorey, K., Grant, R., and Ewan, B. (1994). A new case of linguistic isolation: preliminary report. Paper presented at the Boston University Conference on Language Development, Boston.

Evans, M. A. and Rubin, K. H. (1979). Hand gestures as a communicative mode in school-aged children. *The Journal of Genetic Psychology*, **135**, 189–96.

Feldman, H., Goldin-Meadow, S., and Gleitman, L. (1978). Beyond Herodotus: the creation of language by linguistically deprived deaf children. In *Action, symbol, and gesture: the emergence of language* (ed. A. Lock), pp. 351–414. Academic Press, New York.

Gershkoff-Stowe, L. and Smith, L. B. (1991). Changes in pointing and labeling during the naming explosion. Poster presented at the biennial meeting of the Society for Research in Child Development, Seattle, March 1991.

Goldin-Meadow, S. (1985). Language development under atypical learning conditions: replication and implications of a study of deaf children of hearing parents. In *Children's Language*, Vol. 5 (ed. K. Nelson), pp. 197–245. Erlbaum, Hillsdale, NJ.

Goldin-Meadow, S. (1993). When does gesture become language? A study of gesture used as a primary communication system by deaf children of hearing parents. In *Tools, language and cognition in human evolution* (ed. K. R. Gibson and T. Ingold), Cambridge University Press, New York.

Goldin-Meadow, S. and Butcher, C. (1998). Pointing toward two-word speech in young children. In *Pointing: where language, culture, and cognition meet* (ed. S. Kita), Cambridge University Press.

Goldin-Meadow, S. and Feldman, H. (1977). The development of language-like communication without a language model. *Science*, **197**, 401–3.

Goldin-Meadow, S. and McNeill, D. (1999). The role of gesture and mimetic representation in making language the province of speech. In *The Descent of Mind* (ed. M. C. Corballis and S. Lea), pp. 137–54. Oxford University Press.

Goldin-Meadow, S. and Morford, M. (1985). Gesture in early child language: studies of deaf and hearing children. *Merrill-Palmer Quarterly*, **31**, 145–76.

Goldin-Meadow, S. and Mylander, C. (1983). Gestural communication in deaf children: the non-effects of parental input on language development. *Science*, **221**, 372–4.

Goldin-Meadow, S. and Mylander, C. (1984). Gestural communication in deaf children: the effects and non-effects of parental input on early language development. *Monographs of the Society for Research in Child Development*, **49**, 1–121.

Goldin-Meadow, S., Alibali, M. W., and Church, R. B. (1993). Transitions in concept acquisition: using the hand to read the mind. *Psychological Review*, **100**, 279–97.

Goldin-Meadow, S., Butcher, C., Mylander, C., and Dodge, M. (1994). Nouns and verbs in a self-styled gesture system: what's in a name? *Cognitive Psychology*, **27**, 259–319.

Goldin-Meadow, S., Mylander, C., and Butcher, C. (1995). The resilience of combinatorial structure at the word level: morphology in self-styled gesture systems. *Cognition*, **56**, 195–262.

Goldin-Meadow, S., McNeill, D., and Singleton, J. (1996). Silence is liberating: removing the handcuffs on grammatical expression in the manual modality. *Psychological Review*, **103**, 34–55.

Goodwyn, S. W. and Acredolo, L. P. (1998). Encouraging symbolic gestures: a new perspective on the relationship between gesture and speech. In *The nature and functions of gesture in children's communications* (ed. J. M. Iverson and S. Goldin-Meadow), pp. 61–73. *New Directions for Child Development* series, no. 79. Jossey-Bass, San Francisco, CA.

Graham, T. (1994). The role of gesture in learning to count. Paper presented at the annual meeting of the Jean Piaget Society, Chicago, May 1994.

Greenfield, P. and Smith, J. (1976). *The structure of communication in early language development*. Academic Press, New York.

Guillaume, P. (1927). Les debuts de la phrase dans le langage de l'enfant. *Journal de Psychologie*, **24**, 1–25.

Iverson, J. M., Capirci, O., and Caselli, M. S. (1994). From communication to language in two modalities. *Cognitive Development*, 9, 23–43.

Jancovic, M. A., Devoe, S., and Wiener, M. (1975). Age-related changes in hand and arm movements as nonverbal communication: some conceptualizations and an empirical exploration. *Child Development*, 46, 922–8.

Kendon, A. (1980). Gesticulation and speech: two aspects of the process of utterance. In *Relationship of the verbal and nonverbal communication* (ed. M. R. Key), pp. 207–28. Mouton, The Hague.

Kuschel, R. (1973). The silent inventor: the creation of a sign language by the only deaf-mute on a Polynesian island. *Sign Language Studies*, 3, 1–27.

Leopold, W. (1949). *Speech development of a bilingual child: a linguist's record*, Vol. 3. Northwestern University Press, Evanston, IL.

Macleod, C. (1973). A deaf man's sign language: its nature and position relative to spoken languages. *Linguistics*, 101, 72–88.

Masur, E. F. (1982). Mothers' responses to infants' object-related gestures: influences on lexical development. *Journal of Child Language*, 9, 23–30.

Masur, E. F. (1983). Gestural development, dual-directional signaling, and the transition to words. *Journal of Psycholinguistic Research*, 12, 93–109.

Mayberry, R. I. (1992). The cognitive development of deaf children: recent insights. In *Handbook of neuropsychology*, Vol. 7: *Child neuropsychology* (ed. S. Segalowitz and I. Rapin), pp. 51–68. Elsevier, Amsterdam.

McNeill, D. (1992). *Hand and mind: what gestures reveal about thought.* University of Chicago Press.

Meadow, K. (1968). Early manual communication in relation to the deaf child's intellectual, social, and communicative functioning. *American Annals of the Deaf*, 113, 29–41.

Morford, J. P. (1996a). Insights to language from the study of gesture: a review of research on the gestural communication of non-signing deaf people. *Language and Communication*, 16, 165–78.

Morford, J. P. (1996b). Tendance d'ordre dans un système de signes domestiques. In *Spécificités de la recherche linguistique sur les languages signées* (ed. C. Dubuisson and D. Bouchard), pp. 5–16. Association Canadienne–Française pour l'Avancement des Sciences, Montréal.

Morford, J. P. (1998). Gesture when there is no speech model. In *The nature and functions of gesture in children's communications* (ed. J. M. Iverson and S. Goldin-Meadow), pp. 101–16. *New Directions for Child Development* series, no. 79. Jossey-Bass, San Francisco, CA.

Morford, M. and Goldin-Meadow, S. (1992). Comprehension and production of gesture in combination with speech in one-word speakers. *Journal of Child Language*, 9, 559–80.

Morford, J. P. and Goldin-Meadow, S. (1997). From here and now to there and then: the development of displaced reference in home sign and English. *Child Development*, 68, 420–35.

Morford, J. P., Singleton, J. L., and Goldin-Meadow, S. (1995). From home sign to ASL: identifying the influences of a self-generated childhood gesture system upon language proficiency in adulthood. In *Proceedings of the 19th Boston University conference on language development*, Vol. 2 (ed. D. MacLaughlin and S. McEwen), pp. 403–14. Cascadilla Press, Somerville, MA.

Newport, E. L. (1990). Maturational constraints on language learning. *Cognitive Science*, 14, 11–28.

Newport, E. L. and Meier, R. P. (1985). The acquisition of American Sign Language. In *The cross-linguistic study of language acquisition*, Vol. 1: *The data* (ed. D. J. Slobin), pp. 881–938. Erlbaum, Hillsdale, NJ.

Perry, M. and Elder, A. D. (1996). Knowledge in transition: adults' developing understanding of a principle of physical causality. *Cognitive Development*, **12**, 131–57.

Perry, M., Church, R. B., and Goldin-Meadow, S. (1988). Transitional knowledge in the acquisition of concepts. *Cognitive Development*, **3**, 359–400.

Petitto, L. A. (1988). 'Language' in the pre-linguistic child. In *The development of language and language researchers: essays in honor of Roger Brown* (ed. F. Kessel), pp. 187–221. Erlbaum, Hillsdale, NJ.

Singleton, J. L., Morford, J. P., and Goldin-Meadow, S. (1993). Once is not enough: Standards of well-formedness in manual communication created over three different timespans. *Language*, **69**, 683–715.

Stone, A., Webb, R., and Mahootian, S. (1991). The generality of gesture–speech mismatch as an index of transitional knowledge: evidence from a control-of-variables task. *Cognitive Development*, **6**, 301–13.

Tervoort, B. T. (1961). Esoteric symbolism in the communication behavior of young deaf children. *American Annals of the Deaf*, **106**, 436–80.

Zinober, B. and Martlew, M. (1985). Developmental changes in four types of gesture in relation to acts and vocalizations from 10 to 21 months. *British Journal of Developmental Psychology*, **3**, 293–306.

CHAPTER 8

Do signers gesture?

Karen Emmorey

Laboratory for Cognitive Neuroscience, The Salk Institute for Biological Studies

Introduction

Before answering the title question 'Do signers gesture?' we must first answer the question 'What makes sign language different from gesture?' This analysis depends entirely upon one's definition of gesture. If gesture is defined sufficiently broadly, then the answer is 'nothing'. For example, Armstrong *et al.* (1995) define gesture as 'a *functional* unit, an equivalence class of coordinated movements that achieve some end (p.46; emphasis in the original).' Under this definition, speech itself, the gesticulation accompanying speech, pantomime, emblems, and sign language are all examples of gesture. However, the aim of this chapter is to explore whether we observe in signing a parallel to the gestures that hearing people use when they talk. Kendon (1980) refers to this phenomenon as *gesticulation* which is distinct from pantomime and emblems (conventionalized gestures such as the 'thumbs-up' sign). In this chapter, we will compare sign language primarily to the gestures (gesticulation) that accompany speech, rather than to pantomime, the early gestures of children, gesture 'systems' like home sign, or conventional emblematic gestures.

Some properties found in sign languages but absent in gestures accompanying speech

A review of significant differences between sign language and gesture provides an important backdrop for investigating whether and how gestures might accompany sign. Many authors have described the relation between sign language and gesture (e.g., Klima and Bellugi 1979; Kendon 1988; McNeill 1993), and the following lists some of the clearest distinctions, with specific examples from American Sign Language (ASL).

Sublexical (phonological) structure

Signs exhibit a systematic patterning of form (a phonology) not found in gesture. Signs participate in a system of minimal contrasts at the level of form, rather than

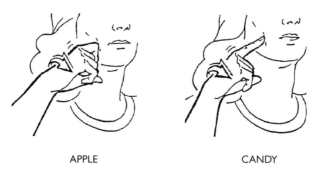

APPLE   CANDY

Fig. 8.1 Illustration of two ASL signs that contrast in handshape: APPLE (left) and CANDY (right).

meaning. For example, the signs APPLE[1] and CANDY differ only in handshape (see Fig. 8.1), but these handshapes do not themselves convey meaning (just as the /p/ and /b/ sounds in 'pat' and 'bat' are not meaningful). The 'X' handshape of APPLE is also found in the sign KEY, but does not contribute to the meaning of either sign. ASL contrasts about 36 different handshapes (Wilbur 1987), but not all sign languages share the same inventory. For example, the 't' handshape in ASL (the thumb is inserted between the index and middle fingers of a fist) is not found in Danish Sign Language. Swedish Sign Language contains a handshape not found in ASL: all fingers are extended except for the ring finger which is bent.

Like words, the articulation of signs is governed by a system of rules and form constraints. An example of a phonological rule in American English is the 'flap rule' in which /t/ and /d/ are pronounced as a flap when they occur between a stressed and an unstressed vowel (the tongue quickly hits the ridge of the mouth behind the teeth). Thus, a flap (rather than /t/) occurs in words like 'writer' and 'later' (compare with 'write' and 'late').

The following is just one example of a phonological constraint in ASL: 'secondary movement' (e.g., finger wiggling, circling, bending, hooking) can only occur at a particular time during the articulation of a sign. Perlmutter (1993) discovered that secondary movement is permitted only during the path movement of a sign or when a sign is held in space (with no preceding or following path movement). Figure 8.2a shows the correct form of GO-UP-IN-FLAMES in which finger wiggling must stop at the end of the sign when the sign is produced phrase-finally, and the ill-formed sign in which wiggling continues throughout the sign. Figure 8.2b shows the sign GERMANY also produced in a phrase-final position. In this case, wiggling must be executed throughout the sign's articulation, and the form parallel to GO-UP-IN-FLAMES is incorrect. Perlmutter accounts for the differences between these two forms by proposing that secondary movement can occur only on the nucleus (the peak) of a sign syllable (defined in terms of movement (M) and position (P) segments). Regardless of whether Perlmutter's syllabic analysis turns out to be correct, the point is that there are non-obvious constraints

(a)

GO-UP-IN-FLAMES   Ill-formed

(b)

GERMANY   Ill-formed

Fig. 8.2 Illustration of a sublexical (phonological) constraint in ASL (see text). Correct forms of (a) GO-UP-IN-FLAMES and (b) GERMANY are shown on the left, with ill-formed versions on the right. Illustrations reproduced, with permission, from Perlmutter, D. (1993). Sonority and syllable structure in American Sign Language. In *Phonetics and phonology: Current issues in ASL phonology* (ed. G. R. Coulter), pp. 227–61. Academic Press, Inc., San Diego.

on the form of signs and that signers have clear intuitions about what is permissible and what is ill-formed. Such is not the case for gesture, and it may be the case that these types of form constraints are not observed even in the most 'language-like' gesture systems, such as home sign. Thus far, there is little evidence that home sign gestures are composed of combinations of meaningless elements or that systematic restrictions on form apply to such elements (see Chapter 7, this volume, for a discussion of home sign systems).

Lexical structure

Like words in all human languages, but unlike gestures, signs belong to lexical categories or basic form classes such as noun, verb, modal verb, adjective, adverb, pronoun, and determiner. Sign languages have a lexicon of sign forms and a system for creating new signs in which meaningful elements (morphemes) are combined. For example, Fig. 8.3 provides illustrations of the sign GIVE with various movement patterns which indicate different temporal aspects (ways of performing an action). Sign languages tend to use non-concatenative combinatorial processes (similar to Semitic languages) rather than prefixation or suffixation. ASL exhibits the same types of morphological processes found in spoken languages, e.g., noun–verb derivation (Supalla and Newport 1978), compounding (Klima and Bellugi 1979), numeral incorporation (Chinchor 1983), and reduplication (Klima and Bellugi 1979), just to name a few.

These morphological processes are governed by constraints on ordering and on their application to particular forms. For example, in Fig, 8.3d the durational inflection applies after the exhaustive inflection to yield a form meaning 'give to each in turn, over a long time'. Such a verb could be used to describe someone at Halloween giving out candy to children, again and again, throughout the evening. In contrast, if the durational inflection applies prior to the exhaustive, as in Fig. 8.3e, the meaning of the verb is 'give continuously to each in turn', which could be used to describe a teacher who takes a long time to pass out papers to students (the papers are passed out once, but it takes a long time). Finally, the durational inflection can apply recursively, before and after the exhaustive, as in Fig. 8.3f. A verb inflected in this way could be used to describe a teacher passing out several papers to each student, and this action occurs throughout the day (e.g., for each class). Thus, lexical meaning is dependent upon the order of application of morphological inflections.

Morphological processes are also sensitive to the phonological form of a sign. For example, the nature of the reduplication that occurs after compounding is

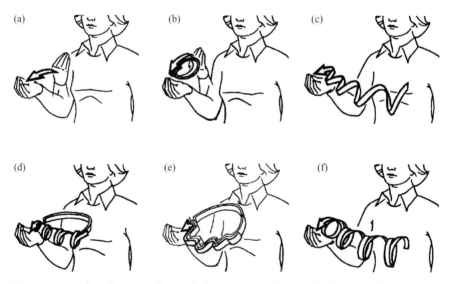

Fig. 8.3 Examples of aspectual morphology in ASL. The panels illustrate the sign GIVE with various movement patterns which indicate different temporal aspects. (a) GIVE (uninflected); (b) GIVE$_{[Durational]}$; (c) GIVE$_{[Exhaustive]}$; (d) GIVE$_{[[Ex.]Dur.]}$; (e) GIVE$_{[[Dur.]Ex.]}$; (f) GIVE$_{[[[Dur.]Ex.]Dur.]}$.

dependent upon the phonological form of the compound. Sandler (1989) found that whether the entire compound is reduplicated or only part of the compound depends upon whether the compound contains one or two independent movements. For example, the signs MIND and BLOW-UP can be combined to mean 'blow one's top,' and the resulting compound has two movements. Reduplication only applies to the second part of the compound. In contrast, the compound FAINT (derived from MIND and DROP) contains only one movement, and the entire form is reduplicated. Sandler suggests that morphological reduplication applies to the final syllable of a sign (MIND+BLOW-UP is bisyllabic and FAINT+DROP is monosyllabic). Note that reduplication adds the same meaning (repeated action) to both verb compounds as a whole—the meaning change is not restricted to the part of the compound that is reduplicated.

These examples show that the formation of signs is governed by a system of constraints which are sensitive to phonological form, lexical category, rule ordering, and semantics. Again, these properties are not found even in the most language-like gesture systems (pantomime and home sign). Even though gesture classes have been observed in various home sign systems (Goldin-Meadow *et al.* 1994), and home sign gestures have been argued to have a 'morphological' structure in which a gesture can be broken down into meaningful components (Goldin-Meadow *et al.* 1995), the gesture lexicon of home signers does not exhibit the hierarchical constraint-based system of generative lexical processes found in signed (and spoken) languages.

Syntactic structure

Gestures that accompany speech rarely occur in combination, and successive gestures do not form a larger hierarchical structure (McNeill 1992). In contrast, signs combine to form sentences which are governed by phrase structure rules and syntactic principles. For example, signers judge MAN OLD SLEEP-FITFULLY ('The old man sleeps fitfully') as grammatical, but OLD SLEEP-FITFULLY MAN as an ill-formed sentence. This judgement is not based on meaning—signers judge IDEA BLUE SLEEP-FITFULLY ('The blue idea sleeps fitfully') as also well-formed grammatically, but nonsensical. The basic word order of ASL is subject–verb–object (Fischer 1974), but other word orders can be derived through topicalization (Liddell 1980):

Basic word order:

(1) DOG CHASE CAT.   'The dog chased the cat.'

Topicalized object:

$$\overline{\qquad}^t$$
(2) CAT, DOG CHASE.   'As for the cat, the dog chased it.'

Topicalization (indicated above by the 't') is marked by a nonmanual signal that is timed to co-occur with the manual sign(s). The ASL topicalization marker is a combination of a backward head tilt and raised eyebrows. Topicalization in ASL is subject to the same universal 'island constraints' that apply to spoken languages (Lillo-Martin 1991):

Ungrammatical subject extraction:

$$\overline{}^{\,t}$$
(3) *MOTHER, I DON'T-KNOW 'WHAT' LIKE.

The above sentence violates the so-called 'WH island constraint', which states that an element (e.g., MOTHER) cannot be extracted from within an embedded clause of a certain type. Note that a resumptive pronoun 'saves' the sentence (from Lillo-Martin 1991):

Subject extraction with a resumptive pronoun:

$$\overline{}^{\,t}$$
(4) MOTHER, I DON'T-KNOW 'WHAT' PRONOUN$_a$ LIKE.
    'As for mother, I don't know what she likes.'

The presence of a resumptive pronoun permits the long distance dependency between elements in the matrix and subordinate clauses. Fischer (1974) has shown that ASL also obeys the 'complex NP constraint' (an element cannot be extracted from a complex noun phrase), and Padden (1988) showed that ASL obeys the 'coordinate structure constraint' (a dependency cannot occur between one element within the conjunct of a coordinate structure and another element outside that structure).

These few examples illustrate that ASL not only has rules for constituent ordering, but also exhibits subordinate clause structure and long distance dependencies, and follows universal constraints on syntactic form. Again, although Goldin-Meadow and Mylander (1990) found that home signing children combine gestures into sequences with a characteristic order (patient, action) and may even exhibit subordination, there is little evidence that home sign systems are subject to syntactic structure constraints found in spoken and signed languages, such as the 'island' constraints mentioned above, constraints on the distribution of various types of pronouns (e.g., rules regarding when reflexive and personal pronouns are allowed to be co-referential with a noun), or head feature conventions which state that a syntactic feature (such as tense) must be shared by a head node (e.g., a VP) and its head daughter (e.g., a V) within a syntactic tree. Clearly, the gestures that accompany speech do not have such syntactic properties and are not governed by these constraints.

Standards of form and a community of users

Finally, sign languages belong to a community of users who are systematic in their judgements of phonological, lexical, and syntactic form (with some limited individual and dialectal variation). In contrast, the gestures that accompany speech are idiosyncratic with no agreed standards of form. Speakers vary in their tendency to gesture, and different individuals

create their own gesture symbols for the same event, each incorporating a core meaning but adding details that seem salient, and these are different from speaker to speaker

McNeill (1992), p.41

Furthermore, McNeill finds that in general, the gestures of people speaking different languages are no more different than the gestures of people speaking the same language. In contrast, sign languages used by deaf people in distant geographic locations may vary dramatically from one another.

Even for home sign, the standard of form is idiosyncratic, belonging to the individual. Goldin-Meadow and Mylander (1990) demonstrated that deaf home signers' gestures are quite different from their parents' gestures (see also Chapter 7, this volume). In particular, the parents' gestures lack the combinatorial properties found in the children's gestures. In addition, Kegl and McWhorter (1997) argue that home sign alone is not sufficient to support the spontaneous generation of a signed language. Kegl and her colleagues are documenting the emergence of Nicaraguan Sign Language (Senghas 1995; Kegl *et al.* 1999). At the earliest stage of development, there were only deaf home signers who came together in the schools in Managua in the early 1980s. However, these original home sign systems, even when used by adults, were not examples of spontaneously generated languages. Although these home sign systems were communicative, they often were no more than list-like labelling. Kegl and colleagues discovered that there was a stage of development that intermediated between various idiosyncratic home sign systems and the emergence of a full-fledged sign language. This intermediate stage was a pidgin which arose from the intercommunication among this critical mass of home signers. When young deaf children were exposed to this pidgin form of the language, creolization began to take place, and the kinds of grammatical properties described above for signed languages began to emerge. The Nicaraguan data indicate that the emergence of a true language is dependent upon a community of users and does not arise spontaneously in individuals.

Some properties found in gestures accompanying speech but absent in sign languages

In this section, we explore the nature of gestures that speakers use when they talk, focusing on aspects of gesticulation that do not appear to have a parallel in sign language. Most of the description of the relation between gesture and speech is from McNeill (1992).

Holistic form

Gestures are argued to have a 'global' and 'synthetic' form because their meanings are derived from the whole, not the parts, and many meanings can be synthesized into a single gesture. The following example, from McNeill (1992), illustrates these properties (brackets show the extent of the gesture):

(5) [and he's trying to run ahead of it]
     Hand moves forwards at chin level while fingers wiggle.

The gesture is symbolic of a character running at a particular height (in this case, a cartoon character running along a wire above the street). McNeill (1992, pp. 20–21) argues that:

'this gesture–symbol is 'global' in that the whole is not composed of separately meaningful parts. Rather, the parts gain meaning because of the meaning of the whole. The wiggling fingers mean running only because we know that the gesture, as a whole, depicts someone running. It's not that a gesture depicting someone running was composed out of separately meaningful parts: wiggling + motion, for instance.

In contrast, to describe someone running, an ASL signer might use a classifier construction (a predicate in which handshape denotes an object of a specific type), or a lexical verb could be used. For the classifier construction, the meaning is derived from the combination of the handshape and its motion, and there are language-internal constraints on the nature of the combination. For example, signers could use either an inverted 'V' handshape denoting legs or a two-handed body-part classifier with '1' handshapes in which each index finger denotes a leg. However, only the V classifier can be combined with path motion; if the body-part classifier is used to indicate running, then the height and forward path of motion must be indicated by a separate verb (Supalla 1990). This constraint is relatively arbitrary, based on a distinction between ASL manner and path verbs.

The gestural depiction in (5) of running along a path is only understood as symbolic of this event by virtue of its relation to the speech. In contrast, signs do not take their meaning from another communicative signal. Figure 8.4 provides

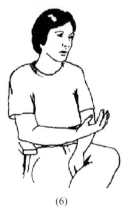
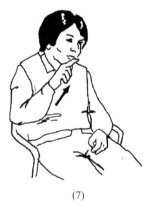

(6)   (7)

Fig. 8.4 Illustration of the iconic gestures in examples (6) and (7). Reproduced, with permission, from McNeill, D. (1992). *Hand and mind. What gestures reveal about thought.* Copyright The University of Chicago Press, Chicago, Illinois.

further examples of the holistic and idiosyncratic nature of gestures (from McNeill 1992). Both speakers are describing a scene in a cartoon in which Sylvester the cat climbs up through a drainpipe in an effort to catch Tweety Bird. As in (5), the meaning of these gestures is only interpretable with respect to the accompanying speech, and the 'parts' of the gesture (e.g., handshape and motion) do not have meanings that are independent of the gesture as a whole.

(6)   and he goes [up through] the pipe this time
      Hand rises up in basket-like shape, depicting the character rising up and the interiority of the pipe

(7)   he tries [climbing] up the rain barrel
      Hand flexes backwards, showing the character rising upwards

Types of gesture

Examples (5)–(7) are iconic gestures which display concrete aspects of a scene described in speech. Similarly, signs are also very often iconic, i.e., some aspect of their physical form bears a resemblance to their referent. Iconicity is more prevalent than earlier researchers acknowledged (see Taub (1997) for an excellent analysis of the role of iconicity in both spoken and signed languages). Gestures can also be metaphoric; in these cases, the gesture represents an 'image' of abstract concepts and relationships that refer to the discourse metastructure. Figure 8.5 is an example from McNeill (1992) in which the speaker refers to a transition in the film he is retelling:

(8)   and now [we get] into the story proper
      Hands supporting an object (conduit image) rotate (three times) and move forwards (spatial image).

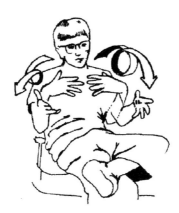

Fig. 8.5 Illustration of the abstract gesture in (8). Reproduced, with permission, from McNeill, D. (1992). *Hand and mind. What gestures reveal about thought.* Copyright The University of Chicago Press, Chicago, Illinois.

Fig. 8.6 Illustration of the beat gesture in example (9). Reproduced, with permission, from McNeill, D. (1992). *Hand and mind. What gestures reveal about thought.* Copyright The University of Chicago Press, Chicago, Illinois.

McNeill analyses this gesture as a metaphoric gesture for transition or process. The gesture also contains a conduit metaphor in which the concept of the film is represented gesturally as a bounded container. The forward motion of the gesture represents the concept of entering, and the rotation indicates transition and change. The gesture *in toto* conveys an image of the transition into the main part of the film. Signs can also convey metaphoric images of abstract concepts (see particularly Wilcox (1993) and Taub (1997)), and there may be some interesting parallels between metaphoric gestures and the nature of metaphor in sign language (for example, certain abstract concepts can be represented as containers using classifier constructions).

Another type of gesture that can accompany speech is called a 'beat' or a 'baton'. Unlike iconic and metaphoric gestures, beats tend to have the same form regardless of the speech content. The typical beat is a quick flick of the hand or fingers up and down, or back and forth. Beats mark the accompanying word or phrase as significant for its discourse-pragmatic content, rather than for its semantic content (McNeill 1992). Figure 8.6 provides an illustration from McNeill (1992):

(9) when[ever she] looks at him he tries to make monkey noises
     Hand rises short way up from lap and drops back down.

In this example, the speaker is referring to the theme of an episode, and not to a particular event, as indicated by his use of the word 'whenever'. The beat gesture is associated with this word, emphasizing its metanarrative function of summarizing (i.e., the speaker is not narrating a chain of events, but summarizing a set of events). Beats tend to be associated with metanarrative functions such as introducing new characters, summarizing actions, introducing new themes, and signalling changes in narrative structure. There does not appear to be a clear parallel between beat gestures and signs (although of course, signs, like words, convey metanarrative information).

A final type of gesture that accompanies speech can be categorized as deictic.

Deictic gestures are pointing gestures that function to indicate objects or events in the physical environment surrounding the speaker. However, deictic gestures can also be abstract, for example, pointing to a location in gesture space that stands for an abstract concept or relationship described in speech (McNeill 1992). There is no doubt that pointing signs have deictic functions, and later we will examine the distinction between pronominal deixis and gestural deixis in our discussion of whether signers gesture.

Co-expressive synchronous timing

Gestures are integrated into the accompanying speech, and almost all gestures (around 90%) occur when the person is actually speaking (McNeill 1985). Gestures are rarely produced by listeners. The 'stroke' phase of a gesture expresses the meaning of the gesture and is synchronized with the linguistic elements that are co-expressive with it (Kendon 1980). The gesture and the speech are co-expressive in the sense that they both refer to the same referent (i.e., the same event, object, relation, etc.)—gesture and speech form a composite expression (see Clark 1996). The brackets in the above examples indicate the speech co-occurring with the stroke of the gesture. Gesture preparation (e.g., the hand rises up into 'gesture space') can precede speech and is optional, but the stroke is obligatory and timed to occur at the same time as the prosodic stress peak of the associated utterance (McNeill 1992). The gesture stroke never follows the related speech. Of course, the articulation of signs is not timed to coincide with a structural element of a separate co-expressive system.

Function

The extent to which sign language is communicative has never been questioned; however, the extent to which the gestures that accompany speech are communicative is a topic of much debate. Some researchers argue that the primary function of gesture is to convey information to the addressee (e.g., Cohen 1977; Kendon 1983). Others argue that the primary function of gesture is to facilitate lexical retrieval (Rauscher *et al.* 1996; see also Chapter 6, this volume), while still others suggest that gestures are linked to speech hesitations and repair (Butterworth and Beattie 1978).

In particular, Krauss and colleagues question the communicative function of gestures that co-occur with speech (Krauss *et al.* 1991, 1995). Krauss *et al.* (1995) point out that even though people gesture more when they are face-to-face, speakers nonetheless produce gestures when they cannot be seen by their addressee, e.g., when speaking on the telephone or through an intercom. Such gestures cannot perform a communicative function since they cannot be seen. In addition, there appears to be only weak evidence that preventing gesture impairs communicative success, and the ability to see a speaker's gestures does not appear to enhance comprehension by an addressee (Krauss *et al.* 1995). Therefore, Krauss and colleagues have concluded that the primary function of gestures is to facilitate speech production. Evidence for this hypothesis stems from the effect of preventing gesture on speech and from the temporal relation of gesture to speech. The initiation of gestures almost always precedes the word associated with that gesture (its 'lexical affiliate'), and such temporal coincidence would be necessary if gesture production is to aid word retrieval (Morrel-Samuels and Krauss 1992). In addition, preventing gestures and creating word finding difficulties by forcing subjects to use constrained speech both lead to the same types of speech dysfluencies, suggesting that the prevention of gesture leads to difficulties in lexical retrieval (Krauss *et al.* 1995). Obviously, signs *are* lexical items and do not facilitate the production of another communicative channel.

Clark (1996) argues that although gestures may be facilitative, their main function is in fact communicative. Clark suggests that iconic gestures are either component or concurrent gestures. Component gestures are embedded as part of the utterance, and are patently communicative. For example: 'The boy went [rude gesture] and ran away.' However, these are not the gestures that concern Krauss and colleagues. Concurrent gestures, on the other hand, are produced at the same time as the speech utterance. Clark argues that these gestures often convey information that is not present in the speech and that this information is in fact informative. For example, Engle (1998) finds that when explaining how locks work, speakers often produce gestures that convey information related to but not present in the accompanying speech. Clark suggests that the facilitative role of gestures may be an epiphenomenon of their communicative function.

Finally, McNeill (1992) suggests that gestures are not only an act of communication, but also an act of thought. He argues that gestures occur because of the speaker's ongoing thought process—thought is not worked out and then translated into speech and gesture; rather, words and gestures arise from a shared computational stage that precedes articulation. McNeill argues that spontaneous gestures reflect the early 'primitive' stage of an utterance, in which one dimension of thought is a global-synthetic image. In contrast, words reflect the final stage of the utterance and are governed by linguistic structure. McNeill (1993, p.156) writes:

one supposes that for the deaf and others who make use of conventional sign languages the primitive stages of their sentences also include global-synthetic images, just as in the case of spoken languages, but their signs, unlike the spontaneous gestures of the hearing, do not, cannot, reflect this stage. The kinesic–visual medium is grammatical and socially regulated for the deaf, and this shifts the overt performance of deaf signers to the final stage of the internal temporal evolution of utterances.

Thus, according to McNeill, signs cannot reflect the early imagistic aspects of thought in the way that gestures do.

Do signers gesture?

After laying out the differences between sign language and the gestures that speakers use when they talk, we are in a position to tackle the question 'Do signers gesture?' I suggest the answer is 'Yes, but not the way speakers do.' The major difference is that signers do not produce idiosyncratic, spontaneous movements of the hands and arms while they are signing. The constraint on such movements is fairly obvious: Both hands are involved in producing the linguistic utterance, and constraints on bimanual coordination and motor resources prevent the production of a lexical sign with one hand and the production of a holistic non-linguistic gesture with the other.

Manual gestures

However, I will argue that signers do produce *component* gestures, to use Clark's terminology (Liddell and Metzger (1998) describe such gestures as 'constructed action'). Such manual gestures are produced as a separate component of a signed utterance, and signers stop signing while they produce the gesture. Figure 8.7 provides an illustration in which the signer (B.D.) produces a sign (RUN), holds the sign with the dominant hand, and produces a gesture meaning something like 'stop' (the left hand waves towards the location of an antagonist), and then returns to the sign. The signer in Fig. 8.7 is retelling a scene from the *Frog, where are you?* story (Mayer 1969).[2] The images in the following ASL figures are video frames from the signer's actual narration. In the scene described, a dog is running along side a deer who is carrying away the boy to whom the dog belongs. In the following examples, gestures are described in lower case and bracketed by back slashes (see note 1 pp. 158–159 for other conventions used here).

(10) #DOG CL:RUN$_{[hooked V hs]}$/hand waves towards location of deer/
         CL:RUN$_{[hooked V hs]}$
         'The dog is running (gestures 'stop') and running.'

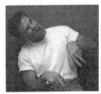

| #DOG | CL:RUN | /stop/ | CL:RUN |

Fig. 8.7 Illustration of the signs and gesture in example (10).

Manual gestures may also be strung together, as in the example shown in Fig. 8.8. In this example, the signer is describing a scene in the 'Frog' story in which the boy peers over a log, sees a group of baby frogs, and gestures to the dog to be quiet and come over to the log. The sequence is purely gestural with no hierarchical or componential structure.

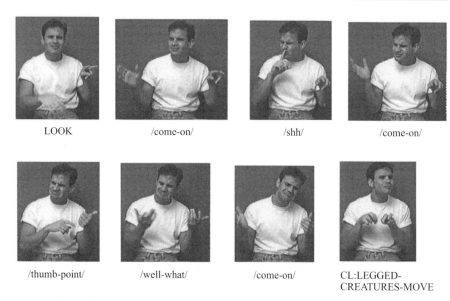

| LOOK | /come-on/ | /shh/ | /come-on/ |

| /thumb-point/ | /well-what/ | /come-on/ | CL:LEGGED-CREATURES-MOVE |

Fig. 8.8 Illustration of the signs and gestures in example (11).

(11) LOOK/come-on, shh, come-on, thumb-point, well what?, come-on/
      CL:TWO-LEGGED-CREATURES-MOVE[hooked V hs]
      'Look over here. (gesture: come-on, shh, come-on, thumb-point, well
      what?, come-on). The two crept over (to the log).'

Notice that the signs RUN and LOOK in examples (10) and (11) remain
loosely articulated on one hand while the signer produces the gesture with the
other hand. This is as close as one gets to simultaneous gesture and signing.
However, such examples differ crucially from concurrent speech and gesture
because, although co-temporal, the signs and gesture are not co-expressive. That
is, the sign LOOK does not refer to the same referent as the 'come-on' or 'shh'
gesture. In addition, LOOK was not initially produced at the same time as the
gesture; rather, LOOK was first signed and then maintained while the gestures
were produced.

Examples (12)–(15) below provide further illustrations of gestures alternating
with signs. As with examples (10) and (11), the gestures do not appear to have
lexical affiliates, i.e., specific signs with which the gesture is associated.

The following examples are from a signer (S.S.) telling James Thurber's
'Unicorn' story (Thurber 1940):

(12) CL: RUN[two-handed body-part classifier, 1 hs]/taps as if to wake imagined body/WIFE
      THAT_a/taps repeatedly at location a/
      'He ran' (gesture: taps location where wife is sleeping). 'His wife is there'
      (gesture: taps imagined body more vigorously).

(13) CL: KNEEL-ON-SURFACE[hooked V hs on flat B hs]/rests head on his hand/
   'He knelt down' (gesture: head rests on his hand and his face has a
   contemplative expression).

Examples (14) and (15) are from another signer (O.C.) telling the 'Frog' story:

(14) BOY/hands fly upward, palms out, as if losing his balance/CL:FALL-FROM-
   TREE[V hs moves down from l hs]
   'The boy (gesture: loses balance, falling backward) fell out of the tree.'

$$\overline{\qquad\qquad}wh$$

(15) CL: HOLD-OBJECT-WITH-FISTS[both hands with S hs] WHERE /flat hand to
   forehead as if searching/
   '(The boy) holds onto something (branches). 'Where (is the frog)?'
   (gesture: searching)'

The meanings of these manual gestures tend to be fairly clear even outside of the sign context, and this is true for the majority of manual gestures that occur in alternation with signing. In contrast, the gestures of speakers are generally un-interpretable without the accompanying speech (Krauss *et al.* 1991). The manual gestures that occur with signing tend to be more mimetic and conventional than the gestures that are concurrent with speech.

In fact, it is not a simple matter to determine whether a given manual ex-pression is a gesture or a sign. This question arises primarily with respect to the possibility that a potential gesture may be an ASL classifier predicate—the lexical status of signs such as APPLE (see Fig. 8.1) are not questioned. Marschark (1994) seems to suggest that if a manual expression looks the same as a gesture produced by a speaker, then that expression can be considered gesticulation rather than signing. He provides the following as an example of gesticulation and signing (p. 213): 'a deaf child tracing the shape of a suspension bridge after signing 'I SAW BRIDGE THERE'.' However, it is quite possible that this expression was an ASL tracing construction. Unlike a tracing gesture, the ASL construction is subject to linguistic constraints. For example, 'the tracing movement always starts with both hands together in one place; then one hand moves away in one direction, or both hands move in opposite directions' (for a symmetrical object) (Supalla 1982). When only one hand moves, it must be the dominant hand, and handshape specifies the nature of the object traced, e.g., an 'I' handshape for an outline, a 'G' handshape for a thick line, or a 'B' handshape for a surface; further constraints apply to the nature of contact between the two hands and the morphological status of the handshapes (see Emmorey and Casey 1995). The deaf child may have produced such a construction, a gesture that had the same form, or an incorrect attempt at the ASL tracing construction (e.g., deleting the non-dominant 'anchor' hand).

Thus, particularly for children, it may be difficult to determine whether a given manual expression is truly a holistic, non-linguistic gesture or a morphologically complex classifier predicate. Such ambiguity is particularly prevalent for 'instru-ment' classifier handshapes in which the handshape indicates how the human hand holds an object (as in example (15)). A possible parallel ambiguity in spoken language might occur between an onomatopoetic word and a 'vocal gesture,' e.g., an imitation of a sound such as a barking dog or a clanking automobile. Is the expression a word or a vocal demonstration of a sound?

In sum, unlike the manual gestures of speakers, the gestures of signers occur in alternation with the linguistic signal (rather than concurrently with it), and signers' gestures tend to be more conventional and mimetic, rather than idiosyncratic. I would predict that if viewers were shown signers' gestures in isolation from the surrounding signs, they would be much more accurate in interpreting their semantic characteristics than would viewers shown gestures in isolation from speech. Finally, signers' manual gestures are not synchronized to co-occur with a particular sign related to the gesture's meaning; rather, these gestures can function as components of an utterance or as an independent expression.

Deictic pointing gestures

Pointing gestures look pretty much like ASL indexical pronouns: the index finger points towards a person, object, or location in the real world or towards a location in gesture/signing space. What is the difference? In ASL, the pointing sign (i.e., the 'I' handshape) is part of an intricate system in which handshape distinguishes case (e.g., reflexive, possessive, or indexical), orientation distinguishes person (first or non-first), and movement indicates number (plural or singular). Pronouns can be directed towards locations in signing space to refer to nominals associated with those locations. We will return to this type of pronoun in our discussion of gesture and signing space. Pronouns can also be directed towards physically present people or objects, and of course, signers also use non-linguistic pointing gestures. How can one tell the difference between a pronoun and a gestural point?

One possibility is that there is an articulatory distinction between the two forms. One of our ASL consultants suggested that pointing gestures can be distinguished from ASL deictic pronouns by subtle differences in movement. Pronouns may be characterized by a single motion towards a person or a location in space; whereas, a pointing gesture can have short repeated motions towards a person or location. Such repeated motion is judged as odd when it occurs with a form that is unambiguously an ASL deictic pronoun (e.g., the possessive 'B' handshape or the SELF pronoun directed towards a physically present person). Further research may reveal whether or not there are articulatory or rhythmic differences between pointing gestures and indexical pronouns.

Another difference is that pronouns occur in rule-governed positions within a sentence where gestures do not occur. For example, 'subject pronoun copy' is a syntactic rule in which a pronoun copy of a subject appears at the end of the clause, and it is used to add emphatic meaning (Padden 1988). The following discussion illustrates that this rule applies to deictic pronouns and not to deictic gestures.[3] In the examples below, the subscript 'Bob' indicates that the pronoun was directed towards a person (Bob) who was physically present during the conversation.

(16) PRONOUN[Bob] LIKES COFFEE.
'He (Bob) likes coffee.'

(17) /Thumb point towards Bob/LIKES COFFEE.
'(Bob) likes coffee.'

The gesture in (17) is similar to the thumb-point gesture shown in Fig. 8.8, and is not part of the ASL pronominal system. The pointing gesture in (17) is not the subject of the sentence; rather, ASL permits null subjects in tensed clauses, particularly when the subject is clear from the discourse context (Lillo-Martin 1986). In a sense, the thumb-point gesture co-occurs with the null subject. It is possible that the form glossed as PRONOUN in (16) is actually a non-linguistic pointing gesture co-occurring with a null subject. However, examples (18) and (19) illustrate that the 'subject pronoun copy' rule applies only to ASL deictic pronouns and not to deictic gestures (question marks before an example indicate that signers find the example odd or unacceptable):

(18) PRONOUN[Bob] LIKES COFFEE PRONOUN[Bob].
'He (Bob) likes coffee, he does.'

?? (19) /Thumb-point towards Bob/LIKES COFFEE/thumb-point towards Bob/.

The main point here is that signers produce both pointing gestures and pronouns that are directed towards physically present people or objects. Although these forms may look identical, only the pronouns are part of a syntactic representation, governed by linguistic rules and constraints of the sort that do not apply to gesture (for example, the 'pronoun copy' rule is subject to the syntactic island constraints mentioned earlier).

Body gestures

Thus far, we have focused our discussion on manual gestures that accompany speech, but the face, body, and voice can also be gestural. Clark and Gerrig (1990, p.782) provide the following example of a component body gesture which completes an utterance:

(20) I got out of the car, and I just [demonstration of turning around and bumping his head on an invisible telephone pole].

Examples (21) and (22) provide illustrations of body gestures that are concurrent with signing, rather than components of the signed utterance (brackets mark the extent of the gesture during signing):
From signer S.S. telling the 'Unicorn' story:

(21) [CL: SIT-ON-SURFACE[hooked V hs on loose U hs] ROCK-IN-ROCKING-CHAIR. HUSBAND WONDER REALLY HAPPY FINISH] FROM-NOW-ON

Body rocks back and forth as if in a rocking chair
'He sits and rocks in his rocking chair. The husband thinks back. I'm really happy it's all over for good.'

From signer P.C. telling the 'Cinderella' story:

(22) DECIDE DANCE. [DANCE^{+++}] THEN GIRL THINK, 'I MUST GO HOME, I MUST GO HOME.'
Body sways as if to music.
'They decide to dance. They dance all around, and then the girl realizes, 'I must go home, I must go home.'

These body motions (e.g., rocking or swaying) are not linguistic. That is, they are not grammaticized movements like the inflections shown in Fig. 8.3, and they are not part of the phonologically specified movement of the signs with which they co-occur. Unlike manual gestures, body gestures can be expressed simultaneously with signing. Body gestures express how referents move their bodies during the action described by the concurrent signing. The duration of the body motion does not necessarily correspond to the actual duration of the referent's motion, e.g., in example (22), the girl is still dancing while thinking 'I must go home', but the signer does not sway during the quotation. Finally, body gestures can also co-occur with manual gestures which alternate with ASL. For example, in (14) the signer's body moves backwards along with the manual gesture indicating a loss of balance.

Facial gestures

Although most research has focused on manual gestures, speakers (and signers) also produce facial gestures. Chovil (1991/1992, p.177) provides the following example in which a facial gesture is used for emphasis:

(23) This is [really] silly.
Raises eyebrows

Example (24) below from Chovil (1991/1992, p.180) illustrates a 'personal reaction display' in which the speaker conveys information about an emotion or an evaluation about something said. In this example, the speaker is talking about how her son's constant questioning could irritate her. In example (25), the speaker produces a facial expression that conveys dislike (from Chovil 1991/1992, p.184).

(24) . . . Sometimes I find them amusing, other times I find them [exasperating].
Raises her eyebrows; widens and rolls her eyes.

(25) [Basic steamed white rice]
Squints her eyes and wrinkles her nose.

ASL signers also produce such facial gestures. However, it is important to distinguish between affective or evaluative expressions and grammatical facial expressions. Linguistic and affective facial expressions differ in their scope and timing and in the facial muscles that are used (Reilly *et al.* 1990a,b). Grammatical facial expressions have a clear onset and offset, and they are coordinated with specific constituent structures. Affective or attitudinal expressions have more global and inconsistent onset and offset patterns, and they are not timed to co-occur with specific signs or constituents. Examples of linguistic facial expressions include marking for adverbials, topics (examples (2)–(4)), 'wh' questions (example (15)), conditionals, rhetorical questions (example (26) below), and relative clauses (Liddell 1980; Baker-Shenk 1983). Linguistic facial expressions are phrasal morphemes that mark lexical and syntactic structures.

In contrast, affective and evaluative facial expressions are not morphemic and convey information about emotion or attitude (Liddell 1980). Example (26) is from a lecture on sign language aphasia in which the signer (N.F.) describes how a person might come to be brain damaged. The facial expression that co-occurs with her signing conveys compassion or sympathy. To be consistent with the treatment of affective facial expressions as a type of gesture, the extent of the facial expression will be marked with brackets, and the expression itself will be described in italics. This transcription method also serves to clearly distinguish between affective and grammatical facial expressions.

        ____rh-q

(26) HOW? [CAN B-E STROKE. CAN B-E CAR ACCIDENT. DIFFERENT^{+++}]
REASON INDEX-ORDINAL-TIP-LOCI.
Mouth turns down slightly, compassionate expression
'How (can it happen)? It can be a stroke. It can be a car accident. There are many different reasons.'

When describing the actions of a character in a story, a sign narrator can portray the facial expression, eye gaze, or head and body movements of the character performing the actions they describe (Liddell 1980; Engberg-Pedersen 1993). For example, in Fig. 8.7, the signer's head and face portray the dog looking up at the deer and barking. Figure 8.9 and example (27) provide another example from signer O.C. who is describing a scene in the 'Frog' story in which a beehive falls from a tree, and the bees swarm out and chase the dog.

(27) LARGE-ROUND-OBJECT-FALLS$_{[2 \text{ hands with C hs}]}$. [CL:SWARM. MAD.]
Eyes squint, angry expression
[#DOG CL:RUN$_{[\text{hooked V hs}]}$.]
Tongue out, fearful expression
[BEE CL:SWARM-MOVES]
Eyes squint, angry expression
'The beehive fell to the ground. The bees swarmed out. They were mad. The dog ran away, and the bees chased him.'

In example (27), the signer rapidly alternates between a facial expression that depicts the anger of the bees and one that depicts the fear of the dog. The sentences in (27) are examples of what sign linguists term 'referential shift' or role shift (e.g., Padden 1986). Referential shift is indicated by a break in eyegaze with

CL:ROUND-OBJ   CL:SWARM   MAD

#DOG   CL:RUN   BEE   CL:SWARM-MOVE

Fig. 8.9 Illustration of the signs in example (27).

the addressee, a shift in head and body position, and a change in facial expression (only the break in eyegaze is obligatory). A referential shift indicates that the following discourse should be understood from the point of view of the referent associated with the shift. In (27), the facial expressions produced by the signer are understood as reflecting the attitude of the bees or the dog—the signer herself is neither angry nor afraid. Referential shift is a linguistic device that can disambiguate the point of view associated with a facial expression, but the facial expression itself is non-linguistic.

Some researchers have suggested that during a referential shift, signers systematically use a facial expression or posture that uniquely identifies the character associated with the shift (Loew *et al.* 1997). However, although skilled storytellers might use caricatures that identify a specific character (e.g., a sneer for an evil person), such caricatures are not the norm.[4] Rather, ordinary signers produce facial expressions that depict selective aspects of what someone or something did or said—they are demonstrations in the sense of Clark and Gerrig (1990). That is, these facial expressions are not set 'character expressions', but serve to illustrate the current emotion or attitude of the character whose actions, thoughts, or words, are being described by the narrator (the person signing).

Facial gestures do not necessarily illustrate only an emotional state or evaluation. In example (27), the signer sticks her tongue out slightly when describing the dog running. This aspect of her facial gesture depicts the panting of the dog rather than an emotion. In example (28), signer S.S. depicts the mouth movements of a hearing person on the phone (the wife in the 'Unicorn' story):

(28) [PHONE-TO-EAR]
      Mouths unintelligible words with an angry expression
      'She spoke angrily into the phone.'

Although English speakers produce affective facial expressions and other facial gestures during narratives, they do so much less frequently than ASL signers. Provine and Reilly (1992) found that English speaking mothers produced significantly fewer affective facial expressions than signing mothers when telling the same story to their children. Instead of using their face, speakers rely more heavily on intonation and voice quality to convey affective and evaluative information. Furthermore, just as speakers vary in their tendency to use their voice to depict different characters or to convey affective information, signers vary in the extent to which they use affective facial expressions. However, signers do not vary in their use of obligatory grammatical facial expressions.

Gesture versus signing space

ASL, and other signed languages, have classes of signs which can be directed towards locations within signing space (e.g., pronominals, spatial verbs, indicating (agreement) verbs, and classifier predicates). For example, the sign LOOK in example (11), Fig. 8.8, is directed towards the location associated with the baby frogs, and the classifier predicate glossed as SWARM-MOVES in example (27) moves from the location associated with the beehive towards the location associated with the dog. In a series of recent papers, Liddell (1994, 1995, 1996, in press) has argued that such locations in signing space are not morphemic or part of the syntactic representation of the sentence. Liddell observes that when signs are directed towards physically present people or objects (such as the pronouns in examples (16) and (18)), the direction of motion is not lexically fixed, but depends upon the actual location of the referent ('Bob' in our examples). Since a referent can be in an unlimited number of physical locations, there are no linguistic features or discrete morphemes that can specify the direction of the sign. Liddell argues that the same is true for signing space: there are an unlimited number of locations in signing space towards which a pronoun (or other sign which 'uses space') can be directed. Furthermore, just as 'Bob' in examples (16) and (18) is not part of the syntactic representation of the sentence, Liddell argues that the locations within signing space are similarly not syntactic. Thus, reference is deictic, rather than anaphoric, for both physically present and non-present referents.

Liddell (in press) proposes that these types of signs (i.e., pronominals, agreeing verbs, etc.) are combinations (blends) of linguistic and gestural elements. He writes,

The handshapes, certain aspects of the orientation of the hand and types of movement are all describable by discrete linguistic features. The direction and goal of the movement constitute a gestural component of the sign.

                                                      Liddell (in press), p.17

Spoken utterances can also exhibit a composite of linguistic and gestural elements, but it is easy to distinguish between the linguistic signal and deictic gesture because they occur in different modalities. In addition, the gestural component does not influence the form of individual spoken words as it does for signed languages. Liddell (in press, p.26) explains that

the one difference [he is] proposing between signed languages and spoken languages, is that signed languages have all developed in ways which allow the gestural component to combine with the linguistically specified features of some classes of signs without interfering with the ability to recognize the signs themselves.

Both speakers and signers produce utterances that combine words concurrently with gestures; but for signed languages the deictic gesture is superimposed on the word and thus alters its form, since the word and gesture are in the same modality.

If Liddell is correct, then signing space *is* gesture space.[5] Furthermore, Liddell's proposal suggests that signers are constantly producing signs with a gestural component—the signs relevant to his proposal are extremely common and pervade the language. The analogous deictic gestures of speakers are much rarer. Under this proposal, signers must rapidly and frequently integrate linguistic representations with non-categorical representations of spatial locations (i.e., where the hands are directed in signing or real space). Thus, for sign languages there may be a very intimate connection between linguistic structures and non-linguistic representations of spatial relations (see also Emmorey 1996). Listeners must also be able to integrate linguistic representations and spatial information conveyed by the gesture of a speaker, but such integration is not an integral part of comprehension. That is, speech is quite comprehensible even when gestures cannot be seen, but sign language comprehension *requires* the interpretation of the gestural component.

Function

Do gestures perform the same function for signers that they do for speakers? It seems unlikely that the manual, body, or facial gestures produced by signers function to facilitate lexical access. These gestures are not tied to a particular lexical item, and the body and facial gestures do not have the spatiodynamic features that would be needed to prime an associated lexical representation. Signers simply do not produce the type of gesture that has been purported to aid lexical retrieval, namely, manual gestures concurrent with (or slightly preceding) associated lexical signs.

Signers' gestures certainly appear to be communicative. For the most part, the gestures presented here depict how someone's hands or body move during an event described by the signer. Further research may reveal other types of manual and body gestures. In particular, it seems likely that signers produce interactive gestures during conversations. Bavelas and her colleagues describe a type of gesture which makes reference to the interlocutor, rather than to the topic of the discourse (Bavelas *et al.* 1992, 1995). For example, interactive gestures help coordinate turn-taking during a dialogue. Speakers may gesturally transfer a turn by producing a gesture towards the addressee (often with the palm up, a type of 'giving' gesture) or may take the turn by producing a gesture towards themselves (Bavelas *et al.* 1995). Similarly, signers produce a well-known waving gesture which can be used to request a turn within a conversation: the open hand (palm down) is directed towards the interlocutor and the wrist oscillates up and down. This gesture indicates a desire for the floor (it is also used generally as a gesture to gain attention.) Further research may reveal other manual and non-manual interactive gestures. Eyegaze and head motions are particularly good candidates for non-manual gestures that may perform some of the interactive functions which Bavelas has uncovered for the manual gestures of speakers.

As noted earlier, speakers produce gestures even when they cannot be seen by their addressee. This phenomenon has been taken as evidence that gestures perform a cognitive function, as well as a communicative one. McNeill (1992, p.109) suggests that gestures reveal

aspects of [the speaker's] inner mental processes and points of view towards events when these are not articulated in speech. In gestures we are able to see the imagistic form of the speaker's sentences. This imagistic form is not usually meant for public view, and the speaker him- or herself may be unaware of it or think that it has been well hidden, but it is visible to those who would look at the gestures.

Are the gestures of signers similarly revealing? Elisabeth Engberg-Pedersen (personal communication) provides an anecdote which suggests that they may be, if the use of signing space is taken to be gestural. Engberg-Pederson videotaped a signer describing a yearly meeting of the National Association of the Deaf. The signer indicated that normally only the same group of people came to these meetings, but that particular year was quite different, and many ordinary deaf people attended. When Engberg-Pederson showed this tape to a group of deaf people, they started laughing at this point. When she asked them why, they said that the signer had revealed her true opinion about these 'ordinary deaf people' by using a very low spatial location for them. In this example, signing space carried meaning beyond the association between a referent and a location in space. The use of a low spatial location reflected the general cognitive metaphor 'high status is up and low status is down' (Lakoff and Johnson 1980). In this example, the signer's 'unwitting' use of space revealed her inner thoughts.

To conclude, signers do gesture, but not in the same way that speakers do. Signers do not produce spontaneous idiosyncratic hand gestures that are concurrent with signing. However, they frequently produce facial and body gestures that are articulated simultaneously with signing (particularly during narratives). Signers produce manual gestures that alternate with signing, and these gestures are often iconic and can be metaphoric, e.g., the 'well-what' gesture in example (11), Fig. 8.8, is an abstract gesture in which information (what can be seen behind the log) is supported by the hands (the conduit metaphor). The manual gestures of signers differ from those of speakers in that they tend to be more conventional, are not tied to a particular lexical sign, and have different timing properties. Signers also do not produce manual beat gestures, although it is possible that such gestures are produced non-manually. The gesture space of signers may be much richer than that of speakers, particularly if Liddell's hypothesis is correct. Finally, the gestures of signers perform some, but not all, of the functions that have been proposed for the gestures of speakers.

References

Armstrong, D. F., Stokoe, W. C., and Wilcox, S. E. (1995). *Gesture and the nature of language.* Cambridge University Press.

Baker-Shenk, C. (1983). A microanalysis of the nonmanual components of questions in American Sign Language. Unpublished D.Phil. thesis. University of California, Berkeley, CA.

Bavelas, J. B., Chovil, N., Lawrie, D., and Wade, A. (1992). Interactive gestures. *Discourse Processes*, **15**, 469–89.

Bavelas, J. B., Chovil, N., Coates, L., and Roe, L. (1995). Gestures specialized for dialogue. *Personality and Social Psychology Bulletin*, **21**, 394–405.

Butterworth, B. and Beattie, G. (1978). Gesture and silence as indicators of planning in speech. In *Recent advances in the psychology of language: formal and experimental approaches* (ed. R. N. Campbell and P. T. Smith), pp. 347–60. Plenum Press, New York.

Chinchor, N. (1983). Numeral incorporation in American Sign Language. In *Proceedings of the third international symposium on sign language research* (ed. W. Stokoe and V. Volterra), pp. 159–60. Linstok Press, Silver Spring, MD.

Chovil, N. (1991/1992). Discourse-oriented facial displays in conversation. *Language and Social Interaction*, **25**, 163–94.

Clark, H. (1996). *Using language.* Cambridge University Press.

Clark, H. and Gerrig, R. (1990). Questions as demonstrations. *Language*, **66**, 764–805.

Cohen, A. (1977). The communicative function of hand gestures. *Journal of Communication*, **27**, 54–63.

Emmorey, K. (1996). The confluence of space and language in signed languages. In *Language and space* (ed. P. Bloom, M. Peterson, L. Nadel, and M. Garrett), pp. 171–209. MIT Press, Cambridge, MA.

Emmorey, K. and Casey, S. (1995). A comparison of spatial language in English and American Sign Language. *Sign Language Studies*, **88**, 255–88.

Engberg-Pedersen, E. (1993). *Space in Danish Sign Language.* Signum-Verlag, Hamburg.

Engle, R. (1998). Not channels, but composite signals: speech, gesture, diagrams, and object demonstrations are integrated in multimodal explanations. Presentation at the Twentieth Annual Meeting of the Cognitive Science Society, August, Madison, WI.

Fischer, S. (1974). Sign language and linguistic universals. In *Proceedings of the Franco-German conference on French transformational grammar.* Athaenium, Berlin.

Goldin-Meadow, S. and Mylander, C. (1990). Beyond the input given: the child's role in the acquisition of language. *Language*, **66**, 323–55.

Goldin-Meadow, S., Butcher, C., Mylander, C., and Dodge, M. (1994). Nouns and verbs in a self-styled gesture system: what's in a name? *Cognitive Psychology*, **27**, 259–319.

Goldin-Meadow, S., Mylander, C., and Butcher, C. (1995). The resilience of combinatorial structure at the word level: morphology in self-styled gesture systems. *Cognition*, **56**, 195–262.

Kegl, J. and McWhorter, J. (1997). Perspectives on an emerging language. *Proceedings of the Stanford child language research forum* (ed. E. Clark), pp. 15–36. Center for the Study of Language and Information, Palo Alto, CA.

Kegl, J., Senghas, A., and Coppola, M. (1999). Creation through contact: sign language emergence and sign language change in Nicaragua. In *Language creation and language change: Creolization, diachrony, and development* (ed. M. DeGraff), MIT Press, Cambridge, MA.

Kendon, A. (1980). Gesticulation and speech: two aspects of the process of utterance. In *The relationship of verbal and nonverbal communication* (ed. M. R. Key), pp. 207–27. Mouton, The Hague.

Kendon, A. (1983). Gesture and speech: how they interact. In *Nonverbal interaction* (ed. J. M. Weimann and R. P. Harrison), pp. 12–45. Sage, Beverly Hills, CA.

Kendon, A. (1988). How gestures can become like words. In *Cross-cultural perspectives in nonverbal communication* (ed. F. Poyatos), pp. 131–41. Hogrefe and Huber, Göttingen.

Klima, E. and Bellugi, U. (1979). *The signs of language.* Harvard University Press.

Krauss, R., Morrel-Samuels, P., and Colasante, C. (1991). Do conversational hand gestures communicate? *Journal of Personality and Social Psychology*, **61**, 743–54.

Krauss, R., Dushay, R. A., Chen, Y., and Rauscher, F. (1995). The communicative value of conversational hand gestures. *Journal of Experimental Social Psychology*, **31**, 533–52.

Lakoff, G. and Johnson, M. (1980). *Metaphors we live by.* University of Chicago Press.

Liddell, S. (1980). *American Sign Language syntax.* Mouton, The Hague.

Liddell, S. (1994). Tokens and surrogates. In *Perspectives on sign language structure: papers from the fifth international symposium on sign language research*, Vol. 1 (ed. I. Ahlgren, B. Bergman, and M. Brennan), pp. 105–119. International Sign Language Association, University of Durham.

Liddell, S. (1995). Real, surrogate, and token space: grammatical consequences in ASL. In *Language, gesture, and space* (ed. K. Emmorey and J. Reilly), pp. 19–41. Erlbaum, Hillsdale, NJ.

Liddell, S. (1996). Spatial representations in discourse: comparing spoken and signed languages, *Lingua*, **98**, 145–67.

Liddell, S. (in press). Blended spaces and deixis in sign language discourse. *Language and gesture: window into thought and action* (ed. D. McNeill).

Liddell, S. and Metzger, M. (1998). Gesture in sign language discourse. *Journal of Pragmatics*, **30**(6), 657–97.

Lillo-Martin, D. (1986). Two kinds of null arguments in American Sign Language. *Natural Language and Linguistic Theory*, **4**, 415–44.

Lillo-Martin, D. (1991). *Universal grammar and American Sign Language.* Kluwer Academic, Dordrecht.

Loew, R., Kegl, J., and Poizner, H. (1997). Fractionation of the components of role play in a right-hemisphere lesioned signer. *Aphasiology*, **11**, 263–81.

Marschark, M. (1994). Gesture and sign. *Applied Psycholinguistics*, **15**, 209–36.

Mayer, M. (1969). *Frog, where are you?* Dial Books for Young Readers, New York.

McNeill, D. (1985). So you think gestures are nonverbal? *Psychological Bulletin*, **92**, 350–71.

McNeill, D. (1992). *Hand and mind: what gestures reveal about thought.* University of Chicago Press.

McNeill, D. (1993). The circle from gesture to sign. In *Psychological perspectives on deafness* (ed. M. Marschark and D. Clark), pp. 153–83. Erlbaum, Hillsdale, NJ.

Morrel-Samuels. P. and Krauss, R. M. (1992). Word familiarity predicts temporal asynchrony of hand gestures and speech. *Journal of Experimental Psychology: Learning, Memory, and Cognition*, **18**, 615–22.

Padden, C. (1986). Verbs and role-shifting in ASL. In *Proceedings of the fourth national symposium on sign language research and teaching* (ed. C. Padden), National Association of the Deaf, Silver Spring, MD.

Padden, C. (1988). *Interaction of morphology and syntax in American Sign Language.* Garland Outstanding Dissertations in Linguistics, Series IV, Garland, New York.

Perlmutter, D. (1993). Sonority and syllable structure in American Sign Language. In *Phonetics and phonology: current issues in ASL phonology* (ed. G. R. Coulter), pp. 227–61. Academic Press, San Diego, CA.

Provine, K. and Reilly, J. (1992). The expression of affect in signed and spoken stories. Presentation at the Fourth Annual Meeting of the American Psychological Society, October 1992, San Diego, CA.

Rauscher, F., Krauss, R., and Chen, Y. (1996). Gesture, speech, and lexical access: the role of lexical movements in speech production. *Psychological Science*, **7**, 226–31.

Reilly, J., McIntire, M., and Bellugi, U. (1990a). Faces: the relationship between language and affect. In *From gesture to language in hearing and deaf children* (ed. V. Volterra and C. Erting), pp. 128–41. Springer-Verlag, New York.

Reilly, J., McIntire, M., and Bellugi, U. (1990b). Conditionals in American Sign Language: grammaticized facial expressions. *Applied Psycholinguistics*, **11**, 369–92.

Sandler, W. (1989). *Phonological representation of the sign: linearity and nonlinearity in American Sign Language.* Foris Publications, Dordrecht.

Senghas, A. (1995). Children's contribution to the birth of Nicaraguan Sign Language. Unpublished D.Phil. thesis, MIT.

Supalla, T. (1982). Structure and acquisition of verbs of motion and location in American Sign Language. Unpublished D.Phil. thesis, University of California at San Diego.

Supalla, T. (1990). Serial verbs of motion in ASL. In *Theoretical issues in sign language research*, Vol. 1: *Linguistics* (ed. S. Fischer and P. Siple), pp. 27–52. University of Chicago Press.

Supalla, T. and Newport, E. (1978). How many seats in a chair? The derivation of nouns and verbs in American Sign Language. In *Understanding language through sign language research* (ed. P. Siple), pp. 91–132. Academic Press, New York.

Taub, S. (1997). Language in the body: iconicity and metaphor in American Sign Language. Unpublished D.Phil. thesis, University of California at Berkeley.

Thurber, J. (1940). The unicorn in the garden. In *Fables for our time, and famous poems*, Hamish Hamilton, London.

Wilbur, R. (1987). American Sign Language: linguistic and applied dimensions. Little, Brown, and Co., Boston, MA.

Wilcox, P. (1993). Metaphorical mapping in American Sign Language. Unpublished D.Phil. thesis, University of New Mexico.

Notes

1. Words in capital letters represent English glosses for ASL signs. Multiword glosses connected by hyphens are used when more than one English word is required to translate a single sign. Gestures that occur in alternation with signs are described in lowercase and bracketed by backslashes. A subscript word(s) following a sign gloss indicates a morphological inflection. Letter subscripts indicate specific locations in

signing space. A superscript '+++' indicates repetition. A # sign indicates a fingerspelled loan sign. A line above a sign(s) indicates the scope of the facial expression named at the end of the line. Classifier forms are abbreviated with CL, and a description of the classifier form may be given as a bracketed subscript (hs stands for 'handshape'). English glosses are given in quotations.

2. The 'Frog' stories by signers B.D. and O.C. were collected by Judy Reilly.
3. Examples (16)–(19) were worked out in collaboration with Edward Klima.
4. This point was brought to my attention by Judy Reilly.
5. Gesture space excludes location distinctions that are specified in the lexicon. Liddell (in press) notes that the signs POINT and GOAL are the only ASL signs distinguished by where they are articulated within signing space. Such location distinctions would be specified lexically and would not constitute a gestural use of signing space.

CHAPTER 9

Signs, gestures, and signs

William C. Stokoe and Marc Marschark

Gallaudet University and National Technical Institute for the Deaf

Introduction

This chapter is intended to clear up several sources of confusion that have—or should have—surfaced at various points in this book about the relations among signs, gesture, and language. We understand the frequent perplexity on this issue, and place the blame for it squarely in the lap of the historical study of language and gesture. At the same time, because the confusion is not new, we believe that this clarification will be helpful. While weaving together several psychological, linguistic, and historical threads into a coherent discourse on the sometimes fuzzy relations of gesture and language, we hope also to provide new insights into both the phylogenetic and the ontogenetic development of language.

Given our own interests, special consideration will be given here to sign languages and, to a lesser extent, people who use those languages. It would be nice to think that we would have reached these conclusions eventually even if we did not have prior interest in these areas; but, in reality, both of us have come to gesture from studies of sign language. At this point, our interests in language-at-large help us to get our arms around gesture, speech, and sign and see them as an integrated whole rather than as three separate areas of enquiry. Over the course of this chapter, we therefore will argue that gestures, spoken words, and sign language have much in common. Gestures, however, unlike the other two, will be shown to be grounded in physical and psychological dimensions that make them in some sense both more primitive and potentially more expressive then either spoken or signed languages.

In seeking to take the theoretical bull by the horns, we need first to wrestle down the terminological bull that frequently obscures rather than clarifies issues in this area—and hence the title of this chapter. We (e.g., Marschark 1994; Armstrong *et al.* 1995), McNeill (1992), and others have used the term *gesture* with somewhat different meanings; and the polysemy of the word *sign* only makes matters worse. So, let's take our title from left to right. At the simplest level, a sign (in the semiotic sense) is anything that can be perceived to denote something else to some interpretant (see Sebeok 1994). This is the sense of arbitrary, socially agreed-upon signs like road signs, piles of rocks, and words, as well as non-arbitrary signs like pheromones, the first morning light, and many gestures.

Organisms of greater neural complexity interpret various kinds of signs with well-differentiated sensory systems; and their brains provide them with a flexibility of responding that simpler life forms lack. Brains will be important later in this discussion, but for the present purposes, signs that are in the metaphorical hands of Mother Nature, the sign painter, or the (simple or sophisticated) engineer will not be of interest to us. Instead, we will focus on the signs produced using either the vocal apparatus or the manual–brachial–facial apparatuses of human beings (and some other primates) for the purposes of social communication. Included within that category are the signs of sign language: linguistic elements that semantically and syntactically comprise countless social communication systems around the world and may have had special significance in the origins of human language (Armstrong *et al.* 1995). Also included here are gestures, although for the present purposes we consider only those of the manual–brachial variety.

Gestures and signs

Moving to the right in our title, the difference between garden-variety gestures and the signs of sign language lies very deep indeed, even if they may sometimes appear identical (Marschark 1994). No single field or discipline can take us all the way to the heart of the matter. Researchers in anthropology, anatomy and physiology, cognitive science, epistemology, linguistics, semiotics, sociobiology, and other fields have often set out to find what makes the difference between gestures and language. The search inevitably requires travelling into the distant past; and when the going gets difficult, searchers are likely to put up a signpost marking the path as forking into branches called 'verbal' and 'nonverbal'. These labels appeal to the obvious fact that only humans speak, while many other animals use gestures. Nevertheless, assuming that the path divides here may be a serious mistake.

When we examine what really is meant by 'verbal' and 'nonverbal', we find semantic as well as logical confusion. *Verbum* is the Latin word for 'word', and 'verbal' commonly means 'of, pertaining to, or associated with words'. Unfortunately, so used, 'verbal' often is burdened with the gratuitous implication that words can be found only in spoken/written languages. Committing the costly error of mixing logical types, the signpost erectors are tacitly taking 'speech' and 'language' as different names for the same thing. That line of argument is obviously flawed, however, as genuine sign languages do exist. Besides, everyone has at some time seen and used gestures in place of unspoken words, confident that the identical meaning will be expressed by either one. If anything should be called verbal, such gestures surely should (McNeill 1985).

Let us pave that path a bit further. Since about 1960, studies have shown that items in the vocabularies of many sign languages are 'verbal', even if they are nonvocal (e.g., Stokoe 1960; Stokoe *et al.* 1965). Those studies often have been focused on the similarity between the grammars of sign language and spoken language, a domain in which we have failed to find any real differences (see

Marschark *et al.* 1997, for reviews). Such null findings, however, say little about the ontological status of verbal (linguistic) systems and their component parts (see Emmorey, Chapter 8, this volume; Messing, introductory chapter, this volume). The situation becomes even more fuzzy when it is recognized that sign languages often include movements of the vocal apparatus as components of what are often referred to as 'manual' signs.

A variety of researchers, such as Baker (Baker and Padden 1978; Baker and Cokely 1980; Baker-Shenk 1983), McIntire and Snitzer Reilly (1988), and Liddell (1986) have described various roles of nonmanual features in American Sign Language (ASL). Marschark *et al.* (1998) explored several possible roles of mouth movement in ASL and described a variety of obligatory and optional mouth movements that serve adverbial, adjectival, and pronominal functions. Such 'oral gestures' allow the producer to provide emotional, prosody-like highlighting to elaborate on a message or comment on ongoing signed productions in ways that can make signs (or, similarly, gestures) more expressive than mere words (Marschark *et al.* 1987). Over time, some mouth movements that are part of redundant signs (e.g., the puffed cheeks in the sign FAT) have gained the privilege of possible stand-alone status and are now sometimes seen linked to other signs as adjectives or adverbs. Other sign-detached mouth movements are more recent and may be limited in their use to standing in for the complete sign (e.g., the raised corner of the mouth to indicate recency). The roots of such reductions seem to correspond to the evolution of gestural and linguistic communication and so reflect the natural way of such things.

Marschark *et al.* (1998) also considered the possible interplay of manual and oral articulators in communication as a function of phylogenetic, neuropsychological, and historicolinguistic change. In that context, they speculated about the form of communication among our early ancestors and the environmental and evolutionary pressures that led to spoken and signed languages as we know them now. It is in this direction that some of the most interesting recent work on gesture has been done. Along a slightly different path than the one we are taking here, both Kendon (e.g., 1988) and McNeill (1985) have described how speaking and gesturing are manifestations of a single, verbal system. If evolution has indeed equipped humans with a single 'central processor' for thinking, for knowing, and for communicating with others about these important cognitive activities, it certainly would be in keeping with the natural tendency toward economization of effort.

McNeill's work (summarized by McNeill 1992) is focused on hearing speakers' gestures and so does not explain how some human movements can be gestures while similar-looking movements can be signs of a sign language. Nor does it explain, or seek to explain, the functional role of gestures that are embedded within sign language productions of deaf individuals. Such issues cloud the distinction between gestures and signs, a distinction that we are tempted to allow to fade. Nevertheless, the relation of signs and gestures continues to arise in a variety of psychological, linguistic, and developmental contexts because of the impression that gesture is somehow a more essential part of sign language than it is of speech-based communication (see Bonvillian and Folven 1993; Marschark 1994). The issue therefore seems worthy of at least some consideration, if only to make perfectly clear how fuzzy the distinction really is.

The nature of the relation of gestures and signs is of interest to investigators in several different areas. Perhaps the most basic of these concerns for psychologists and linguists is the historical and, at times, still contentious debate over the extent to which manual gestures should be considered verbal in the first place (see Chapters 1 and 5, this volume). If we accept McNeill's (1985, 1992) contention that gesture and speech derive from the same internal processes—and we do—we can dismiss this as a non-issue. As other chapters in this book will show, the dissimilarity of manual and oral modes in the production of gesture and speech may make this a difficult relationship for some to accept (see also Feyereisen and de Lannoy 1991). On the other hand, it is precisely the similarity of gestures and signs that makes their distinction difficult. In both signed and spoken languages, gesture serves as a complement to, and in many ways an essential component of, linguistic communication. Insofar as spoken and signed languages represent co-ordinate, functionally equivalent modes of communication, gesture should serve the same psychological and linguistic roles in both. Indeed, such interactions only serve to reinforce our belief that in many ways the verbal–nonverbal distinction is more apparent than real.

Origins of gestures and the descent of language (or is it the other way around?)

Perhaps it is time to take down the verbal–nonverbal signpost and recognize that the path to what we are looking for does not fork there at all. We are all travelling the human path, a path that branched from the nonhuman tangle millions of years ago. If there is nonverbal communication along the way, we will find it in the behaviour of creatures who lack the capacity for verbal communication; that is, for language. Perhaps it is even time to abandon the road metaphor. Clearly we have bodies and brains that are at least homologues of primate and mammalian bodies and brains. Taking an economical view of the human species, therefore, it makes sense to assume that we used those bodies and brains in an earlier way of representing concepts or mental images and communicating about them. Eventually, over a considerable period of time, we turned them into the now million-year-old but still not yet thoroughly understood system we call language.

Difficulty clearly arises when one seeks to specify when this change might have occurred. The vocal articulatory apparatus is extremely complex both in its structure and in its brain wiring (e.g., some movements need to begin earlier than others even though they have a later impact on articulation). Although language leaves little hard evidence behind and requires some rich interpretation, anatomical structures used in producing language are something that we can know about with some certainty. For example, investigators have argued for some time that, because the vocal tract of Neanderthals apparently included a larynx with a different shape than ours, they could not have produced the range of vowels that we can (Byrne 1995). In the spring of 1998, however, investigators examining the size of the hypoglossal canal (which carries nerve fibres that control the tongue) in modern humans and our ancestors determined that Neanderthals would indeed have had the ability to talk, even if they perhaps did not sound much like us (Kay *et al.* 1998). Findings suggested that while the hypoglossal canals of australopithecines, human ancestors who died out about one million years ago, did not differ significantly from those of chimpanzees, species of the *Homo* genus living as much as 400,000 years ago might have been able to articulate spoken language.

The relationship between human and Neanderthal vocal productions may be moot, as recent reports indicate that analyses of DNA samples revealed Neanderthals not to be direct ancestors of *Homo sapiens sapiens*. Nevertheless, the underlying issue—the relationships among 'humanness', language, and speech— clearly lies deep in the theoretical psyches of many investigators. Edelman (1992, p.125), for example, equates language and speech when he argues that the of origin of language lies 'specifically in the evolution of the vocal tract and the brain centers for speech production and comprehension'. Support for such a position appears to come from findings indicating that chimpanzees have a larger voluntary (i.e., not autonomic) vocal repertoire than was previously assumed (see Feyereisen and de Lannoy 1991, Chapter 1, for discussion). However, there are now neuro-anatomical data to suggest that gestural and guttural signals both probably served as the earliest 'linguistic units', even if the gestural modality may have been the primary route to syntax and hence eventually to language (Armstrong *et al.* 1995). Such data would be consistent with our suggestion that language may be closer to 1,000,000 than 50,000 years old; and even that lower limit, frequently assumed to be required if language had its origins in guttural communication, has been shattered since we started writing this chapter. Simply put, it seems dangerous to place ad hoc limitations on our ancestors.

Setting aside the possibility that speech and gesture may have changed signifi-cantly over the millennia, there are other kinds of evidence that point to possible dates for the origins of language. Byrne (1995, p.162), for example, has argued that

'the sudden appearance of cave painting, mass destruction of big game, cultural variation, and ocean travel, is evidence for a recent origin for language in anatomically modern humans within the past 200 thousand years.'

Lieberman (1991) leans towards language being even older, suggesting that the full archaeological record strongly implies that humans had the kind of con-ceptual ability or cognitive power only conferred by language about a million years ago. In any case, it seems likely that social and environmental factors created a greater selection pressure for human intelligence and human language, as well as their associated neocortical correlates, rather than the other way around (see Marschark and Everhart (1997) for the parallel argument with regard to child development). In Byrne's (1995, p.233) words, the issue is this:

Over the years, linguists have always hotly debated the origins of language and whether there are precursors of language in other species' communication. In the main, their answer has been 'no' but they may have asked the wrong question. Asking instead whether there are precursors of language in other species' *cognition* gives a different answer: there are several precursors of language evident in the behavior of all great apes. These include attribution of intentions and beliefs to others ... comprehension of cause and effect, and the hierarchical structure in behavior; and rudimentary anticipatory planning.

A great deal of further investigation will be needed to test the present hypothesis, or more properly, the linked hypotheses that compose the scenario proposed here. But at least this approach gets closer to the heart of the matter. Rather than posting a 'keep out' sign, we assume, first, that as the human line (actually, the orangutan–human line) emerged with larger neocortices, the typical higher primate way of watching what others do and learning from it led to socialized gestural communication, just as it does in chimpanzees (Byrne 1995). These gestures, by the responses they elicit, can be reliably interpreted as specific requests (e.g., 'share that food' or 'groom me here'). In hominids, from the same ancestor as chimpanzees, many more such gestures would have been made and understood (King 1994).

Second, we suggest that gestures made by the hands and arms and head and face—body parts significantly different in humans than in our nearest primate relatives–emerge naturally from human physiology and its interactions with the world. The visual system, especially in primates, is closely linked to the motor system (Kimura 1975, 1981, 1993). To realize how close this coordination must be, one need only consider the interplay of vision and movement necessary for the gymnastic–acrobatic lifestyle primates evolved during eons of living in treetops. Consider too the difference between a chimpanzee's aggressive display and its submissive begging for food. In the former case, the upper arm is raised, the forearm nearly vertical and pronated to turn the hand into position for striking or pushing away. In the latter, the upper arm is pulled back, the forearm is horizontal and supinated to bring the hand palm upward, ready to receive the begged-for food. Both the hand–arm configuration and the hand–arm movement signify, but each signifies something different, because the two visual scenes are interpreted differently. The hand, arm, and movement in the chimpanzee threat gesture add up to a message like, 'I'll bash you!' In the begging gesture, hand, arm, and movement transmit something else: 'Let me have some of that food, if you will' (both accompanied by appropriate facial expressions). Only an instant later the visual system reads the movement and is able to 'interpret' the entire gesture: in one case with the hands/arm outward from the source, and in the other moving inwards. Let us consider the real-world interaction of the vision–movement–communication conglomerate in a bit more depth.

Syntax of action, and structure of the world

Kimura (1993, p.8) noted that

... the great apes can employ, at the very least, a rudimentary manual sign language when constrained to do so, demonstrating that the capacity is there to be selected, as it appears to have been in humans.

Chimpanzee gestures may be interesting, but language is surely something else. Both may have the same biological foundations—*pace* Lenneberg (1967)—and both clearly are shaped by the nature of the world and the ability of an organism to perceive it or otherwise interact with it. Unpacking this notion we see at least two different dimensions worth pursuing:

(1) the link between the syntax of action and the syntax of language; and

(2) the way in which our sense organs divide up the world and the reflection of those divisions in language.

We will take each of these issues in turn.

One of the fascinating things about both human and chimpanzee gestures is their physical/physiological structure, which frequently has the same underlying structure as sentences. This structure may be best described in terms of the symbolic formula so dear to linguists,

$$S \rightarrow NP + VP$$

That is to say, a sentence (S) can broken down into a noun phrase (NP) plus a verb phrase (VP). For example, in the sentence 'The chimp bit the linguist', 'the chimp' is the NP and 'bit the linguist' is the VP. But the bases of these linguistic abstractions of abstractions of abstractions are physiological and psychological, not linguistic. The foundation of language is natural, merging with human anatomy and human function: The hands are seen by foveal vision to have a distinctive configuration, and their movement is seen by peripheral vision to have a distinctive speed, direction, path, and manner. The human brain, which has circuits dedicated to interpreting each kind of information, does not confuse them (Swisher 1993). Thus, a hand's configuration, as seen in foveal vision, denotes or connotes something else by resembling it or some significant part of it. Almost simultaneously, hand movement, seen by the other kind of vision, represents action by reproducing it or suggesting a change or happening in some relation to (e.g., 'in', 'of', 'from', or 'to') that something.

The parallels here are unmistakable:

handshape	+	action
visible detail	+	visible movement
subject	+	predicate
noun	+	verb

These pairs are all congruent—naturally, because that is the way mind and nature work. They are also systematic pairings: There would be no gesture without a body part *and* its movement; there would be no language without subject *and* predicate, noun *and* verb.

What has this to do with the difference between a gesture and a sign? Everything. Over the course of many hundreds of thousands of years, creatures that saw this double signifying nature in gestures had, as the fossil record testifies, larger brains than chimpanzees. Presumably, members of this orangutan–human line also used their brains in different ways. With gestures they could have begun language—not 'protolanguage' but the real thing. Their first sentences would have consisted simply of a subject or noun (the hand or hands) naturally, physically, and conceptually joined to a predicate or verb (the movement) (see Edelman 1992).

This may look like a poverty stricken language if we compare its simple sentences with the elaborate syntax used by speakers and writers of modern world languages. It looks even more impoverished if we compare it with the rules of universal grammar as they are now conceived and constantly added to by contemporary grammarians in addressing both spoken language and sign language (e.g., Lillo-Martin 1997). Yet gestures of this basic, noun–verb kind would have been signs of a language, because several essential relationships can be represented gesturally by hands and hand actions. These include at least:

(1) actor–action (e.g., CHIMP CLIMBS);

(2) actor–action–patient (e.g., HAND TOUCHES FRUIT);

(3) experiencer or patient and change of state (e.g., FRUIT FALLS).

In this sense, some gestures can be seen as sentences, regardless of whether they are gestures of our ancestors or those of hearing, speaking contemporary humans who may never have seen deaf people's language and who can never have seen archaic humans using language. Both gestures of this garden-variety kind and the signs of a sign language may well have developed from the gestures made perhaps a million years ago by early humans—movements which turned certain natural gestures into signs of human language. Although some may still believe that language has never been other than spoken and heard, the fact remains that the configuration and movement of the hands and arms can resemble the appearance of things and their actions. Language needs both subjects and predicates, and gestures of this kind (not coincidentally) have two analogous parts.

Once *Homo erectus* or *Homo sapiens* had begun to see/understand implicitly both sentence-like and word-like meanings in gestures and to see explicitly that configurations and movements were linked but also separable, they would have been able to change them and make permutations of them based on patterns (1) to (3) above. They could do this by forming the same handshape while making a different movement, and conversely, by using the same movement with different handshapes. Thus, even at this early stage, the productivity of language would have been present. Like the child with a 'pivot-class open-class' grammar, they would have been able to make many *meaningful* visible utterances (Braine 1963; Brown 1973).

The next step might have been to form the handshape with its resemblance to something or to a visible feature of something, and then, instead of making the usual movement, to hold or display or shake the handshape, and so call attention to the thing itself, not as part of an action but as a name for the thing, a noun. Likewise, a movement that because of its appearance, indicates going away, coming forward, falling, or grasping, could have been performed with a noncommittal handshape, thus separating out from the primordial sentence the action as a verb.

Just to be explicit here: in recognizing that there is a syntax to action that is mirrored by the syntax of language, we do not mean to imply that this is in any way an accident. Rather, we assume that the nature of the world, together with the biological organisms in it, requires that it be carved up in particular ways, notwithstanding minor differences across cultures and languages (see Marschark and Everhart 1997). In this, both gesture and language play essential roles.

One of the spoils of the cognitive revolution has been general acceptance of the assumption that language development ontologically (and, we assume, phylogenetically) is facilitated by the availability of a primitive conceptual system in which concepts and linguistic units are in roughly a one-to-one correspondence. In the case of children acquiring their first language, the situation results from the fact that the language used by adults in the environment is already keyed to dividing up the world in ways that make cognitive and culturally/environmentally relevant sense (Bronowski and Bellugi 1970; Macnamara 1977). The underlying conceptual system is unlikely to be language-specific or even specific to a particular mode of language, although particular concepts may well vary in their availability or ease of communication in one language (or language mode) or another. It thus seems safe to assume that the more directly communication—whether by gesture, spoken language, or sign language—maps onto the world, the easier it will be to comprehend.

The degree of such mapping, of course, depends on both the language–world correlation and the perceiver who stands between them. That is, such mapping is very much in the eye of the beholder. This situation is readily apparent in regard to iconic signs, signs that look like what they represent (e.g., TENNIS or CAMERA in ASL). Such signs appear to be easier for adults to learn relative to arbitrary signs, but the two are learned with equal facility by children acquiring a signed language as their first language. The problem is that adults map iconic signs like TENNIS onto the concept because they recognize and remember the obvious relationship between the movement of the sign and the playing of tennis (although they could assume that it means 'badminton' or 'racquetball'). Young children do not yet have that correlation and therefore cannot use it in the language learning process. They do, however, have other correlations available to them by virtue of biology, physics, and the nature of the world.

Clark (1973) discussed this situation explicitly in terms of the way in which children map dimensional adjectives onto the world. Clark suggested that there is a perceptual space ('P-space') that is defined by gravity, the existence of ground level, and the asymmetry in perception created by the location of the perceiver within the environment. P-space thus consists of three reference planes with three associated, primary directions: ground level as a reference for up, the body-based vertical left–right plane as a reference for forwards and backwards, and the body-based vertical front–back plane as a reference for leftwards and rightwards. The organized semantic structure of English spatial terms, or language space ('L-space') clearly maps onto P-space.

As Clark noted, the most obvious property of English adjectives and propositions is the requirement of points of reference, which match exactly with those in L-space. In particular, the terms used to describe either locations or movements to/from locations (or events in time) are determined by the relative positions of the perceiver/speaker and the objects or locations of interest. Such relations are obvious in spoken language, they are even more so in sign language and in gesture. After age three or four, few language users would think of asking why the words *up* and *down* mean 'up' and 'down'. If we should ask, we are likely to get an answer like 'They just do', or 'These words came into English from other languages which pronounce them ...', and it is doubtful that any spoken language in the world could yield better answers to why their particular words mean 'up' and 'down'.

In contrast, no user of a sign language (at least of ASL, British Sign Language, or Italian Sign Language, those with which we are most familiar) ever needs to ask why the signs for 'up' and 'down' are what they are, and no one who studies gesture needs to ask why pointing gestures look and move as they do (see Goldin-Meadow, Chapter 7, this volume). Both are so obvious that the answer is over-looked. Overlooked, that is, by those who seek to define language in such a way that it cannot have developed from any 'original' sign system. But *up* and *down*, *here* and *there*, *in* and *out*, *in front of* and *behind*, *close* and *far*, and other dimensional conceptions are inseparable from our existence in a three-dimensional world with physically determined reference planes and reference points. Whether or not we are dealing with an egocentric (self-based) or altocentric (other-based) P-space or L-space in any particular situation, our perception of the world, and the language or gestures we use to describe it, are governed by some fundamental constancies. Why must we assume that linguistic rules are as they are for some reason separate from the rules of perception and physics?

To this point, we do not think we have said anything radical, and all of our conjectures thus far have contained at least some hard cores of fact. The complex of human hands, fingers, forearms, and upper arms can indeed be made to resemble a great many visible things in the environment and do directly map locations in it. That situation is not too different now from what it was 50,000 or 950,000 years ago. Very likely, one of the pressures towards language was the ability, observable in humans and their nearest relatives, to see similarity in things and so to form concepts and classes (Bronowski and Bellugi 1970; Edelman 1989). The arms, hands, and fingers can be moved in ways that express a great many observable actions, just as animal faces and posture have been expressing emotions since mammals emerged (Darwin 1872). When used with manual sentence-embodying gestures, however, human facial displays add to the gesture or signed sentence what most languages need adjectives and adverbs and adverbial phrases to express (Marschark *et al.* 1998).

Of brains, gestures, and language development

It is now well-established that as humans we have at least equal potential for the natural acquisition of spoken or signed languages, and that there may even be an advantage for language in the visuospatial modality through the one-word stage of language development (Meier and Newport 1990; Bonvillian and Folven 1993; Lillo-Martin 1997; Siple 1997; but cf. Volterra and Iverson 1995). How then does it happen that spoken language is the dominant form of communication for humans who can hear? Although there is considerable debate concerning the origins of sign language use among people who are deaf, there is no doubt that signs and gestures have long served a variety of purposes among hearing people in situations where there was no common spoken language (e.g., between some Native American tribes), where spoken language would be disruptive (e.g., in the theatre or among would-be thieves), or where it was forbidden (e.g., in monasteries) (see Bragg 1997; Daniels 1997). Native American tribes, for example, had sign languages that varied considerably in their signs for familiar things (Mallery 1881), and we know that there is much less consistency across modern sign languages than meets the eye of the naïve observer. Nevertheless, users of different sign languages find it much easier to establish cross-language communication with others than do users of spoken languages (Battison and Jordan 1976; Jordan and Battison 1976).

As we suggested earlier, the availability of both gestural and guttural modes of communication may go back even further, to a point where the two may have overlapped during the formative years (millennia) of language. Setting aside the question of exactly when language *qua* language might be said to have 'begun', considerable support for gestural origins for language has come from neuro-psychological and neuroanatomical sources. For example, the areas of the brain involved in language processing *per se* differ from those controlling vocal communication in nonhuman primates, and the human vocal tract evolved relatively late compared with the musculature involved in the gestures described earlier (Feyereisen and de Lannoy 1991). There also is considerable overlap in the neurological and behavioural mechanisms of the manual movements required for gesture and sign and the oral movements required for spoken language (Kimura 1975, 1981; McNeill 1992).

Kimura (1975, 1981), for example, demonstrated that stroke patients with language dysfunction showed correlated disruptions to fine manual motor movements that would be consistent with a motoric rather than a linguistic basis for Broca's aphasia. Results of a more fine-grained study by Hickok *et al.* (1996) show that the current neurological processes underlying sign language and non-linguistic hand movements are independent. Strong claims that the dominance of the left hemisphere for language is more a motor than a linguistic phenomenon thus may be unfounded. Tzeng and Wang (1984), in contrast, argued that the common neurocognitive roots of language, gesture, and sign might lie in the fine temporal resolution ability of the left hemisphere, a mechanism essential for and apparent in production in all three domains. Assuming an early form of gestural communication, the advent of tool use in human evolution (where the right hand/left hemisphere would have controlled tool movement while the left hand/right hemisphere held the object of tool use) would have occupied the hands with other matters, thus creating evolutionary as well as practical pressure for conversion to guttural communication (see also Armstrong *et al.* 1995; Byrne 1995).

Regardless of the evolutionary origins of speech and manual movements, it is clear that there is a contemporary link between spoken language and the gestures that frequently accompany it; hence McNeill's (1985, 1992) convincing argument that both speech and gesture derive from the same underlying verbal system. In several studies, McNeill and his colleagues have found that gesture and speech bear similar logical and behavioural relations, follow similar development courses, and are affected in similar ways following cerebral lesions and in aphasia. Marschark (1994) provided a related analysis in which he examined the functional roles of gestures embedded within sign language productions of deaf children and adults as compared with those embedded within spoken language productions of hearing children and adults. The point was not to draw an artificial line between gesture and language, but to point out that the same gestures occur in both deaf and hearing language users, lending credence to views of language origins that entail the involvement of both gestural and guttural communication.

Marschark described how deaf and hearing individuals use gestures in the context of narrating real and fictional events, in making their goals, wants, and desires known, and in discussing abstract ideas. In his research on storytelling by deaf and hearing mothers and children (e.g., Marschark *et al.* 1986, 1987), for example, deaf and hearing children as well as adults were found to use gestures to supplement linguistic productions and to replace them, and there were comparable, consistent relationships between the use of gestures and language acquisition in young deaf and hearing children. In very young children, for example, gestures primarily serve semantic functions, relating to either instrumental or emotional needs. As vocabularies develop, however, gestures take on a supplementary role, highlighting or elaborating accompanying speech or sign, while occasionally standing in for words or signs that are either unknown or temporarily unavailable. Eventually, gestures serve both semantic and pragmatic functions and can occur at both the content level and at an interpersonal level between 'speaker' and 'listener'.

Marschark found that arbitrary gestures, iconic gestures, and pantomime all occur in the productions of both deaf and hearing populations. The one obvious point of linguistic divergence in their gestures lies in the commonest form of gesticulation, deictic pointing. Deixis is lexicalized in ASL, and it typically replaces verbal statement in referencing people, places, or things previously identified; whereas it remains largely supplementary for most hearing speakers. Importantly, it is possible to distinguish nonlexicalized pointing from the acquisition of lexicalized deixis in young deaf children (Petitto 1987) adding to confidence in differentiating gesture from sign.

Marschark pointed out that prelingual and language-delayed children use gestures all the time to try make themselves understood. When excessive gesture is seen in older hearing children, the usual assumption is one of deficiency, either in language, cognition, or both. Recognition that this is not the case with regard to deaf children does not require the assumption that all 'manual communication' produced by deaf children must be classified as 'sign language', other than in the broadest and least informative senses of both 'sign' and 'language'. The goal of both the gesture and sign used by deaf children is the achievement of some social end, even if that end is only to be understood. Just as gesture in hearing adults provides support and elaboration of ongoing speech, so gesture in deaf children can provide support and elaboration of ongoing sign language. Consistent with the arguments of McNeill (1985, 1992), Marschark (1994) therefore argued that gesture provides us with alternate access both to the verbal system underlying speech and sign and to a 'speaker's' understanding of social and referential communication. In neither sense, he claimed, should deaf people be fundamentally different from hearing people.

More generally, the relationship of first words and early gesture has been of interest for a long time with regard to hearing children. Piaget (1962) and Werner and Kaplan (1963), for example, suggested that related words and gestures should emerge at about the same time in development, because both are reflections of children's underlying conceptual representations. Such productions were seen to indicate a transition from sensorimotor to symbolic functioning. If particular gestures depict object-related behaviours as primitive forms of symbolic representation, one would expect that growth in speech and sign repertoires would be linked to reduction in gestural similarity and frequency as symbols and referents become decontextualized. In contrast, if gestures and words are serving similar functions, one would expect a positive relationship between gestural and language production both in terms of frequency and in the shift away from being contextually bound to particular referents (Acredolo and Goodwyn 1988).

There is now considerable evidence that gestural and spoken/sign language competencies do not emerge in parallel in the strong sense implied by Piaget and by Werner and Kaplan (see Petitto 1987; Bates *et al.* 1989; for discussion). However, the precise linkage and potential comparability of gesture and speech or sign in children is not quite as clear. In their pioneering work on the relationships on gesture and early language, Bates *et al.* (1977) described a developmental sequence of prespeech gestural production that predicted the emergence of the first words.

Bates *et al.* found that 'showing gestures' and 'ritual requests' for attention or instrumental action are used by children at about 9–10 months of age. These are followed by 'giving gestures' at around 12 months and 'communicative pointing' or deixis at around 13 months.

These gestural schemes were reliably correlated both with each other and with the size of children's vocabularies within this age range. Taken together, as a 'gestural complex', they accounted for the largest proportion of variance observed among all of their gestural communication measures. Insofar as the components of the gestural complex appeared just as regularized in form and to carry the same referential and communicative intentions as later emerging speech, Bates and her colleagues suggested that their findings reflected decontextualization of children from their communicative referents, consistent with the spirit of Werner and Kaplan's (1963) notions. Moreover, their results indicated that gesture is a precursor of first words and signs, providing social and symbolic structure for them. This conclusion meshes well with our phylogenetic argument as well as the longstanding observation that the gestural systems of younger deaf children, as well as older ones with impoverished language input, are systematic and consistent (see Goldin-Meadow, Chapter 7, this volume).

How easy to lose the way

One error that frequently prevents our being able to get to the heart of the language matter is the tacit assumption that we are smarter, more intelligent, than our prehistoric ancestors. In some broad sense, however, the reverse may in fact be true, as our brains have more knowledge to work with, more things done for them through technology, while theirs had to do the whole job. If intelligence is defined as the ability, in any conceivable circumstance, to see and do whatever must be done to live well and survive, and defined further as the ability to perceive some priority in performing these tasks, then surely we are inferior to *Homo erectus* and *Homo sapiens*. They not only survived in circumstances that would be the death of any of us, but they gave rise to our species.

It seems that similar errors are being made by modern scholars who dismiss the idea that language evolved from something that appears to be as deceptively simple as gestures. By insisting that language, from its beginning, had to have the full panoply of phonological, morphological, syntactic, and semantic rules which language scholars keep finding in present spoken languages, such theorists are (possibly unconsciously) implying that early humans could not have had anything like the skills, the brain modules, or the language organ they imagine we presently have (see Lillo-Martin 1997 for discussion). Confusing sophistication with intelligence can lead to extinction, as both natural history and world history reveal.

Let us therefore now fast-forward over some number of millennia, as language was being gesturally performed and visually received. Most likely, vocal sounds were being uttered at the same time that visual signs were being produced. Except for some onomatopoetic words in spoken languages, there is nothing that can make a direct connection between a vocal sound and a concept, thing, or action. However, if vocalizations produced along with gestural communication gradually became differentiated, it would eventually be noticed that certain sound patterns came out regularly paired with particular sign–meaning dyads. It then would only have been a matter of time until the sounds were recognized as symbols for the meanings, even though the visible actions that had directly represented them were missing. And so, the present arbitrary nature of sound–meaning relationship was born as it is reborn again and again as generations of human children learn language. Yet even today, ordinary gestures go along with speaking whether or not there is a receiver–perceiver present to benefit from them (witness the frequency with which people make gestures while talking on the telephone).

How long this stage of language evolution—language that was seen as well as heard—might have lasted is another puzzle, but it would appear to have ended between 400,000 and 50,000 years ago, as the shapes of human skulls indicate the emergence of fully modern speech tracts, quite unlike that of human neonates and nonhuman primates. Having learned how to express language with voice more or less decoupled from manual activity, the human race evidently went over to the new system pretty completely. Nevertheless, just as there was nothing to rule out vocalizing while information was being communicated gesturally, there is even less reason to suppose that when spoken language came to be the norm that visible activity ceased forthwith. In fact, we know that gesturing never has disappeared. We are generally most familiar with the gestures we see others using in our everyday lives, but seem to be somewhat less knowing about our own gesturing. An interesting experiment might seek to find whether subjects know that they themselves are making as many gestures as they see their interactive partners and others making. Our informal observations suggest that they do not.

Obviously, gesturing is now much influenced by culture. A common perception is, 'Foreigners gesture a lot, but we don't.' There may be a grain of truth in this, if the perceiver belongs to an Anglo-American or Japanese culture. These cultures boast of long histories of literacy as well as traditions in which the only 'proper' way of speaking is in sentences like those found in well-edited journals or historical books and scrolls. Earlier, however, the Greek and Roman oratorical traditions taught gesture as an adjunct to speaking. Gestures were regarded as a way of making a favourable impression on judges or an audience, and there still exist cultural traditions almost the opposite of Western civilizations. Instead of treating gestures as extras, as decorative touches on the main pattern of communication, the people having these traditions keep manual gestures closer to their original function. In aboriginal Australia, in North and South America, and in Africa, for example, there are peoples who preserve sign languages, and use them in some circumstances instead of their spoken languages, treating each mode as a perfectly reasonable alternative way of communicating (e.g., Kendon 1988). Italians may not go that far, but people from more southern parts of Italy, in particular, maintain a variety of gestures in their repertoires, some of which are intended to accompany or replace spoken language (e.g., the gesture for *furbo*, the index finger pulling down on the outer corner of the eye to indicate something like 'sly' or 'clever').

Towards an integrated view of language

In many ways, the proposals we have put forward here are consistent with Gibson's (1966) notion of the senses as perceptual systems. Hearing, he pointed out, is much more than sound waves detected by the ears. It is one channel of several by which organisms actively and systematically extract information from their environment that they need for survival. The ears are only a part of the whole receptive system that involves not only end organs and nerves but such physical actions as orienting the head or body or both to maximize the sound input, and the mental action of 'tuning out' unwanted sounds by concentrating attention on the information wanted.

Gibson's treatment of the senses as systems, and thus as much more than collections of parts, suggests a more productive, synergistic, way than those now in vogue for considering language and thought. All organisms make proactive use of their whole bodies to gain visible, audible, tactile, olfactory, and gustatory information. Organisms of a social species will also use these systems naturally to gain and communicate social information. So considered, human cognition–communication is a multimodal system of systems. It integrates the sensory systems and much else. The systems have evolved from much simpler ones (e.g., vision from the eyespots of the jellyfish, orientation in three dimensions from the statocyst) (Edelman 1989, 1992). Likewise, cognition, language, consciousness —what it takes to be human—also evolved. Otherwise, one would have to explain how it could have been bestowed all at once and from nowhere on a single species.

The suggestion here is that among the signs (in the general semiotic sense) that hominids used for sharing information, one kind alone had a structure that turns out to be the central structure of language. This kind of sign was gestural, but its use and development would hardly have led to the disappearance of other kinds of signs. While any English speaker can say, 'I am very angry,' the chances are that this sentence of the English language seldom needs to be spoken—the appearance of the angry person makes the situation perfectly clear.

Here it is necessary to be specific once again about the term 'gesture', which we have been using primarily as meaning upper limb movements that denote or connote information. The motions of an angry person's face and body do not precisely fit the usual dictionary definition of a 'movement of the body or limbs as an expression of feeling' (*Oxford English Dictionary*, Shorter, Third edn).

Saying, 'I am very angry', does express a thought (and satisfies the textbook definition of a complete sentence); but this particular 'thought' is the report of a felt emotion, more deeply seated and temporally prior to the operation of speaking about it. In any case, this is not the kind of gesture we are concerned with here. We are more interested in the kind that is made by moving hands and arms, because that kind is built exactly as basic sentences are: by joining predication (hand movement) to a substantive (handshape).

A sign-language sign is a gesture in the sense of a hand–arm action used to express a sentence or some part of a sentence. But sign-language signs, or the earlier signs from which they derive, have been part of the human communication repertoire for approximately a million years. The gesture commonly encountered therefore is now a vestige, a relic from the remote past. Once of the same nature as those movements by which language was first (and continues to be) expressed, the ordinary gesture, now that most languages are expressed with voices, retains its pre-language power: the ability to represent globally but not yet grammatically.

Gestures and signs differ in their futures as well as their pasts. Sign-language signs comprise an essential subsystem of a living language. They continually undergo changes both in form and meaning as productive, creative, and evolving symbols. Gestures, in contrast, serve us best by not changing. Those gestures that are obvious imitations of instrumental activities, like eating, or using a hammer, are common across cultures that share similar activities and are thus 'naturally' protected against change. More arbitrary gestures are protected more by their frequency of use than their iconicity. Such gestures need to be predictable within the community that uses them, and their existence and evolution is more social in nature. New gestures thus appear and older ones disappear, but this is more of a generational phenomenon than anything inherent in the gestures themselves. Meanwhile, it is usually the spoken (or signed) vocabulary of a community, and not its gesture repertoire, with which teenagers enjoy messing about.

Sign-language signs, as parts of language systems, change more quickly than gestures, but in predictable ways (Frishberg 1975; Battison 1978). The greatest difference, however, would seem to be that those actions generally termed gestures exist as individually signifying actions. There are few or no constraints on how or whether these gestures can be performed in sequence with others like them, used with speech or without, and so on. The main criterion for their use seems to be that what they signify should be appropriate in context and not violate the 'rules of engagement'; for example, intimate conversations admit the use of gestures that would be outrageous in formal interactions. Sign-language signs, in contrast, are parts of a system, and exactly like the words of a spoken language, they must be used according to the rules of the system. Sign-language signs can be used alone as words can, but that usage does not free them of their connections to the system.

For the diligent scholar engaged in the task of analysing sign language in actual use, recognizing an ordinary gesture amid a signer's signs will still be difficult. Sometimes, it may even be impossible (see Marschark 1994). If McNeill (1992) is right, and gestures and speech are outputs from the same verbal system, gestures and sign-language signs are even more likely to be from the same source. Then, because the whole performance is visible, if the emotional tone and emphasis are correctly interpreted, it should not matter much whether a particular manual action belongs in the canonical lexicon of that sign language or is treated as an ad hoc representation of meaning or affect.

Before too many hairs are split and resplit, it is well to remember that all this precision about language, its levels, systems, grammar, and lexicon, competence, and performance did not arise when languages were first spoken, and certainly not when they were first expressed gesturally. It was only long after a system of phonetic or alphabetic writing had been invented and writing things down had become common practice that the roles of grammarian and linguist became possible. Asking, 'Is gesture language or not language?' may be trying in vain to make a (tightly Aristotelian) science of something that simply is not made that way.

In our view, language had to begin with gestures. It had to start with gestures, because only gestures can look like or point to or hold up or otherwise visibly reproduce what they mean. On the other hand, vocal sounds alone cannot connect to meanings unless the makers and hearers of the sounds have agreed on the rules for connecting them. Even with a convention to link vocalizations to concepts, however, there is nothing in unaided sound to show that what is meant is a noun or verb or something else. Words get to be nouns and verbs only by being, or having been, parts of sentences. To put it bluntly, *speech depends on language but language does not depend on speech.*

Once creatures very much like us could see that the familiar gestures they were using stood for objects, events, and ideas, a critical mass for an explosion into language was at hand. Its first expression would have been gestural sentences and familiar and limited contexts. Only later would their users begin to make some gestures into words to stand for things and others into words that stand for actions. These gesture words would have naturally carried with them the character of noun or verb conferred on them by their original function in a gestural sentence. Language then would have happened when a community of hominids about to be human took a new look at the gestures that they and other hominids had been making for millions of years. All at once, the moment they saw that these gestures could represent more than their usual meanings (e.g., 'gimme food' or 'come closer') language began.

This scenario requires rethinking what we have probably always supposed to be the way things are. We usually think of words as like bricks or the different pieces of a construction toy. We may imagine that we select them from a lexicon, like a box of pieces, and put them together to make sentences. But looking at gestures with more than usual attention, we can quite easily see that all by itself a single visible action (which always includes more than hands) may represent a whole, a complete, a genuine sentence; for example, 'I don't know' 'He dropped it' 'You're wrong.' With the help of biology, physics, and the human ability to discern consistency in inconsistency, language has a synergy that bricks do not. Let us not sell short our 'simple' ancestors or their 'simple' gestures.

References

Acredolo, L. and Goodwyn, S. (1988). Symbolic gesturing in normal infants. *Child Development*, **59**, 450–66.

Armstrong, D. F., Stokoe, W. C., and Wilcox, S. E. (1995). *Gesture and the nature of language*. Cambridge University Press, New York.

Baker, C. and Cokely, D. (eds) (1980). *American Sign Language: a teacher's resource text on grammar and culture*. TJ Publishers, Silver Spring, MD.

Baker, C. and Padden, C. (1978). Focusing on the nonmanual components of ASL. In *Understanding language through sign language research* (ed. P. Siple), pp. 27–57. Academic Press, London.

Baker-Shenk, C. (1983). A microanalysis of the non-manual components of questions in ASL. Unpublished Ph.D. dissertation, University of California, Berkeley, CA.

Bates, E., Benigni, L., Bretherton, I., Camaioni, L., and Volterra, V. (1977). From gesture to the first word: on cognitive and social prerequisites. In *Interaction, conversation, and the development of language* (ed. P. Siple), pp. 247–308. Academic Press, New York.

Bates, E., Thal, D., Whitesell, K., Fenson, L., and Oakes, L. (1989). Integrating language and gesture in infancy. *Developmental Psychology*, **25**, 1004–19.

Battison, R. (1978). *Lexical borrowing in American Sign Language*. Linstok Press, Silver Spring, MD.

Battison, R. and Jordan, I. K. (1976). Cross-cultural communication with foreign signers. *Sign Language Studies*, **10**, 53–68.

Bonvillian, J. D. and Folven, R. J. (1993). Sign language acquisition: developmental aspects. In *Psychological perspectives on deafness* (ed. M. Marschark and M.D. Clark), pp. 229–65. Erlbaum, Hillsdale, NJ.

Bragg, L. (1997). Visual–kinetic communication in Europe before 1600: a survey of sign lexicons and finger alphabets prior to the rise of deaf education. *Journal of Deaf Studies and Deaf Education*, **2**, 1–25.

Braine, M. D. S. (1963). On learning the grammatical order of words. *Psychological Review*, **70**, 323–48.

Bronowski, J. and Bellugi, U. (1970). Language, name, and concept. *Science*, **168**, 669–73.

Brown, R. (1973). *A first language*. Harvard University Press, Cambridge, MA.

Byrne, R. (1995). *The thinking ape: evolutionary origins of intelligence*. Oxford University Press.

Clark, H. (1973). Space, time, semantics, and the child. In *Cognitive development and the acquisition of language* (ed. T.E. Moore), pp. 27–64. Academic Press, New York.

Daniels, M. (1997). *Benedictine roots in the development of deaf education*. Bergin and Garvey, Westport, CT.

Darwin, C. ([1872], 1973.) *The expression of the emotions in man and animals*. Random House, New York.

Edelman, G. M. (1989). *The remembered present: A biological theory of consciousness*. Basic Books, New York.

Edelman, G. M. (1992). *Bright brilliant fire*. Basic Books, New York.

Feyereisen, P. and de Lannoy, J.-P. (1991). *Gestures and speech*. Cambridge University Press, New York.

Frishberg, N. (1975). Arbitrariness and iconicity: historical change in American Sign Language. *Language*, **51**, 696–719

Gibson, J. J. (1966). *The senses considered as perceptual systems*. Houghton Mifflin, Boston, MA.

Hickok, G., Bellugi, U., and Klima, E. S. (1996). The neurobiology of sign language and its implications for the neural basis of language. *Nature*, **381**, 699–702.

Jordan, I. K. and Battison, R. (1976). A referential communication experiment with foreign sign language. *Sign Language Studies*, **10**, 69–80.

Kay, R. F., Cartmill, M., and Balow, M. (1998). The hypoglossal canal and the origin of human vocal behavior. *Proceedings of the National Academy of Sciences of the USA*, **95**, 5420.

Kendon, A. (1988). How gestures can become like words. In *Cross-cultural perspectives in nonverbal communication* (ed. F. Poyatos), pp. 131–41. Hogrefe, Toronto.

Kimura, D. (1975). The neural basis of language *qua* gesture. In *Studies in neurolinguistics* (ed. H. Avakian-Whitaker and H. A. Whitaker), pp. 145–56. Academic Press, New York.

Kimura, D. (1981). Neural mechanisms in manual signing. *Sign Language Studies*, **33**, 291–312.

Kimura, D. (1993). *Neuromotor mechanisms in human communication*. Oxford University Press, New York.

King, B. J. (1994). *The information continuum: evolution of social information transfer in monkeys, apes, and hominids*. SAR Press, Santa Fe, NM.

Lenneberg, E. (1967). *Biological foundations of language*. Academic Press, New York.

Liddell, S. (1986). Head thrust in ASL conditional marking. *Sign Language Studies*, **52**, 243–62.

Lieberman, P. (1991). *Uniquely human: the evolution of speech, thought, and selfless behavior*. Harvard University Press, Cambridge, MA.

Lillo-Martin, D. (1997). The modular effects of sign language acquisition. In *Relations of language and thought: the view from sign language and deaf children* (M. Marschark, P. Siple, D. Lillo-Martin, R. Campbell, and V. S. Everhart), pp. 62–109. Oxford University Press, New York.

Macnamara, J. (1977). Cognitive basis of language learning in infants. *Psychological Review*, **79**, 1–13.

Mallery, G. (1881). *Sign language among North American Indians, compared with that among other peoples and deaf-mutes*. Mouton, The Hague.

Marschark, M. (1994). Gesture and sign. *Applied Psycholinguistics*, **15**, 209–36.

Marschark, M. and Everhart, V. S. (1997). Relations of language and cognition: what do deaf children tell us? In *Relations of language and thought: the view from sign language and deaf children* (M. Marschark, P. Siple, D. Lillo-Martin, R. Campbell, and V. S. Everhart), pp. 3–23. Oxford University Press, New York.

Marschark, M., West, S. A., Nall, S. L., and Everhart, V. (1986). Development of creative language devices in signed and oral production. *Journal of Experimental Child Psychology*, **41**, 534–50.

Marschark, M., Everhart, V. S., Martin, J., and West, S. A. (1987). Identifying linguistic creativity in deaf and hearing children. *Metaphor and Symbolic Activity*, **2**, 281–306.

Marschark, M., Siple, P., Lillo-Martin, D., Campbell, R., and Everhart, V. S. (1997). *Relations of language and thought: the view from sign language and deaf children*. Oxford University Press, New York.

Marschark, M., LePoutre, D. and Bement, L. (1998). Mouth movement and signed communication. In *Hearing by eye: the psychology of lipreading and audiovisual speech* (ed. R. Campbell and B. Dodd), pp. 243–64. Taylor, London.

McIntire, M. L. and Snitzer Reilly, J. (1988). *Nonmanual behaviors in L1 and L2 learners of American Sign Language*: Linstok Press, Silver Spring, MD.

McNeill, D. (1985). So you think gestures are nonverbal? *Psychological Review*, **92**, 350–71.

McNeill, D. (1992). *Hand and mind.* University of Chicago Press.

Meier, R. P. and Newport, E. L. (1990). Out of the hands of babes: on a possible sign advantage in language acquisition. *Language*, **66**, 1–23.

Oxford English Dictionary, Shorter, 3rd edn. (1989.) Oxford University Press.

Petitto, L. A. (1987). On the autonomy of language and gesture: evidence from the acquisition of personal pronouns in American Sign Language. *Cognition*, **27**, 1–52.

Piaget, J. (1962). *Plays, dreams, and imitation in childhood.* W. W. Norton, New York.

Sebeok, T. A. (1994). *Signs: an introduction to semiotics.* University of Toronto Press.

Siple, P. (1997). Universal, generalize ability, in the acquisition of signed language. In *Relations of language and thought: the view from sign language and deaf children* (Marschark, M., Siple, P., Lillo-Martin, D., Campbell, R., and Everhart, V.S.), pp. 24–61. Oxford University Press, New York.

Stokoe, W. C. (1960). Sign language structure: an outline of the visual communications systems. *Studies in Linguistics*, Occasional Papers **8**. University of Buffalo, Buffalo, NY.

Stokoe, W. C., Casterline, D.C., and Croneberg, C.G. (1965). *A dictionary of American Sign Language on linguistic principles.* Gallaudet College Press, Washington, DC.

Swisher, V. (1993). Perceptual and cognitive aspects of recognition of signs in peripheral vision. In *Psychological perspectives on deafness* (ed. M. Marschark and D. Clark), pp. 209–28. Erlbaum, Hillsdale, NJ.

Tzeng, O. J. L. and Wang, W. S.-Y. (1984). Search for a common neurocognitive mechanism for language and movements. *American Journal of Physiology*, **246**, R904–R911.

Volterra, V. and Iverson, J. M. (1995). When do modality factors affect the course of language acquisition? In *Language, gesture, and space* (ed. K. Emmorey and J. Reilly), pp. 371–90. Erlbaum, Hillsdale, NJ.

Werner, H. and Kaplan, B. (1963). *Symbol formation.* Wiley, New York.

CHAPTER 10

Two modes—two languages?

Lynn S. Messing

Gesture and Movement Dynamics Laboratory of the University of Delaware and the duPont Hospital for Children

Introduction

People who know only spoken languages are anatomically incapable of communicating in more than one language at a time; it is impossible to articulate two different spoken languages simultaneously with a single vocal tract. In contrast, it is theoretically possible for people to produce a spoken language and a different signed language at the same time; except for some facial expressions (such as using pursed lips), there are no anatomical conflicts between the two languages. If people do not so communicate, it must be for more interesting cultural or cognitive reasons.

This chapter will discuss the behaviour of people who know both a spoken and a signed language. The behaviour of this population will be contrasted with that of bilinguals knowing two spoken languages. In principle, the actions of dual modality bilinguals while speaking can be broken into two categories: the bilinguals can use their hands and faces in a non-linguistic manner to gesture, or they can use them to communicate linguistically in a natural signed language, in a manual code of a spoken language or in a variety of contact signing.[1] In practice, as will be seen below, the boundary between these two categories is fuzzy at best, and can disappear entirely in some circumstances.

The most studied phenomenon involving a signed and a spoken language is simultaneous communication (simcom). The introductory chapter of this book contains a brief introduction to simcom, and an understanding of that information is presupposed in this chapter. Bimodal communication (BC), a phenomenon similar to simcom, will be presented in this chapter.

This chapter will address the following questions:

(1) How do sign and speech develop in monolingual and bilingual children?

(2) What interactions occur between sign and speech in hearing bilingual, bimodal adults?

(3) How do the functions of the bilingual, bimodal interactions mentioned in question two compare with those of code-switching by individuals who are bilingual in two spoken languages?

Let us begin with a discussion of childhood acquisition of languages in two modes.

Child language acquisition

All children with normal limb functioning gesture, and children exposed to signed languages from an early age naturally learn to sign. How and when does such a child make the transition into a linguistic use of the gestural modality?

Before discussing child bilingual language acquisition or even the learning of a signed language, let us lay a groundwork by discussing the simpler and more often studied situation of a child learning only one language, which both the family and the community share.

Monolingual language acquisition

A child learning a spoken language typically goes through several phases: In the latter half of the first year, the child's babbling becomes more complex and sounds increasingly like the spoken language being learned. The child begins to utter individual words around the time of its first birthday. Approximately 6 months later, the child begins to combine words into two-word phrases. Such phrases are telescopic, and listeners must rely heavily upon context to distinguish their meaning. For example, 'Mommy sock' may indicate that a sock the child is holding belongs to its mother, or it could be a request for the mother to look at, put on, or take off a sock. Around the child's second birthday, the child's mean length of utterance again increases, and during the following year, the child's sentence structures become increasingly like those used by adults.

Newport and Meier (1985) reviewed the literature on child acquisition of signed languages and found that, with one possible exception, children learning to sign go through the same phases, at the same times, as children learning to speak. Just as infants learning a spoken language engage in a period of vocal babbling, infants learning a signed language engage in manual babbling (Petitto 1988; Petitto and Marentette 1991). (Interestingly enough, preliminary work by Meier and Willerman (1995) revealed that infants learning a spoken language may also engage in manual babbling.) Signing children begin to combine two signs together, and to express the same types of meanings and relationships between the signs, at an age similar to when speaking children begin to combine two words. More complex morphology and syntax also appeared at comparable ages, and followed similar developmental paths, for the speaking and signing children. The only potential difference observed in the development of language was that signing children may make their first signs at a younger age than that at which speaking children utter their first words.

When do babies learning a visual language make the transition from 'merely' using their hands and faces for gesturing and babbling to using them to articulate real signs? This question is still debated. Some researchers, such as Meier and Newport (1990), Orlansky and Bonvillian (1985), and Bonvillian *et al.* (1990) have suggested that children learning to sign utter their first signs at an earlier age than children who are learning to speak say their first words. A few explanations for the precociousness of the signs are given by Meier and Newport; namely, that the motor coordination necessary for signing may be achieved at an earlier age than that needed for speaking, signs may be more easily perceived than words by the child, and adults may more readily identify children's attempts at forming signs than they do at producing words. Incidentally, the signs so articulated are not especially iconic. Other scientists, including Volterra and Iverson (1995) and Petitto (1988), believed that first signs appear at about the same age as first words. Much of the debate hinges on the criteria used to differentiate signs from gestures or manual babbling, and words from vocal babbling. Some criteria used include:

- phonetic similarity to adult forms
- reasonably consistent phonetic form
- contextually appropriate use
- spontaneous articulation
- use in different contexts and with different communicative intents
- use which distinguishes it from a proper noun (i.e., it must be more than a label for a specific entity).

Even using strictly defined criteria, it is not always easy to determine whether particular manual movements should be considered signs. Petitto (1988) hypothesized that the reason why some studies indicate that children enter the one-sign stage earlier than their counterparts enter the one-word stage is that both researchers and parents may be over-eager to interpret gestures as signs. She points out that many of these early 'signs' are also made by children learning only spoken languages. Both groups of children open and close their hands, but only in the latter is such a movement interpreted as the American Sign Language (ASL) sign MILK. This view is buttressed by an experiment she conducted in which she asked a deaf colleague to transcribe all the signs she saw a videotaped infant (aged 10 and 11 months in different tapes) producing. Unbeknownst to the transcriber, the boy was a hearing child not exposed to any signed languages. Nevertheless, over 100 signs, and some rather complex sign combinations, were recorded. Although this demonstration, with its small corpus and lack of independent coders, cannot be considered definitive, it nevertheless indicates that caution should be taken in interpreting actions as signs. Similarly, Volterra and Iverson (1995) noted that children, regardless of the language(s) they are learning, point to objects of interest to them; but only with children learning to sign are these points, made alone or in conjunction with one other sign, interpreted as pronouns. Volterra and Iverson consider such early gestures to be communicative, but not linguistic.

By contrast, Petitto (1983, 1990) documents one quite dramatic transition from gesture to sign. She compared the pointing gestures and the pronoun use of children learning signed and spoken languages. All of the infants started off pointing to the people and things that interested them some time around 9 months of age. At approximately 22 months of age, children learning spoken language, having already used the word 'me', began to use the word 'you'; however, some of them used these terms in a manner precisely opposite to that of adults. That is, they used 'you' to refer to themselves, and 'me' to refer to the person they addressed. In ASL, the pronouns YOU and ME are nearly identical to the pointing gestures the children had started using. Both have as a handshape a fist with an extended index finger. The tip of that finger points to the person to whom they are referring. These signs are among those whose meanings are most transparent to hearing adult non-signers. Nevertheless, at about the same age that some children learning English confused 'you' and 'me,' some of Petitto's subjects learning ASL also seemed to confuse YOU and ME. They pointed to their interlocutors to refer to themselves, and they seemed to avoid using any sign or gesture whatsoever to refer to their interlocutors. At about 25–27 months old, both the signing and speaking subjects learned to use the pronouns according to adult conventions.

Bilingual, bimodal language acquisition

In what ways do children growing up in a bilingual, bimodal environment differ in their behaviour from those growing up in households with two spoken languages? The behaviour and abilities of children growing up bilingual, regardless of their languages' modalities, depend greatly on several factors; among them: the language(s) each family member or caregiver uses with each other and with the child, the language(s) used in the community, the amount of exposure the child has to each of the languages, the age at which such exposure begins, and the similarity of the languages. This chapter only has room to touch upon child bilingualism, and so will focus primarily on the case where each parent uses a different language, the parents use only that language with the child and with each other, and one of those languages is the dominant language of the community.

Bilingual children and adults have been shown to use code-shifting, code-switching, and borrowing. The precise definitions for these terms have been debated in the bilingualism literature, but the following definitions will suffice for this chapter. Code-shifting is the practice of changing languages between sentences or utterances. One common reason for code-shifting is to address different individuals in the language(s) with which they are most comfortable. Code-switching occurs when the change between languages happens within a given sentence. Borrowing also occurs within sentences. A code-switch draws upon the lexicon and the morphology (i.e., word structure) or the syntax (sentence structure) of both languages, whereas a borrowing involves the introduction of an individual, unanalysed, word from one language into a sentence which is otherwise in the other language.

Hearing children growing up with two spoken languages seem to begin with a non-redundant bilingual lexicon. So for example, they might consistently refer to the concept of 'milk' via the vocabulary item drawn from one language, and to 'daddy' via the other language's lexical item. Therefore, their version of the English phrase 'daddy milk,' would be an utterance which a bilingual adult would interpret as a code-switch. (e.g., Leopold 1939–1949; Hatch 1978; Grosjean 1982). It is a matter of debate whether children at this stage have two separate language systems or one mixed one. Hearing children growing up with a signed and a spoken language similarly appear to begin by articulating a bilingual, bimodal, non-redundant vocabulary (Griffith 1985). Hearing children learning two spoken languages begin to differentiate between them in their own speech production somewhere in or around their third year of life (Leopold 1939–1949; McLure 1977; Volterra and Taeschner 1978). By the time they are four, they learn to code-shift, or at least code-switch, depending on the command they have of each language, to accommodate to the linguistic preferences of the person they are addressing (Hakuta 1986). Several researchers (e.g., Meadow 1972; Schlesinger 1972; Schiff and Ventry 1976; Prinz and Prinz 1981; Griffith 1985; Gaustad 1988) have examined the code-shifting ability of hearing children with at least one deaf parent. They found that by the time their subjects were between 2 and 2½ years old, they were sensitive to the language used by others, and they tailored their own language to the language others used; i.e., they signed more when other people signed to them, and they spoke more when others spoke to them. They initiated conversations with people they knew in the preferred communication mode(s) of the other conversant. Griffith (1985) noted that her subjects primarily used the mode(s) appropriate to the other conversant; however, both her subjects and those of Volterra (1981) sometimes began an utterance in sign and finished it in English. Prinz and Prinz (1981) also gave examples of this kind of code-shift. The reverse order never seemed to occur. There is an unfortunate paucity in the literature of borrowing and code-switching by children learning a signed and spoken language. Prinz and Prinz (1981) implied that as their subjects acquired a greater command of their languages, and as they grew more competent in code-shifting and in tailoring their communications to meet the needs of their interlocutors, they used increasingly less borrowing and code-switching.

This discussion barely scratches the surface of the literature on child signed language acquisition. Although there are many worthwhile books and articles that address this topic to varying extents, the interested reader is especially referred to Volterra and Erting (1990) and Newport and Meier (1985).

Adult language in two modes

Borrowing

As often happens in a situation of language contact, borrowing occurs between ASL and English. Battison (1978) showed how certain fingerspelled English words have been borrowed into ASL, with a consequent restructuring in order to obey ASL phonological constraints. Some of these fingerspelled words also underwent morphological or semantic revisions in the borrowing process. Johnson (1994) disagreed with Battison at the point at which a word becomes borrowed into ASL via fingerspelling, but did not disagree that such borrowing does in fact occur.

Although no studies have been done on borrowing from ASL to English, the phenomenon of bimodal communication to be examined below, may be considered to be a type of borrowing or code-switching. Also, the use of the English word 'sign' by ASL signers to mean 'signed language' may be one such borrowing. The ASL sign SIGN also means 'signed language'. Similarly, during the debriefing portion of the experiment described below, subjects commented on using calques of ASL in English. For example, they would say, 'For for', to mean 'why'. (One way to translate 'why' into ASL is with a reduplicated version of the sign FOR.) The subjects seemed to use such borrowings only informally and in jest.

Code-switching

The intermodal code-switching which has been documented differs in one important respect from what is typical of intramodal code-switching. In the latter, the information content of the sentence is usually divided relatively non-redundantly between the two languages. In the former, however, the information presented in one of the languages is typically information also presented in the other language. Bernstein *et al.* (1985) discussed intermodal code-switching. Although they did not cite examples, they claimed that at times their subjects would use simcom, then would stop speaking and utter something in ASL. After this, they would stop signing long enough to translate what they signed into spoken English. They would then begin to use simcom again. Davis (1989) examined the output of simultaneous interpreters who were interpreting from English to ASL. He found that they often employed code-switching and borrowing from English, in the form of manually coded English (MCE), when they signed. One strategy which they used was to form an ASL sign before or after fingerspelling its English equivalent. Another strategy used was to sign in ASL and to mouth an English word. Adults have been found to use intramodal code-switching in spoken languages for a variety of reasons, which Messing (1996, p.114) categorized as follows:

Strategic negotiation: Code-switching can be used strategically in negotiating one's relationship with one's conversational partner.

Identity marker: Code-switching can be used as an identity marker, to indicate such things as one's ethnicity or amount of education.

Domain marker: If each of the languages is typically used in a certain place, or for discussing certain topics (i.e., in a certain domain), code-switching can be used when the domain changes or when more than one domain is involved.

Compensation: Code-switching is sometimes used when the speaker in the conversation either does not have the ability to discuss a topic in one of the languages, or simply cannot access the necessary vocabulary rapidly enough on a given occasion.

Accommodation: Another use of code-switching is to accommodate conversational partners whom the speaker believes do not have the ability to converse comfortably in at least one of the languages. This becomes especially likely if there is no one language in which all of the conversants are fluent.

Stylistic effect: Code-switching can be used for stylistic effect, either to employ the *mot juste*, or to provide emphasis.

Many of these functions have also been seen to be used in intermodal interactions. These will be discussed later in this chapter.

Clearly, phenomena which researchers in bilingualism find to be common between two spoken languages can and do also occur between a spoken and a signed language. Let us now compare speakers' use of signs and gestures.

Signs and gestures with speech

Processing simultaneous communication

Simultaneous communication (simcom) presents several processing difficulties. First, individual words can be produced much faster than can signs, due to the large articulator movements required to sign (Bornstein 1979). Many researchers (e.g., Bellugi and Fischer 1972; Bornstein and Pickett 1976; Grosjean 1979) found that speakers can utter between two and three words in the time it takes a signer to articulate one sign. Despite this fact, Bellugi and Fischer determined that English speakers require the same amount of time as ASL signers to communicate propositions.

This seeming paradox can be explained by the fact that ASL makes extensive use of the simultaneous articulation of several morphemes, whereas English generally requires morphemes to be communicated sequentially. So, for example, the basic sign GIVE can be inflected to mean something which can be translated into English by the phrase 'he continually gives you'. However, MCEs, which utilize English morpheme structure, must also convey morphemes sequentially. Therefore, it ought to take at least twice as long to communicate a proposition using an MCE, either by itself or with voice, as it would using either English or ASL alone.

Lieberman (1975) stated that if propositions are conveyed too slowly, the message becomes hard to process. Therefore, people will not succeed in speaking at a comfortable pace and signing an MCE simultaneously. They will not be able to sign everything they say in English, or they will have to employ the simultaneity of morphemes found in ASL, or else they will violate Lieberman's constraint on proposition speed.

All of these strategies have been documented. Marmor and Petitto (1979), Strong and Charlson (1987), Kluwin (1981), and Crandall (1974) all found that users of simcom do not convey all of their English morphemes in sign. Kluwin ascertained that only deaf users of simcom and, to a lesser degree, experienced hearing signers, make use of ASL grammatical structures involving the simultaneity of morphemes. Maxwell and Bernstein (1985) verified that while 89% of their deaf subjects' simcom utterances did not have all of the English morphemes signed, only 14% of the utterances did not convey equivalent propositions.

Baker (1978) and Cokely (1979) conducted joint research on the rate of production of speech, sign, and simcom by hearing and deaf individuals. They noticed that when hearing individuals use simcom, they both sign and speak more slowly than they do using either mode by itself. Even so, they do not sign many of the morphemes they speak. Deaf signers speak even more slowly than their hearing counterparts do when using simcom. They omit few or none of the signs necessary to convey the English proposition in the contact signing. In order to convey all of the English morphemes in both speech and sign, these individuals violate Lieberman's constraint on the speed of proposition articulation.

Strong and Charlson (1987) examined the communication strategies used by three hearing teachers. They found five different strategies which all of the teachers employed. The first strategy is to speak and sign unmodified English. This strategy is used in 5–12% of all of the teachers' utterances. It is only used with simple sentences without pronouns and with no multimorphemic words. The next tactic is to speak unmodified English, and sign a modified English. The modified sign has redundant elements deleted. For example, one might say 'two trees' and sign TWO TREE. Although simple ASL structures are used with this strategy, complex structures are avoided. Third, the teachers sometimes sign and speak ungrammatical English. Both modes incorporate a mixture of ASL and English syntax. Next the teachers sometimes speak or sign incomplete English; i.e., important, non-redundant, information is deleted in one or both modes. Finally, the teachers repeat information in one or both modes. This information can either be simple words, or entire propositions. In addition to the difficulty of articulating the sign equivalents of English morphemes rapidly enough, users of simcom have another difficulty. The requirement of constructing a message and encoding and articulating it in two different modes simultaneously appears to overload the cognitive capacity. Marmor and Petitto (1979) found that when their subjects were reading 'aloud' in an MCE, they omitted fewer English morphemes in their signing than they did when they were conversing, i.e., when they were required to construct their message as well as transmit it.

There are two possible reasons for the signed messages being incomplete. Researchers have not yet provided any evidence in support of either hypothesis. The first one is that cognitive overload results in certain morphemes not being retrieved from the lexicon to be signed. In other words, the message is incompletely coded into the MCE. The second possibility is that all of the sign equivalents of English morphemes are retrieved, but not all are signed. That is, the message is completely coded into the MCE, but it is not completely articulated.

The timing of gestures and signs with speech

It is interesting to compare the timing of signs and speech in simcom with that of gestures and speech in non-signed, spoken conversations. It is overly simplistic, however, merely to categorize all non-signed, communicative movements of the hands and arms under the rubric of 'gesture'. McNeill (1992) formulated the following continuum, based on the work of Kendon (1988b), of different types of gesture:

gesticulation → language-like gestures → pantomimes → emblems → sign languages

Gestures are placed in different parts of the continuum based on how linguistic they are. As one moves rightwards in the continuum, the gestures become increasingly systematic and conventionalized, and decreasingly associated with speech.

Kendon (1980) and McNeill (1992, and, to a lesser extent, Chapter 5, this volume) have discussed the phases of gestures and the relationship of the timing of gesticulations to the speech which they accompany. The point most relevant to this chapter is that the main movement of a gesture, the stroke phase, typically co-occurs with the meaning unit with which it corresponds; it occasionally precedes it, but it follows only rarely.

Part of Kendon's (1988a) work which McNeill used in devising the continuum dealt with the signs and gestures used by Warlpiri women. During periods of mourning, these aboriginal Australians are not supposed to speak, and so they use a signed language to communicate. But at other times, they sign even while they are speaking. In addition to the aforementioned differences between signs and gesticulations, these signs also differ from gesticulations in their timing. The stroke phase of the Warlpiri signs often occurs after the related speech phrases.

Naughton (1996) videotaped a pair of hearing American women who were fluent in ASL, as they conversed in English. She found that they displayed a different behaviour with respect both to the timing and the content of their signs than did Kendon's subjects. The stroke phases of the signs used by Naughton's subjects, unlike those of the Warlpiri women, patterned like gesticulations in their timing.

The content of the signs observed by the two researchers also differed. The Warlpiri signs related closely in meaning to the individual words which were spoken, and most of the signs were straightforward equivalents of them. The only sorts of additional meaning provided were things which the signs obligatorily marked. An example would be the spatial relationships specified by the use of a directional verb. By the directions of their movements, these signs mandatorily incorporate the locations of their subjects and/or objects.

The American Sign Language signs, however, were frequently tied more closely to full phrases or thoughts than to individual words. There were numerous instances of spoken spatial deictics, such as 'here', whose referents could only be found in the accompanying signs. For example, one of Naughton's subjects described the layout of a wedding scene by saying, 'And then, so there's, okay, so he's here. And th- those two are sitting here. They're sitting in the seat and then here's all the audience.' The accompanying signs showed the spatial relationships among the individuals involved, including the fact that the seating of the audience consisted of rows separated by an aisle.

Another difference between the two groups of signers is the amount of information they conveyed in each of the two modes. Kendon's subjects conveyed nearly all of their propositions in both sign and speech; they were using a form of simcom. Naughton's subjects, however, did not seem as intent on conveying all information in the visual modality, and frequently used little to no sign in their conversation. This type of occasional sign being introduced into the gestural stream, Messing (1990) has called 'bimodal communication' or BC (Messing 1990). She distinguishes BC from simcom in the following ways:

The simcom user is trying to encode all propositions linguistically in both modes. The user of BC, in contrast, may only be trying to do so in the spoken mode. Occasional signs are interspersed with non-sign gesticulations in the visual mode. Simcom, at least in the United States, most typically occurs between a deaf and a hearing individual. BC most typically occurs between two hearing individuals.

Note that, as Naughton's subjects have shown, the differences are quantitative rather than qualitative. Simcom and BC could be conceived as labels for two parts of a continuum. Studies of simcom examine how much an individual can articulate when attempting to convey complete messages in two modes; in contrast, studies in BC determine how much an individual will articulate in two modes when not making such an attempt.

Bimodal communication

Methods

An experiment was conducted to determine the type and extent of BC used by people of different signing abilities (Messing 1993, 1994, 1995, 1996). The subjects were all white, hearing women who attended either the University of Delaware or Gallaudet University. English was their first language, and they had learned varying amounts of ASL as adults. They were grouped according to their signing abilities: Non-signers knew at most the ASL alphabet and ten other signs. Beginners were enrolled in ASL 1 classes. Intermediate signers were taking ASL 2 or ASL 3 courses, and advanced signers were either in ASL 4 or sign interpretation classes. There were 20 non-signers, 18 beginners, and six each of intermediate and advanced signers. A brief translation task confirmed that the subjects were placed in appropriate groups; i.e., all of the subjects placed in the more skilled groups outperformed all of the subjects placed in the less skilled groups. Non-signers were included in the experiment to determine a 'chance' BC rate; i.e., how many gestures which just happen to look like signs are used by people who do not know ASL.

The subjects were videotaped during and after the performances of five scenarios. Scenarios, or strategic interactions, are activities similar to role-plays. Di Pietro (1987) states several differences between the two activities. The relevant ones here are that in scenarios, unlike in role plays, participants are informed about a situation in which they are to imagine themselves to be. Within this situation, they can 'be themselves'; they are not told what to do or say. Furthermore, each participant in a scenario is typically privy to information not known to the other participant(s).

The subjects were told to try to put themselves into each situation, and to act as they believed they would in real life. No mention was made either of the purpose of the study or of the language they were to use when performing the strategic interactions. On the rare occasion subjects asked about which language to use, the instruction was reiterated to do whatever they think they would do in real life.

Results

The initial hypothesis had been that the relationship between signing skills and amount of BC used would be monotonically increasing. In fact, the relationship proved to be more complex. As Table 10.1 indicates, the inter-scenario BC rates were indeed monotonically increasing (an ANOVA across skill levels resulted in $p < 0.0001$), but a graph of the rates within scenarios across signing levels was closer to an inverse-U. A likely explanation for this change in behaviour came to light in the debriefings. Many of the subjects' families and friends had criticized the subjects for their use of BC. Although the non-signers and the less experienced signers displayed the same sort of behaviour within the scenarios and after them, the most advanced signers behaved quite differently in the two situations. As one of the advanced signing subjects commented, 'I can turn [the use of BC] on and off.' During the scenarios, when the subjects were aware that they were being videotaped for research purposes, they were feeling self-conscious and were on their 'best behaviour'. Although the subject pool was too small to state this with great confidence, the advanced signers certainly appeared to use less BC during scenarios than after them ($t = 2.08$; $_{0.90}t_2 = 1.886$ for a matched-pair t-test). It is interesting to note, however that they nevertheless used far more BC during scenarios than did the non-signers ($t = 8.75$; $_{0.9995}t_{11} = 4.437$). Therefore, even when they had 'turned off' their use of BC, they were continuing to use it.

Moreover, the intermediate and advanced signers often gave the appearance of signing 'despite themselves'. Some of the signs would be made with a greatly reduced motion in a location where it would be less obvious than in the standard, citation form. For example, the citation form of the ASL sign KEY has the hands in contact with each other in neutral space—the area directly in front of the signer between waist and chest height. The forearm of the dominant hand rapidly

Table 10.1 Bimodal communication rates by signing levels

	Between scenarios		Within scenarios	
	X'	S.D.	X'	S.D.
Non-signers	3.33	7.26	3.08	4.43
Beginners	8.70	13.15	8.20	8.13
Intermediates	28.67	49.65	38.33	44.76
Advanced	97.33	27.04	20.67	5.50

pronates and supinates with the dominant hand in a fist closed except for an extended index finger proximal joint. An advanced signing subject had had her arms on top of her chair's armrests, until she started to discuss a key. At that time, she bent her wrists and raised her forearms slightly off the armrests and formed her hands into the appropriate shapes for the sign KEY, and her dominant hand performed the movement appropriate for that sign. Because this particular sign is so distinct, the data coders had had no difficulty whatsoever in identifying this movement as a sign, despite the fact that it was made without the typical hand contact and in lower and more peripheral locations than it would be either in citation form or even in casual signing.

One of the biggest obstacles, and surprises, to the two data coders was that there were several such gestures, especially by advanced signers. Fully 8% of the intermediate signers' signs, and 15% of those of the advanced signers, were 'partially articulated'. Some such signs were not only in a different location than usual, they also had a reduced movement or an 'incorrect' handshape. In some instances, the handshapes used were ones which are not even part of the phonetics of ASL. While some signs, such as KEY, are robust enough to be identifiable even in such varied forms, there were other gestures which both coders questioned whether or not to identify as signs. The coders initially viewed the videotapes independently with the volume off to identify and record signs. They then watched the tapes with the volume up to write down what was being said during the signs. There were times that something about a gesture indicated to both coders that it was a sign, but the gesture deviated sufficiently from the citation form that the identification of which sign was intended could only be achieved once the coders knew what was being said. There were even a few instances in which a coder could not decide, even with the volume up, whether a gesture was a sign. The coders did eventually reach a high inter-coder reliability; of the movements which either coder identified as a sign, there was an 80.26% agreement on identifying them as particular signs. (If the coder had to rely on the accompanying speech to identify a sign, it was counted as a disagreement for the purposes of determining reliability.) This number is actually a gross under-estimate of the true reliability—it counts as incorrect the occasional instance in which both coders recognized something as a sign but disagreed on which sign it was, and it does not take into account that the vast majority of the gestures both coders identified as non-signs. However, achieving this reliability required several sessions of coding parts of the data and discussing the reasons for the coding choices. Deciding whether or not a gesture is a sign can be much harder than one might expect. See Marschark (1994), Emmorey (Chapter 8, this volume), and Stokoe and Marschark (Chapter 9, this volume) for discussions of signs and gestures.

The timing of the signs used by Messing's subjects was far more akin to that of Naughton's subjects than of Kendon's. Instances of BC were coded as occurring before, during, or after their spoken counterpart. Almost all of the signs co-occurred with their spoken counterparts. Only the intermediate and advanced signers made any signs (approximately 8% of their total instances of BC) before their spoken counterparts, and only the advanced signers produced any signs after the corresponding speech. Furthermore, even the advanced signers only made two signs, or 4% of their signs, after their spoken equivalents. Those two signs occurred after the word(s) with which their meaning most closely corresponded, but even they were articulated within the duration of the spoken clause.

The code-switching behaviour of the non-signers and beginners differed greatly from that of the intermediate and advanced signers. The signs categorized as code-switches fell into two classes: either they were multimorphemic and appropriately inflected, or else they were classifiers, a syntactic category found in ASL but not in English. As one would expect, the non-signers and beginning signers did not code-switch, with the notable exception of one time when a non-signer imitated a sign which the researcher accidentally used. The sign must have appeared to the subject to be 'merely' a gesture; however, it happened to be a classifier, and as such had to be coded as a code-switch. In contrast to this, one out of every five instances of BC articulated by the intermediate and advanced signers was a code-switch.

BC and sequential intermodal borrowing and code-switching were employed for several of the same reasons as intramodal code-switching. Let us take those reasons one at a time:

Strategic negotiation: One individual conveyed two very different messages simultaneously. While she used a slang term ('Bogue') to indicate her approval of a witty retort made by her partner, she also signed REVENGE to indicate that she would retaliate.

Identity marker: There were many instances in which signs seemed to be used for no other reason than to indicate that the speaker knew sign; however, the clearest instance of the use of an intermodal, though arguably monolingual, utterance being used as an identity marker was when an advanced signer simultaneously communicated the message, 'I am not signing.' She obviously did not intend this to be a joke, nor did she intend it to be taken as literally true. The full message she wished to communicate seemed to be, 'I won't be signing in the near future; however, this is by choice. I am fully capable of signing.'

Domain marker: No instances of intermodal code-switching for domain marking occurred in this experiment.

Compensation: One subject appeared to be blanking on an English word meaning 'nothing'. She uttered, 'My chance to go to St John's on a honeymoon is, you know, like <pause> nil.' During the pause, it appeared as if she were trying to access an appropriate word. While she was doing this, she made the sign NOTHING, and only after this did she finish the sentence aloud.

Accommodation: Since all of the signing subjects were hearing native speakers of English and had learned, or were learning, ASL as adults, it is not surprising that no instances of intermodal interactions for the purpose of accommodation were found in the data.

Stylistic effect: An advanced signer used a sequential intermodal borrowing for stylistic effect. She said, 'Is this <pause>? You're really <pause>?' During each of the pauses, she signed STRAIGHT. This sign not only conveys the meaning of 'straightforward' or 'truthful', it also carries the broader meaning of living a wholesome life. The utterance was one in which the speaker was questioning not only the veracity of what her partner was saying, but the more general issue of whether her partner (in the role she was playing) was a trustworthy individual. No single word in English would have been able to convey this conglomeration of meanings as succinctly or as inoffensively as did the sign the subject chose to use.

Summary

Let us return now to the three questions posed at the start of this chapter. The first question was, 'How do sign and speech develop in monolingual and bilingual children?' We have seen that children go through the same phases of language acquisition, at approximately the same ages, whether they are learning signed or spoken languages. They babble, make one-word/one-sign utterances, and then two-word/two-sign utterances before the complexity of their utterances increases dramatically. It is still debated whether babies learning a visual language begin making one-sign utterances at a younger age than babies learning a spoken one make one-word utterance. Children growing up bilingual learn to employ code-shifting, code-switching, and borrowing. Although not much research has been conducted on this, it would appear that children learning both a signed and a spoken language decrease their use of bilingual utterances as they mature. (This is often not the case in environments in which children grow up learning two spoken languages.)

In answer to the second question posed above ('What interactions occur between sign and speech in hearing bilingual, bimodal adults?), we can state that hearing adults who have learned ASL as adults have indeed been shown to borrow, code-switch, and code-shift. These individuals also do things impossible to non-signers: they can use simcom and BC. In the latter, signs are interspersed with non-linguistic gestures.

The final question asked how the functions of the bilingual, bimodal interactions compare with those of code-switching by individuals bilingual in two spoken languages. Hearing individuals who know both a signed and a spoken language use bilingual utterances for many of the same functions as people who know two spoken languages. They have been shown to use simcom or BC for strategic negotiation, as identity markers, as compensation, and for stylistic effect. Although they have not yet been reported as using simcom or BC for domain marking or accommodation, this may be due to the brevity and the narrowness of scope of the corpus examined.

References

Baker, C. (1978). How does 'simcom' fit into a bilingual approach to education? In *American Sign Language in a bilingual, bicultural context: proceedings of the second national symposium on sign language research and teaching* (ed. F. Caccamise), pp. 13–26. NAD, Coronado, CA.

Battison, R. (1978). *Lexical borrowing in American Sign Language*. Linstok Press, Silver Spring, MD.

Bellugi, U. and Fischer, S. (1972). A comparison of sign language and spoken language: rate and grammatical mechanisms. *Cognition*, **1**, 173–200.

Bernstein, M., Maxwell, M., and Matthews, K. (1985). Bimodal or bilingual communication? *Sign Language Studies*, **47**, 127–40.

Bonvillian, J., Orlansky, M., and Folven, R. (1990). Early sign language acquisition: implications for theories of language acquisition. In *From gesture to language* (ed. V. Volterra and C. Erting), pp. 219–32. Springer-Verlag, Berlin.

Bornstein, H. (1979). Systems of sign. In *Hearing and hearing impairments* (ed. L. Bradford and W. Hardy), pp. 333–61. Grune and Stratton, New York.

Bornstein, H. and Pickett, J. (1976). Co-ordination of spoken and signed English. Unpublished paper. Gallaudet College, Washington, DC.

Cokely, D. (1979). *Pre-college programs: guidelines for manual communication*. Gallaudet College, Washington, DC.

Crandall, K. (1974). A study of the production of chers and related sign language aspects by deaf children between the ages of three and seven years. Unpublished doctoral dissertation, Northwest University.

Davis, J. (1989). Distinguishing language contact phenomena in ASL interpretation. In *The sociolinguistics of the Deaf community*, (ed. C. Lucas). Academic Press, Inc., San Diego, CA.

Di Pietro, R. (1987). *Strategic interaction: learning language through scenarios*. Cambridge University Press, Cambridge, MA.

Gaustad, M. (1988). Development of vocal and signed communication in deaf and hearing twins of deaf parents. In *Language learning and deafness* (ed. M. Strong), pp. 220–60. Cambridge University Press.

Griffith, P. (1985). Mode-switching and mode-finding in a hearing child of deaf parents. *Sign Language Studies*, **48**, 195–221.

Grosjean, F. (1979). A study of timing in a manual and a spoken language: American Sign Language and English. *Journal of Psycholinguistic Research*, **8**, 379–405.

Grosjean, F. (1982). *Life with two languages: an introduction to bilingualism*. Harvard University Press.

Hakuta, K. (1986). *Mirror of language: the debate on bilingualism*. Basic Books, New York.

Hatch, E. (ed.) (1978). *Second language acquisition: a book of readings*. Newbury House Publishers, Rowley, MA.

Johnson, R. (1994). The structure of fingerspelling American Sign Language. Videotaped lecture presented to Waubonsee Community College on 8 April 1994.

Kendon, A. (1980). Gesticulation, speech, and the gesture theory of language origins. In *Sign and culture* (ed. W. Stokoe), pp. 334–61. Linstok Press, Silver Spring, MD.

Kendon, A. (1988a). How gestures can become like words. In *Cross-cultural perspectives in non-verbal communication* (ed. F. Poyatos), pp. 131–41. Hogrefe, Toronto.

Kendon, A. (1988b) *Sign languages of aboriginal Australia*. Cambridge University Press.

Kluwin, T. (1981). The grammaticality of manual representations of English in classroom settings. *American Annals of the Deaf*, **127**, 417–21.

Leopold, W. (1939–1949). *Speech development of a bilingual child: a linguist's record*, Vols i–iv. Northwestern University Press, Evanston, IL.

Lieberman, P. (1975). *On the origins of language: an introduction to the evolution of human speech*. MacMillan, New York.

Marmor, G. and Petitto, L. (1979). Simultaneous communication in the classroom: how well is English grammar represented? *Sign Language Studies*, **23**, 99–136.

Marschark, M. (1994). Gesture and sign. *Applied Psycholinguistics*, **15**, 209–39.

Maxwell, M. and Bernstein, M. (1985). The synergy of sign and speech in simultaneous communication. *Applied Psycholinguistics*, **6**, 63–81.

McLure, E. (1977). Aspects of code-switching in the discourse of bilingual Mexican–American children. In *Linguistics and anthropology* (ed. M. Saville-Troike), pp. 93–115. Georgetown University Press, Washington.

McNeill, D. (1992). *Hand and mind: what gestures reveal about thought*. University of Chicago Press.

Meadow, K. (1972). Sociolinguistics, sign language, and the Deaf sub-culture. In *Psycholinguistics and total communication: the state of the art* (ed. T. O'Rourke), pp. 19–33. NAD, Silver Spring, MD.

Meier, R. and Newport, E. (1990). Out of the hands of babes: on a possible sign language advantage in language acquisition. *Language*, **66**, 1–23.

Meier, R. and Willerman, R. (1995). Prelinguistic gestures in deaf and hearing infants. In *Language, gesture, and space* (ed. K. Emmorey and J. Reilly), pp. 391–409. Erlbaum, Hillsdale, NJ.

Messing, L. (1990). Bimodal communication. In *The sixteenth LACUS forum 1989* (ed. M. Jordan), pp. 460–9. LACUS, Lake Bluff, IL.

Messing, L. (1993). The use of bimodal communication by hearing, female signers. Unpublished doctoral dissertation. The University of Delaware, Newark, DE.

Messing, L. (1994). Bimodal communication, signing skill, and tenseness. *Sign Language Studies*, **84**, 209–20. Linstok Press, Burtonsville, MD.

Messing, L. (1995). Bimodal communication: what is it, and why study it? In *The twenty-first LACUS forum 1994* (ed. M. Powell), pp. 29–38. LACUS, Lake Bluff, IL.

Messing, L. (1996). What's the use of bimodal communication? In *Proceedings of the workshop on the integration of gesture in language and speech* (ed. L. Messing), pp. 115–24. Applied Science and Engineering Laboratories, Wilmington, DE.

Naughton, K. (1996). Spontaneous gesture and sign: a study of ASL signs co-occurring with speech. In *Proceedings of the workshop on the integration of gesture in language and speech* (ed. L. Messing), pp. 125–34. Applied Science and Engineering Laboratories, Wilmington, DE.

Newport, E. and Meier, R. (1985). The acquisition of American Sign Language. In *The crosslinguistic study of language acquisition*, Vol. 1 (ed. D. Slobin), pp. 881–938. Erlbaum, Hillsdale, NJ.

Orlansky, M. and Bonvillian, J. (1985). Sign language acquisition: language development in children of deaf parents and implications for other populations. *Merrill-Palmer Quarterly*, **31**(2), 127–43.

Petitto, L. (1983). From gesture to symbol: the acquisition of personal pronouns in American Sign Language. *Papers and Reports on Child Language Development*, **22**, 100–7.

Petitto, L. (1988). 'Language' in the pre-linguistic child. *The development of language and language researchers: essays in honor of Roger Brown* (ed. F. Kessel), pp. 187–221. Erlbaum, Hillsdale, NJ.

Petitto, L. (1990). The transition from gesture to symbol in American Sign Language. In *From gesture to language* (ed. V. Volterra, and C. Erting), pp. 153–61. Springer-Verlag, Berlin.

Petitto, L. and Marentette, P. (1991). Babbling in the manual mode: evidence for the ontology of language. *Science*, **251**, 1493–6.

Prinz, P. and Prinz, E. (1981). Acquisition of ASL and spoken English by a hearing child of a deaf mother and a hearing father: phase II, early combinatorial patterns. *Sign Language Studies*, **30**, 78–88.

Schiff, N. and Ventry, I. (1976). Communication problems in hearing children of deaf parents. *Journal of Speech and Hearing Disorders*, **41**, 348–58.

Schlesinger, H. (1972). Language acquisition in four deaf children. *Hearing and Speech News*, **40**, 4–28.

Strong, M. and Charlson, E. (1987). Simultaneous communication: are teachers attempting an impossible task? *American Annals of the Deaf*, **132**, 376–82.

Volterra, V. (1981). Gestures, signs, and words at two years: when does communication become language? *Sign Language Studies*, **33**, 351–61.

Volterra, V. and Erting, C. (eds) (1990). *From gesture to language*. Springer-Verlag, Berlin.

Volterra, V. and Iverson, J. (1995). When do modality factors affect the course of language acquisition? In *Language, gesture, and space* (ed. K. Emmorey and J. Reilly), pp. 371–90. Erlbaum, Hillsdale, NJ.

Volterra, V. and Taeschner, T. (1978). The acquisition and development of language by bilingual children. *Journal of Child Language*, **5**(2), 311–26.

Notes

1. For the purposes of space and clarity of presentation, this chapter assumes that speech and signs are linguistic, and that non-sign gestures are not; however, I believe that in fact the division between what is and is not linguistic is neither so sharp nor so simple. I fully believe that signed languages are just as linguistic as spoken ones, but I am not at all convinced by the conventional wisdom that holds all non-sign gestures to be non-linguistic.

Epilogue
A practical application

CHAPTER 11

Embodied conversational agents: a new paradigm for the study of gesture and for human–computer interface

Justine Cassell

MIT Media Laboratory

Introduction

In this chapter I discuss 'embodied conversational agents' as a way of modelling human gesture–speech behaviour, and as a way of creating a new paradigm for human–computer interaction. In terms of the first goal, I provide evidence that gesture and speech are different communicative manifestations of one single mental representation by attempting to model the interaction between them. Research on the relationship between gesture and speech has been difficult to evaluate because of its descriptive basis. One way to move from descriptive to predictive theories is via formal models, which point up gaps in knowledge and fuzziness in theoretical explanations. We have begun to provide such a model, in the form of a dialogue-generation engine system that drives two animated human figures, thus simulating the generation and carrying out of conversational interaction.

In terms of the second goal, there are three reasons why it might and should occur to us to add nonverbal modalities to human–computer interfaces: one comes purely from the human side of things, the other two come from the interaction between computer and human. First, it occurs to us to add nonverbal modalities to dialogue systems as soon as we take a close look at what really goes on in human–human dialogue. To be sure, we can speak on the telephone with one another and make ourselves understood perfectly well; but when we are face-to-face with another human, no matter what our language, cultural background, or age, we all use our faces and hands as an integral part of our dialogue with others. Second, we may turn to nonverbal modalities when we reflect on the difficulties that interface designers have in getting users to behave as they need to when interacting with perfectly adequate spoken dialogue systems. Users repeat themselves needlessly, mistake when it is their turn to speak, and otherwise behave in ways that make dialogue systems *less* likely to function well (Oviatt 1995). It is in situations just like these in life that nonverbal modalities come into play: in noisy situations, humans depend on access to more than one modality (Rogers 1978). This leads us to the third reason we might wish to add nonverbal modalities to dialogue systems. While humans have long years of practising communication with other humans (some might even say this ability is innate; see Trevarthen 1986), communication with machines is learned. And yet it has been shown that given the slightest chance, humans will attribute social responses, behaviours, and internal states to computers (Reeves and Nass 1996).

If we can skilfully build on that social response to computers, channel it even into the kind of response that we give one another in human conversation, and build a system that gives back the response (verbal and nonverbal) that humans give, then we may evoke in humans the kinds of communicative dialogue behaviours they use with other humans, and thus allow them to use the computer with the same kind of efficiency and smoothness that characterizes their human dialogues. There is good reason to think that nonverbal behaviour will play an important role in evoking these social communicative attributions. We have built such a system which, in the form of an animated human figure, can carry out a dialogue with a human user, using speech, gesture, and facial expression. Our research with this system shows that humans are more likely to consider computers lifelike—humanlike even—when those computers display not only speech but appropriate nonverbal communicative behaviour.

For both the psycholinguistic and interface communities, then, 'embodied conversational agents'—animated autonomous entities that can carry on a conversation using speech, gesture and facial expression—are valuable ways to advance the state of the art. In the remainder of this chapter I first describe how previous researchers have integrated gestures into research on human–computer interface systems. I then turn to the differences between the kinds of gestures most often studied by these computer scientists, and those studied by social scientists. It is the latter group of gestures that underlie my own attempt to simulate human behaviour. I follow that with a discussion of intonation and information structure, which will prove necessary to the modelling of discourse-appropriate gesture, and give a set of rules for gesture generation with respect to those two linguistic variables. I then describe the two systems mentioned above. The first is a conversation simulator comprising a dialogue-generation program, speech and intonation synthesis, gesture integration, and animation interface. The second is work in progress—an embodied conversational agent which can carry out a 'conversation' with a human user.

Background

Although there are many kinds of gesture, the computer science community for the most part has only attempted to integrate 'emblematic' and 'propositional' gestures. Emblematic gestures are culturally specified in the sense that one single gesture may differ in interpretation from culture to culture (Efron 1941; Ekman and Friesen 1969). For example, the American 'V-for-victory' gesture can be made either with the palm or the back of the hand towards the listener. In Britain, however, a 'V' gesture made with the back of the hand towards the listener is inappropriate in polite society. Many more of these 'emblems' appear to exist in French and Italian culture than in America or Britain (Kendon 1993), but in few cultures do these gestures appear to constitute more than 10–20% of the gestures produced by speakers. Despite the paucity of emblematic gestures in everyday communication, it is gestures such as these that have most interested computer scientists. Computer vision systems known as 'gestural interfaces' attempt to invent or co-opt emblematic gesture to replace language in human–computer interaction (see Maggioni 1995). However, in terms of *types*, few enough different emblematic gestures exist to make the idea of co-opting emblems as a gestural language untenable. And in terms of *tokens*, we simply do not seem to make that many emblematic gestures on a daily basis.

The other type of gesture that has been the subject of some study in the human–computer interface community is the so-called 'propositional gesture' (Hinrichs and Polanyi 1986). An example is the use of the hands to measure the size of a symbolic space while the speaker says 'it was this big'. Another example is pointing at a chair and then pointing at another spot and saying 'move that over there'. These gestures are not unwitting and, in that sense, not spontaneous, and their interaction with speech is more like the interaction of one grammatical constituent with another than the interaction of one communicative channel with another; in fact, the demonstrative 'this' may be seen as a place holder for the syntactic role of the accompanying gesture. These gestures can be particularly important in certain types of task-oriented talk. Gestures such as these are found notably in communicative situations where the physical world in which the conversation is taking place is also the topic of conversation. These gestures do not, however, make up the majority of gestures found in spontaneous conversation, and I believe that in part they have received the attention that they have because they are *conscious witting* gestures available to our self-scrutiny.

One of the first human–computer interface systems to integrate propositional gestures was *Put-That-There*, developed by Bolt, Schmandt and their colleagues (Bolt 1980). *Put-That-There* used speech recognition and a space-sensing device with six degrees of freedom to gather input from a user's speech and the location of a cursor on a wall-sized display, allowing for simple deictic reference to visible entities. More recently, several systems have built on this early work. Koons *et al.* (1993) allow users to manoeuvre around a two-dimensional map using spoken commands, deictic hand gestures, and eye gaze. In this system, nested frames are employed to gather and combine information from the different modalities. As in Put-That-There, speech drives the analysis of the gesture: if information is *missing* from speech, then the system will search for the missing information in the gestures and/or gaze. Time stamps unite the actions in the different modalities into a coherent picture. Wahlster *et al.* (1991) uses a similar method, also depending on the linguistic input to guide the interpretation of the other modalities. Bolt and

Herranz (1992) describe a system that allows a user to manipulate graphics with two-handed semi-iconic gestures. Using a cutoff point and time stamping, motions can be selected that relate to the intended movement mentioned in speech. Sparrell (1993) used a scheme based on stop-motion analysis: whenever there is a significant stop or slowdown in the motion of the user's hand, then the preceding motion segment is grouped and analysed for features such as finger posture and hand position. In all of these systems, interpretation is not carried out until the user has finished the utterance, and speech drives the analysis of the gestures.

As far as the *generation* of gesture in human–computer interface systems is concerned, the literature is sparse. Rijpkema and Girard (1991) generated handshapes automatically for an animated character based on the object being gripped in the scene. American Sign Language (ASL) arm gestures have been studied by Loomis *et al.* (1983), and ASL handshapes have been synthesized by Lee and Kunii (1993). Chen *et al.* (1993) developed an animated agent that can shake hands with a human. Calvert (1991) developed a system that generates gestural interaction between two agents as they greet one another, depending on personality variables that have been attributed to the two agents. Perlin and Goldberg (1996) have developed a system allowing for the creation of real-time behaviour based animated actors. The very lifelike motions of the animated actors are due to rhythmic and stochastic noise functions that result in slight but constant changes in appearance, and graceful transitions from one state to another. This system concentrates on posture, walking, and some arm motions. Kurlander *et al.* (1996) also developed a system to generate behaviours in animated actors, in this case avatars in Internet 'chat rooms'. They based their work on conventions from comic book characters, and concentrated on communicative behaviours that might translate chat-room 'emoticons' and fixed expressions such as 'LOL' (laughed out loud). The outcome is engaging. As in Perlin and Goldberg, however, the structure of discourse and the interaction between verbal and nonverbal behaviours is not examined.

Missing from both the understanding and generation systems is a concept of nonverbal function with respect to discourse function. That is, in the systems reviewed, there is no discourse structure (no notion of 'speaking turn' or 'new information' for example). Therefore the role of gesture cannot be analysed at more than a sentence-constituent-replacement level, or in general terms. What is needed is a discourse structure that can take into account turn-taking, and the increasing accumulation of information over a discourse.

In contradistinction to the narrow scope of gestures incorporated into human–computer interface systems, and the narrow interpretation of their meaning, four types of speech-associated gesture (McNeill 1992) have been extensively studied as the focus of the majority of research on the cognitive basis of the gesture–speech relationship, including our own:

Iconic gestures represent some feature of the semantics of the accompanying speech, such as sketching a small rectangular space with one's hands while saying 'Did you bring your **checkbook**?'

Metaphoric gestures represent an abstract feature of the concurrent speech, such as forming a jaw-like shape with one hand, and pulling it towards one's body while saying 'You must **withdraw** money.'

Deictic gestures indicate a point in space. They accompany reference to persons, places and other spatializable discourse entities. An example is pointing to the ground while saying 'Do you have an account at Mellon or at **this** bank?'

Beats are small formless waves of the hand that occur with heavily emphasized words, occasions of turning over the floor to another speaker, and other kinds of special linguistic work. An example is waving one's left hand briefly up and down along with the stressed word in the phrase 'Go **ahead**.'

Evidence from many sources suggests a close relationship between speech and gesture. At the prosodic level, Kendon (1974) found that the stroke phase (the most effortful part) of speech-accompanying gestures tends to occur at the same time as or just before the phonologically most prominent syllable of the accompanying speech. At a cognitive level, Cassell *et al.* (1998) established that listeners rely on information conveyed in gesture as they try to comprehend a story; Alibali *et al.* (1994) showed that children may express in gesture information that they cannot yet express in speech. Other evidence comes from the sheer frequency of gestures during speech. About three-quarters of all clauses in narrative discourse are accompanied by gestures of one kind or another (McNeill 1992), and, perhaps surprisingly, although the proportion of gesture types may change, all of these gestures, and spontaneous gesturing in general, are found in discourses by speakers of most languages.

In this chapter, however, my primary concern is with the semantic and pragmatic relationship between the two media. Gesture and speech do not always manifest the same information about an idea, but what they convey is always complementary. That is, gesture may depict the way in which an action was carried out when this aspect of meaning is not depicted in speech. It has been suggested (Kendon 1994) that those concepts difficult to express in language may be conveyed by gesture. Thus simultaneity of two events, or the respective locations of two objects, may be expressed by the position of the two hands. In this sense, the gesture–speech relationship resembles the interaction of words and graphics in the generation of multimodal text (Feiner and McKeown 1991; Wahlster *et al.* 1991). In storytelling, narrative structure may be indexed by differential use of gesture: iconic gestures tend to occur with plot-advancing description of the action, deictic gestures with the introduction of new characters, and beat gestures at the boundaries of episodes (Cassell and McNeill 1991).

I propose to use the level of 'information structure' to capture regularities such as these. The information structure of an utterance defines its relation to other utterances in a discourse and to propositions in the relevant knowledge pool. Although a sentence like 'George withdrew fifty dollars' has a clear semantic interpretation, the semantics do not indicate how the proposition relates to other propositions in the discourse. For example, the sentence might be an equally appropriate response to the questions 'Who withdrew fifty dollars?', 'What did George withdraw?', 'What did George do?', or even 'What happened?' Which question is asked determines which items in the response are most important or salient, which in turn determines how the phrase is uttered. These types of salience distinctions are encoded in the information structure representation of an utterance.

Following Halliday and others (Halliday 1967; Hajicova and Sgall 1988), I use the terms 'theme' and 'rheme' to denote two distinct information structural attributes of an utterance[1]. Functionally similar distinctions in this context are 'topic/comment', 'given/new', and the scale of 'communicative dynamism'. The theme roughly corresponds to what the utterance is about. The rheme corresponds to what the speaker has to contribute concerning the theme. Depending on the discourse context, a given utterance may be divided on semantic and pragmatic grounds into thematic and rhematic constituents in a variety of ways. For example, given the utterance 'George withdrew fifty dollars', we might consider the theme to be 'How much money George withdrew' and the rheme to be 'fifty dollars.'

Within information structural constituents, I define the semantic interpretations of certain items as being either 'focused' or 'background'. Items may be focused for a variety of reasons, including emphasizing their newness in the discourse or making contrastive distinctions among salient discourse entities. For example, in a theme concerning 'How much money George withdrew' we may say that 'George' may be the focus because it stands in contrast to some other salient discourse entity, say 'Gilbert.' We also mark the representation of entities in information structure with their status in the discourse. Entities are considered either new to discourse and hearer (indefinites), new to discourse but not to hearer (definites on first mention), or old (all others) (Prince 1992).

Distinct intonational tunes have been shown to be associated with the thematic and rhematic parts of an utterance for certain classes of dialogue in certain languages (Steedman 1991; Prevost and Steedman 1993). In particular, we note that the standard rise–fall intonation generally occurs with the rhematic part of many types of utterances. The rise–fall intonation is realized as a pitch peak on the primary-stress syllable of the focused word, followed by an immediate fall to a lower pitch which is then sustained for the duration of the phrase. The rhematic part of yes/no interrogatives is often accompanied by a fall–rise intonation, realized as a low-pitch target on the primary-stress syllable of the focused word, followed by an immediate rise to a sustained higher pitch. Thematic elements of an utterance are often marked by a rise–fall–rise intonation, realized by a rise to a high-pitch target on the primary-stress syllable, followed by an immediate fall to a lower pitch with another pitch rise occurring at the end of the phrase. The following examples illustrate the coupling of tunes with themes and rhemes:

[Q:] Who withdrew fifty dollars?
[A:] (**George**)$_{RHEME}$ (withdrew fifty dollars)$_{THEME}$

[Q:] What did George withdraw?
[A:] (George withdrew)$_{THEME}$ (**fifty dollars**)$_{RHEME}$

Gesture also serves an important role in marking information structure. When gestures are found in an utterance, the vast majority of them co-occur with the rhematic elements of that utterance (Cassell and Prevost, in preparation). In this sense intonation and gesture serve similar roles in the discourse. Intonational contours also time the occurrence of gesture (Cassell and Prevost, in preparation). Thus, based on the research described above, the distribution of gestural units in the stream of speech is similar to the distribution of intonational units, in the following ways:

(1) Gestural domains are isomorphic with intonational domains. The speaker's hands rise into space with the beginning of the intonational rise at the beginning of an utterance, and the hands fall at the end of the utterance along with the final intonational marking.

(2) The most effortful part of the gesture (the 'stroke') co-occurs with the pitch accent, or most effortful part of enunciation.

(3) Gestures co-occur with the rhematic part of speech, just as we find particular intonational tunes co-occurring with the rhematic part of speech. We hypothesize that this is so because the rheme is that part of speech that contributes most to the ongoing discourse, and that is least known to the listener beforehand. This does not mean that one never finds gestures with the theme, however. Some themes are *contrastive*, marking the contrast between one theme and another. An example is 'In the cartoon you see a manhole cover. And then the rock falls down **on that manhole cover**'. When thematic material is contrastive, then gesture may occur in that context.

Implementation

Our study of the literature on the relationship between speech and gesture in human–human conversation led us to build an architecture that integrated the relationship between speech and gesture from the very deepest level of generation onwards. The objective of this project is to provide a testbed in which predictive accounts of gesture, such as the rules given above, can be formalized and evaluated. This goal places certain demands on the generation of content for the 'computational stage' (McNeill 1992) shared by speech and gesture. In particular, the generation process must provide precise and explicit representations of the concepts, such as information structure, to which the theory of gesture refers.

The solution adopted here is to simulate the world and discourse actions of an agent interacting with another agent in the service of accomplishing a goal in a simple environment. For the present implementation, the 'bank domain' was chosen because in it there are two agents who must interact linguistically to accomplish a goal. The complexity of the domain and the steps followed by the agents are analogous to those of Power (1977), but here the model is enriched with explicit representations of the structure of discourse and the relationship of

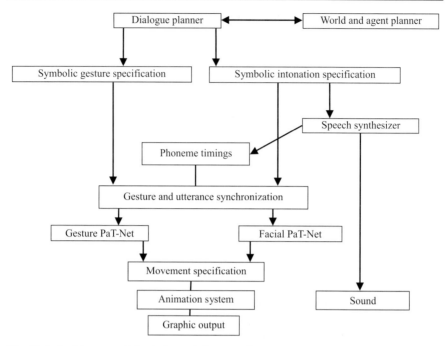

Fig. 11.1 Architecture of the Animated Conversation system.

the structure to the agents' domain plans. The following two sections of the chapter describe the dialogue-generation system in this light.

As shown in Figure 11.1, the selection of content for the dialogue in our system is performed by two cascaded planners. The first is the domain planner, which manages the plans governing the concrete actions the agents will execute; the second is the discourse planner, which manages the communicative actions the agents must take in order to agree on a domain plan and in order to remain synchronized while executing a domain plan.

The input to the domain planner is a database of facts describing the way the world works, the goals of the agents, and the beliefs of the agents about the world, including the beliefs of the agents about each other. The domain planner executes by decomposing an agent's current goals into a series of more specific goals according to the hierarchical relationship between actions specified in the agent's beliefs about the world. An agent's goals may be of one of two forms: to obtain some piece of information, or to ensure that some state holds in the world; questions can be used to achieve either kind of goal, but planning decompositions are only appropriate for the second kind. Once decomposition resolves a plan into a sequence of actions to be performed, the domain planner causes the agents to execute those actions in sequence. As these goal expansions and action executions take place, the domain planner also dictates discourse goals that agents must adopt in order to maintain and exploit cooperation with their conversational partner.

The domain planner transmits its instructions to take communicative actions to the discourse planner by suspending operation when such instructions are generated and relinquishing control to the discourse planner. Several stages of processing and conversational interaction may occur before these discourse goals are achieved. The discourse planner must identify how the goal submitted by the domain planner relates to other discourse goals that may still be in progress. Then content for a particular utterance is selected on the basis of how the discourse goal is decomposed into sequences of actions that might achieve it.

The domain planner and the discourse planner offer a number of explicit representational structures that could serve as input in formulating rules of gesture and intonation. At any point, of course, each agent has a representation of the domain plan that is being executed, and of the constituents of discourse that go into discussion of the plan. Explicit links between these two structures indicate what part of the plan each discourse segment concerns; these links ensure that conversation is coordinated and understood. These three kinds of information form the basis for two additional levels of representation, which are maintained solely for their possible relevance to linguistic processes. First, a model of attention (the attentional state) indicates which entities are known to the participants, which entities have been referred to, and how salient those entities are. The attentional state for some utterance in the discourse consists of a list that contains, for each discourse segment that dominates that utterance, the sets of entities mentioned in that segment. These sets are ordered so that the entities referred to in larger segments are less salient than the entities referred to in segments they dominate. Second, a record of the purposes generated by the planner that initiated discourse actions is kept. Of course, it may happen that only the agent who initiated an action knows this purpose exactly. Accordingly, both parties also separately record the most specific purpose for a segment for which evidence has been given. This architecture of intentional structure, attentional state, and discourse purposes, and the relationship between them was first proposed by Grosz and Sidner (1986); the implementation of these notions here follows their suggestions as closely as possible. We use these representations to reconstruct the information structure of the dialogue as follows:

- Material is classified as *thematic* if it occurs in some part of the speaker's discourse purpose in the current constituent or its ancestors for which evidence has been given.

- Material is classified as *rhematic* if it occurs only in that part of the speaker's discourse purpose in the current segment or its ancestors for which evidence has not been provided.

- Information not meeting either of these criteria constitutes linguistic formulae, which are irrelevant to the speaker's purpose, and are also labelled as thematic.

Focus is assigned to references according to the theory of contrast in Prevost and Steedman (1993), while the discourse status of entities is determined from the agents' knowledge of each other and from the attentional state. Finally, the semantic class of constituents is retrieved from a dictionary associating semantic representations with possible gestures that might represent them. This solution is, of course, provisional: a richer semantics would include the features relevant for gesture generation, so that the form of gestures could be generated algorithmically from the semantics, and much of our current research addresses this problem.

These structures permit the application of the rules for generation of gestures and intonation given above. A variant of Prevost and Steedman's algorithm is used to do this, thus generating English text annotated with intonational cues and gestural instructions from information structures. These intonational and gesture features are attached to words in the dialogue and may alternatively be interpreted as occurring at the start of the associated word, on the stressed syllable of the word, or at the end of the word, depending on the feature. In order for the gestures to appear at the proper times in the animation, the two streams must be synchronized with the synthesized speech.

The intonation stream provides an abstract representation that is automatically translated to a form suitable for input to the speech synthesis component. We used the AT&T Bell Laboratories TTS synthesizer to produce the actual speech wave and phoneme timings (Liberman and Buschbaum 1985). After transforming the utterances into proper input for the synthesizer and generating the speech wave and phoneme timings, the durational outputs from the synthesis are merged by rule with the abstract intonational and gestural notations. This detailed timing information (to the centisecond) allows synchronization of the gestural animations with the speech, as described below.

Gesture integration and animation

In the research presented here the interaction between speech and gesture is modelled in such a form that it can drive an animation system. Note that another model currently in progress generates gaze and head movements, and synchronizes gestures with these facial parameters as well as with movements of the lips (Pelachaud *et al.* 1991, 1996). The input to the animation system should not specify every small movement of the hands because that is determined by semantics rather than physiology, and it should take into account temporal deformations of gestures due to the demands of synchronizing gestures with speech and with one another. We used the following rules:

• Non-beat gestures accompany verb phrases in the rheme and hearer-new references, as follows: words with literally spatial content get iconic gestures; those with metaphorically spatial content get appropriate metaphoric gestures; words with spatializable content get deictic gestures.

- Beat gestures are generated for verb phrases in the rheme and for hearer-new references when the semantic content cannot be represented spatially.

- Beats accompany discourse-new definite references.

- Generated gestures associated with a word are aligned with the stressed syllable of that word. This is a straightforward task for beat gestures, which are simply waves of the hand. In contrast, the other gestures have a preparation phase that occurs before the stroke; accordingly, gestures with a preparation phase must start at the beginning of the intonational phrase in which the associated word occurs to ensure that the stroke can occur on that word.

Gesture production is carried out by a group of parallel transition networks (PaT-Nets), finite state machines, several of which can be run in tandem (Becket 1994). PaT-Nets govern three processes, two of which concern the direct production of gesture through the animation system. The first, 'parse-net', is a control network that parses the output of the speech synthesis module described above. This finite-state machine parses phoneme representations one utterance at a time; in the current domain, this means also that one speaker turn is parsed at a time.

Upon the signalling of a particular gesture, parse-net will instantiate one of two additional PaT-Nets; if the gesture is a beat, the finite-state machine representing beats ('beat-net') will be called, and if the gesture is deictic, iconic, or metaphoric, the network representing these types of gestures ('gest-net') will be called. This separation is motivated by the 'rhythm hypothesis' (Tuite 1993), which posits that beats arise from the underlying rhythmical pulse of speaking, while other gestures arise from meaning representations. In addition, beats are often found super-imposed over the other types of gestures, and such a separation makes super-position easier. Finally, since one of the goals of the model is to reflect differences in behaviour among gesture types, this system provides for control of freedom versus boundedness in gestures (e.g., an iconic gesture or emblem is tightly constrained to a particular standard of well-formedness, while beats display free movement); free gestures may most easily be generated by a separate PaT-Net whose parameters include this feature.

Gesture and beat finite-state machines are built as necessary by the parser, so that the gestures can be represented as they arise. The newly created instances of the gesture and beat PaT-Nets do not exit immediately upon creating their re-spective gestures; rather, they pause and await further commands from the calling network, in this case, parse-net. This is to allow for the phenomenon of gesture co-articulation, in which two gestures may occur in an utterance without inter-mediary relaxation, i.e., without dropping the hands or, in some cases, without relaxing handshape. Once the end of the current utterance is reached, the parser adds another level of control: it forces exit without relaxation of all gestures except the gesture at the top of the stack; this final gesture is followed by a relaxation of the arms, hands, and wrists.

The animation itself is carried out by Jack^{TM}, a program for controlling articu-lated objects, especially human figures. The figures have joints and behaviours designed to generate realistic motion. Additional modules can be added to deal with new domains, such as gesture.

The PaT-Net system issues gesture requests to the animation system, telling the figure to rest, make a beat motion, or make a gesture involving the hand, wrist, and/or arm. Four motion modules have been added to the Jack system: hand motion, wrist motion, arm motion, and beat motion, each of which may be specified separately for each arm. The animation system isolates the higher level PaT-Net system from the details of the human figure's geometry, biomechanical modelling, and joint-control functions.

The hand motions can be specified in terms of an expandable library of handshapes; the current system is based on the American Sign Language alphabet. An additional parameter controls the laxness of the handshape. The animation system moves the fingers from one position to another, attempting to get as close to the goal positions as possible within the constraints of the time allotted and the velocity limits of the finger joints. The result is that as the speed of the gesture increases, the gestures will 'coarticulate' in a realistic manner.

The wrist-position goals are specified in terms of the hand direction relative to the figure (e.g., fingers forward and palm up). The animation system automatically limits the wrist to a realistic range of motion. Beat motions are a specialized form of wrist motion. Rather than having the goal specified, the goal is automatically generated based on the current position of the wrist. The animation system selects the most comfortable way for the figure to gesture in that situation and moves the wrist accordingly. The arm motions are specified in a manner similar to that of the wrists, except that relative spatial positions (e.g., near to the body, far left, and chest high) are given instead of orientations.

Example of output

For this example, imagine that Gilbert is a bank teller, and that George, a customer, has asked Gilbert for help in obtaining $50 (as the dialogue is generated automatically, the two agents have to specify in advance each of the goals they are working towards and steps they are following; this explains the redundancy of the dialogue).

Gilbert:	Do you have a blank check?
George:	Yes, I have a blank check.
Gilbert:	Do you have an account for the check?
George:	Yes, I have an account for the check.
Gilbert:	Does the account contain at least $50?
George:	Yes, the account contains $80.
Gilbert:	Get the check made out to you for $50 and then I can withdraw $50 for you.
George:	All right, let's get the check made out to me for $50.

In this example, as in (American) life, the intonation rises at the end of yes/no questions falls at the end of answers. The most accented syllable is determined by which information is new and salient. Information about which words or phrases are most salient to the discourse, whether words or phrases refer to places in space, or spatializable entities, and which words or phrases end a speaker's turn also determine the placement and content of gestures and facial displays.

In particular, when Gilbert asks a question, his voice rises. When George replies to a question, his voice falls. When Gilbert asks George whether he has an account for the check, he stresses the word 'account'. When he asks whether George has a blank check, he stresses the word 'check'. Every time George answers 'yes' or turns the floor over to Gilbert (at the ends of utterances), he nods his head and raises his eyebrows. George and Gilbert look at each other when Gilbert asks a question, but at the end of each question, Gilbert looks up slightly. During the brief pause at the end of affirmative statements the speaker (always George, in this fragment) blinks. To mark the end of the questions, Gilbert raises his eyebrows. In saying the word 'account', Gilbert forms a kind of box in front of him with his hands: a metaphorical representation of a bank account in which one keeps money. In saying 'check', Gilbert sketches the outlines of a checkbook in the air between him and his listener.

Figures 11.2 and 11.3 reproduce excerpts from the conversation. In Fig. 11.2, panel (a) shows the automatic generation of an iconic gesture representing a check or checkbook, along with the phrase 'Do you have a blank check?'; panel (b) shows the generation of a metaphoric gesture representing supplication, along with the phrase 'Can you help me?' Figure 11.3(a) shows the automatic generation of an iconic gesture indicating writing on something, along with the phrase 'You can write the check','and (b) shows the generation of a beat gesture along with the phrase 'Yes, I have eighty dollars in my account'.

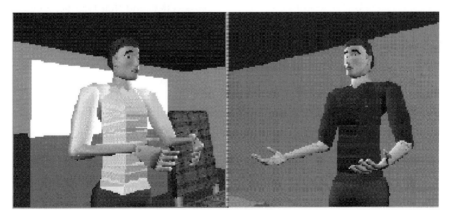

Fig. 11.2 (a) 'Do you have a blank check?'; (b) 'Can you help me?'

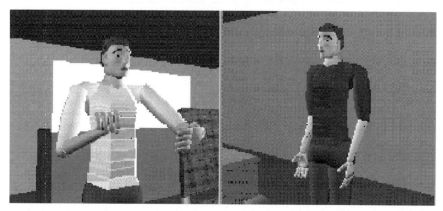

Fig. 11.3 (a) 'You can write the check.' (b) 'I have eighty dollars.'

Lessons learned

In implementing Animated Conversation, three important issues were brought out. First, we realized that while a discourse framework could specify type of gesture and placement of gesture, we would need a semantic framework to generate the *form* of particular gestures. In the Animated Conversation system we were obliged to choose gestural forms from a dictionary of gestures. We were uncomfortable with this. We did not generate the form of the gestures from scratch, and so—although we took advantage of what we knew in terms of temporal integration and discourse integration—we did not exploit rules for semantic integration.

Second, we realized in watching the animation that *too many* nonverbal behaviours were being generated: the impression was of a bank teller talking to a foreigner and trying to enhance his speech with supplementary nonverbal cues. This problem arose because each nonverbal behaviour was generated independently on the basis of its association with discourse and turn-taking structure and timed by intonation, but without reference to the other nonverbal phenomena present in the same clause. Our conclusion was that we lacked two functions in our system: first, a multimodal 'manager' that distributes meaning across the modalities but that is essentially modality-independent in its functioning. Such 'managers' have been described for multimodal integration for generation of text and graphics (Wahlster *et al.* 1991) and multimodal integration in input (Johnston *et al.* 1997). Second, we lacked an understanding of what shape a particular gesture would take: how did we describe which particular gesture would be generated? This is similar to the problem of word choice in text generation (Elhadad *et al.*, to appear).

Third, we realized that by implementing gestures in Animated Conversation deriving solely from a model of discourse structure, we were missing those gestures that depend on turn-taking behaviour. For example, beat gestures may also serve to maintain conversation as dyadic: to check on the attention of the listener, and to ensure that the listener is following (Bavelas *et al.* 1992).

Next steps

In order to continue a study of the issues outlined above, we began implementing our current testbed. In the next section I talk about our plans for the Rea system, which is currently under construction.

The domain which we have chosen is real estate: Rea is capable of interacting with a human concerning the purchase of a home. We chose this domain for the importance that social interaction as well as knowledge plays in the success of a conversation. That is, real estate agents typically come to know the needs and desires of their clients through casual social interaction as well as checklists. Rea engages in social chit-chat, and she will soon be able to take users on 3D walk-throughs of different houses on a large screen. She is able both to answer questions about particular houses and to initiate conversation about the human user's housing needs.

Some of the areas which we are exploring in the Rea architecture are the following:

1. *Use of verbal and nonverbal cues in understanding.* In a multimodal conversation system, the understanding component must not only integrate information from different modalities into a coherent propositional representation of what the user is communicating, but—in order to know what function that information fills in the ongoing conversation—it must also derive the interactional information from the perceptual inputs. Moreover, it must determine when the user has communicated enough to begin analysis and be able to re-analyse input in case it misinterprets the user's turn-taking cues.

2. *The role of nonverbal behaviours in dialogue planning.* The discourse planner for conversational characters must be able to plan turn-taking sequences and easily adapt when those plans are invalidated by nonverbal cues—for example when the human refuses to give over the turn, and continued nonverbal feedback becomes more appropriate than adding new content to the conversation.

3. *Distribution of information in verbal and nonverbal behaviours.* When the discourse plan calls for the generation of interactional information, the character must decide which modality to use, and must take into account interactional information from the user. For example, signalling an interruption or termination may be performed verbally or with a nod of the head depending on whether the user or the character currently has the turn. Crucially, Rea's architecture begins to fill our goal of function-oriented rather than modality-oriented processes. That is, rather than specifying what a gesture will do at any given moment, the system generates a need for a particular function to be filled, or particular information to

Fig. 11.4 Rea has a conversation with a user about a house.

be conveyed, and the modality that is free at that moment (and that the system knows is capable of filling that function) is called into play.

In talking about Animated Conversation, I mentioned that we were dissatisfied with the question of what form to generate for particular gestures, and how to negotiate which content is conveyed in which modality. In Rea, we have begun to work on solutions to these problems. Let us look first at the issue of generating gestural form from scratch. I believe that a key component of a grammar that will be able to handle the issue of semantic form for gesture is a semantic representation scheme located at the sentence-planning stage of generation. This scheme can encode the proper level of abstraction for concepts involving motion so that features such as manner, path, telicity (goal-orientedness), speed, and aspect can be independently applied to the various modalities at hand. In this way we can implement in gesture generation the insights I described above about the role of gesture in describing motion. For example, the gesture module might generate the manner of a motion, while the spoken verb generates the path, or vice versa. Thus, one might say 'I went to the store' but produce a walking gesture with one's index and second finger. In this way, two semantic frames that each contain partial knowledge of the content to be generated are unified.

In order to determine *when* content is distributed across speech and gesture, and when it is conveyed *redundantly* in both speech and gesture, Prevost and I have begun to look at data from human–human conversation (Cassell and Prevost in preparation). We have found that, as we implemented in Animated Conversation, gestures are overwhelmingly found in association with the rheme of an utterance. Within the rheme, however, the question of redundancy is mediated by whether iconic gestures represent information from the point of view of an observer, or the point of view of the speaker. When gestures portray the point of view of an observer, then gestures and speech are almost always redundant. When gestures portray the point of view of a character, or the speaker, then the gesture often conveys information that is not conveyed in the accompanying speech. Results such as these are allowing us to refine the determination of the form and placement of gestures in association with spoken language.

Finally, it should be noted that, unlike what has been posited for humans, the generation of gesture and speech in the systems built to date has been quite linear and unidirectional, without any chance of feedback between the modalities. To address this issue, Scott Prevost and I have been thinking about a way for gesture and intonation to affect one another. Prevost (1996) argues that the determination of focus (and hence pitch accent placement) within thematic and rhematic (old information or new information) constituents should be handled by the sentence planner. Based on this observation and the mapping of triphasic gestures onto intonational tunes described in Cassell *et al.* (1994), we can also assert that the alignment of the three gesture phases with the intonation contour occurs at this level as well. This aspect of our architecture has a strong effect on the interaction between speech and gesture in generation: the choice of gestures and choice of speech form interact such that gesture will actually affect where stress is placed in the utterance. For example, if a sentence such as 'Road Runner zipped over Coyote' is planned, then, depending on the gesture chosen as well as the underlying representation, primary stress will be differently assigned. If the gesture chosen represents driving, then primary stress will fall on 'zipped' (as the reader can see by reading the sentence out loud, it is difficult to imagine performing the gesture along with 'over,' or stressing the word 'over' if the gesture co-occurs with 'zipped'). If, on the other hand, the gesture chosen simply represents motion from point A to point B, then primary stress might fall on 'zipped' or on 'over', depending on which of these terms is focused (or contrastive) in the context of the text. This is an exciting direction to pursue because it means that the generation of one modality can have an effect on the generation of other modalities.

Conclusions

Most research on gesture has been descriptive and distributional. With the evidence available, it is time to attempt predictive theories of gesture use. The research on gesture–speech interaction described above was sufficient to allow us to specify rules and write algorithms that drive an animated model of verbal and nonverbal behaviours in conversational interaction. Formal models such as ours point up gaps in knowledge, and fuzziness in theoretical explanations. In moving from studying conversation between humans to implementing computer conversations, we are moving from a rich description of a naturally occurring phenomenon to a parametric implementation. In the process, certain aspects of the phenomenon emerge as feasible to implement, and certain aspects of the phenomenon emerge as key functions without which the implementation would make no sense.

References

Alibali, M. W., Flevares, L., and Goldin-Meadow, S. (1994). Going beyond what children say to assess their knowledge. Unpublished manuscript, Department of Psychology, University of Chicago.

Bavelas, J., Chovil, N., Lawrie, D., and Wade, A. (1992). Interactive gestures. *Discourse Processes*, **15**, 469–89.

Becket, W. M. (1994). The Jack Lisp API. Technical Report MS-CIS-94–01/Graphics Lab 59, University of Pennsylvania.

Bolt, R. A. (1980). Put-that-there: voice and gesture at the graphics interface. *Computer Graphics*, **14**(3), 262–70.

Bolt, R. A. and Herranz, E. (1992). Two-handed gesture in multi-modal natural dialog. In *Proceedings of the fifth annual ACM symposium on user interface software and technology*, pp. 7–14. Monterey, CA.

Calvert, T. (1991). Composition of realistic animation sequences for multiple human figures. In *Making them move: mechanics, control and animation of articulated figures* (ed. N. Badler, B. Barsky, and D. Zeltner), pp. 35–50. Morgan-Kaufmann, San Mateo, CA.

Cassell, J. and McNeill, D. (1991). Gesture and the poetics of prose. *Poetics Today*, **12**(12), 375–404.

Cassell, J. and Prevost, S. (in preparation). Embodied natural language generation: a framework for generating speech and gesture.

Cassell, J., Pelachaud, C., Badler, N. I., Steedman, M., Achorn, B., Beckett, T., Douville, B., Prevost, S. and Stone, M. (1994). Animated conversation: rule-based generation of facial display, gesture and spoken intonation for multiple conversational agents. *Computer Graphics*, **28**(4), 413–20.

Cassell, J., McNeill, D., and McCullough, K. E. (in press). Speech–gesture mismatches: evidence for one underlying representation of linguistic and nonlinguistic information. *Pragmatics and Cognition*, **6**(2).

Chen, D., Pieper, S., Singh, S., Rosen, J., and Zeltzer, D. (1993). The virtual sailor: an implementation of interactive human body modeling. In *Proceedings of IEEE 1993 virtual reality annual international symposium VRAIS 1993*, pp. 429–35. IEEE Service Centre, Piscataway, NJ.

Efron, D. (1941). *Gesture and environment*. King's Crown Press, New York.

Ekman, P. and Friesen, W. (1969). The repertoire of nonverbal behavioral categories—origins, usage, and coding. *Semiotica*, **1**, 49–98.

Elhadad, M., McKeown, K., and Robin, J. (1997). Floating constraints in lexical choice. *Computational Linguistics*, **23**, 195–240.

Feiner, S. and McKeown, K. (1991). Automating the generation of coordinated multimedia explanations. *IEEE Computer*, **24**(10), 33–41.

Grosz, B. and Sidner, C. (1986). Attention, intentions, and the structure of discourse. *Computational Linguistics*, **12**(3), 175–204.

Hajicova, E. and Sgall, P. (1988). Topic and focus of a sentence and the patterning of a text. In *Text and discourse constitution* (ed. J. Petofi), De Gruyter, Berlin.

Halliday, M. (1967). *Intonation and grammar in British English.* Mouton, The Hague.

Hinrichs, E. and Polanyi, L. (1986). Pointing the way: a unified treatment of referential gesture in interactive contexts. In *CLS 22, part 2: papers from the parasession on pragmatics and grammatical theory* (ed. A. Farley, P. Farley, and K. E. McCullough), pp. 298–314. Chicago Linguistics Society.

Johnston, M., Cohen, P. R., McGee, D., Pittman, J., Oviatt, S. L., and Smith, I. (1997). Unification-based multimodal integration. In *Proceedings of the 35th Annual Meeting of the Association for Computational Linguistics* (ACL-97/EACL-97), pp. 281–8.

Kendon, A. (1974). Movement coordination in social interaction: some examples described. In *Nonverbal communication* (ed. S. Weitz), pp. 150–68. Oxford University Press, New York.

Kendon, A. (1994). Do gestures communicate? A review. *Research on Language and Social Interaction*, **2**(3), 175–200.

Kendon, A. (1995). Gestures as illocutionary and discourse structure markers in southern Italian conversation. *Journal of Pragmatics*, **23**, pp. 247–80.

Koons, D. B., Sparrell, C. J., and Thórisson, K. R. (1998). Integrating simultaneous input from speech, gaze and hand gestures. In *Intelligent user interfaces*, (ed. M. T. Maybury), pp. 53–64. Morgan-Kaufmann, San Mateo, CA.

Kurlander, D., Skelly, T., and Salesin, D. (1996). Comic chat. In *SIGGRAPH '96, Proceedings of the 23rd annual conference on computer graphics*, pp. 225–36. ACM

Liberman, M. and Buschbaum, A. L. (1985). Structure and usage of current Bell Labs text to speech programs. Technical Memorandum TM 11225-850731-11, AT&T Bell Laboratories.

Loomis, J., Poizner, H., Bellugi, U., Blakemore, A., and Hollerbach, J. (1983). Computer graphic modeling of American Sign Language. *Computer Graphics*, **17**(3), 105–114.

Maggioni, C. (1995). Gesture-Computer: new ways of operating a computer. In *Proceedings of the international workshop on automatic face and gesture recognition*, pp. 166–71. Zurich.

McNeill, D. (1992). *Hand and mind: what gestures reveal about thought.* University of Chicago Press.

Oviatt, S. L. (1995). Predicting spoken disfluencies during human–computer interaction. *Computer Speech and Language*, **9**(1), 19–35.

Pelachaud, C., Badler, N., and Steedman, M. (1991). Linguistic issues in facial animation. In *Computer animation '91* (ed. N. Magnenat-Thalmann and D. Thalmann), pp. 15–30. Springer-Verlag, New York.

Pelachaud, C., Badler, N., and Steedman, M. (1996). Generating facial expressions for speech. *Cognitive Science*, **20**(1), 1–46.

Perlin, K and Goldberg, A. (1996). Improv: a system for scripting interactive actors in virtual worlds. In *SIGGRAPH 96, Proceedings of the 23rd annual conference on Computer Graphics*, pp. 205–16.

Power, R. (1977). The organisation of purposeful dialogues. *Linguistics*, **17**, 107–52.

Prevost, S. (1996). An information structural approach to spoken language generation. In *Proceedings of the 34th annual meeting of the Association for Computational Linguistics*, Santa Cruz.

Prevost, S. and Steedman, M. (1993). Using context to specify intonation in speech synthesis. In *Proceedings of the 3rd European conference on speech communication and technology* (EUROSPEECH), pp. 2103–6. Berlin.

Prince, E. F. (1992). The ZPG letter: subjects, definiteness and information status. In *Discourse description: diverse analyses of a fund raising text* (ed. S. Thompson and W. Mann), pp. 295–325. John Benjamins, Amsterdam.

Reeves, B. and Nass, C. (1996). *The media equation: how people treat computers, television and new media like real people and places.* Cambridge University Press.

Rijpkema, H. and Girard, M. (1991). Computer animation of hands and grasping. *Computer Graphics*, **25**(4), 339–348.

Rogers, W. T. (1978). The contribution of kinesic illustrators toward the comprehension of verbal behavior within utterances. *Human Communication Research*, **5**, 54–62.

Sparrell, C. J. (1993). Coverbal iconic gesture in human–computer interaction. Master's thesis, MIT, Cambridge, MA.

Steedman, M. (1991) Structure and intonation. *Language*, **67**(2), 260–96.

Trevarthen, C. (1986). Sharing makes sense: intersubjectivity and the making of an infant's meaning. In *Language topics: essays in honour of M. Halliday*, Vol. 1 (ed. R. Steele and T. Threadgold), pp. 177–200. John Benjamins, Amsterdam.

Tuite, K. (1993). The production of gesture. *Semiotica*, **93**, 1–2.

Wahlster, W., André, E., Graf, W., and Rist, T. (1991). Designing illustrated texts. In *Proceedings of the 5th EACL*, pp. 8–14.

Notes

1. Although note that we drop Halliday's assumption that themes occur only in sentence-initial position.

Index

Note: References to illustrations are given in bold numbers. References to notes are followed by 'n.'